To my loving wife, Nadereh,
who has always stood by with encouragement
while providing direction, insight, and active concern.
To my son and daughter, Arman and Anaheed,
who are both blessed with bright and inquisitive minds
and now, as they near adulthood,
have boundless opportunities before them.

Contents

Foreword

The essence of all successful investing and trading is trend following. Trend following is not just a style or an approach to the market; it is the heart and soul of all profits. There is no way to escape the fact that you must embrace an uptrend of some sort if you hope to eventually recognize a gain.

Even the most long-term dedicated value investors, who focuses on fundamentals and buys out of favor stocks, needs to have his or her insight eventually validated by a positive trend. At the other extreme, the aggressive day trader needs a trend of some sort even if lasts for just for a few minutes. Market success and trend following are inescapably connected.

Despite the essential nature of trend following to the investment process, the literature on the topic is woefully lacking. Platitudes such as "the trend is your friend," "buy low, sell high," and "cut losers and let winners run" constitute much of the discussion about riding a trend.

In many ways trend following is like the famous dicta uttered by Supreme Court Justice Potter Stewart in regards to pornography: "I know it when I see it." Trends are always easy to see in retrospect. They are almost always painfully obvious when we look at charts, but defining them and exploiting them for profit is a daunting task.

Many market players, including me, like to think that our success in identifying and riding trends is some intuitive skill that is akin to artistic talent. We like to believe that trend trading is an art form that can't be easily taught or communicated. L.A. Little crushes that conceit with his systematic approach to trend trading. He uncovers and dissects the many nuances and subtle issues that make trend trading so powerful.

Trend trading isn't just about holding a stock through a series of higher highs and higher lows. That is the easy part. Anyone can hold a stock that goes up endlessly, but, unfortunately, that doesn't happen that much in the real world. We have news events, shifting sentiments, and a host of factors that toss stocks around at random. Only the best stocks will continue to exhibit relative strength and reward us if we stick with them. Knowing when to hold and when to abandon ship is what this book addresses like no other that I have ever read.

The easiest part of the investment or trading process is the buy point. It is not that hard to find a stock that has a positive technical pattern. The hard part is the sell decision and that is what L.A. Little addresses with great precision. He integrates the concepts of volume, swing points, and anchor bars into the analysis, which greatly aids in determining the health of a trend.

In my experience, the most common mistake among active traders is that they don't stick with trends long enough. They simply don't have a good framework for deciding whether a trend will continue and, as the old adage goes, "no one ever went broke" taking a profit. However it can be quite disheartening to look back at how costly premature sales have been.

The great difficulty in trend trading is trying to determine when a trend has ended and it is time to move on versus what is just a healthy correction within a trend. I've heard countless tales about how someone bought a stock like Apple Computers at $7 in 2003 and then sold it for $10.50 and a big fat 50% profit a few months later. That sounds pretty darn good until you look at the current price of Apple Computers at around $340.

There is nothing more valuable in this excellent book than the disciplined structure and set of rules it sets forth for staying with a trend and not selling prematurely. There will be times when the trend is suspect or ambivalent, but L.A. Little develops a clear approach to dealing with those times so that you can stay with the trend and reap the big payoff.

It is obvious to every logical thinker that trend trading is the key to market success. It is the qualification of trends and the execution of the investor that is the key to success. You will not find a better framework for trend trading than that set forth by L.A. Little in this very valuable book.

James "RevShark" DePorre
Shark Investing
Anna Maria Island, Florida

Acknowledgments

The lasting influences in one's life are numerous, but none are more relished than those with close family. To my mother, the first love of my life, I extend an unending gratitude. She always provided rich encouragement laced with discipline.

Professionally I extend special thanks to my publisher for all the wonderful work and opportunities they have provided.

To Elizabeth and Jayanthi from *Stocks and Commodities* magazine, who continue to spread the word of technical analysis far and wide.

To William Hennelly and Poilin Breathnach, managing editors of TheStreet.com and RealMoney.com, whose faith in my writing and technical insight provided a much wider audience for my material.

Finally, to the countless technicians, both contemporary and historical, whose writings inspired and embellished my trading methods, I thank you all.

L.A. LITTLE

Trend Qualification and Trading

Introduction

Unlike men, not all trends are created equal. That simple premise, when fully understood, forever changes how you look at a chart. Trend, as it applies to securities trading, is loosely defined as the proclivity for prices to move in a general direction over a period of time.

Trend direction, although generally understood as a series of higher highs and higher lows (uptrend) or lower lows and lower highs (downtrend), is largely left to the practitioner to identify and interpret, without any system of uniformity and codification. This is a problem.

A more subtle but detrimental problem is the widespread practice of treating all trends as equals. Rarely does one see any discussion or even the recognition that some trends are "better" than others. This monolithic approach to trend combined with a blindness toward quality necessarily results in inferior trading results. To believe that all trends are equal in importance is to ignore reality. They are not.

It is sometimes said that successful traders have a knack for picking the "right" stocks. Although there is a lot more to successful trading than the choice of what to trade, successful traders tend to trade "stronger" trends; their skill, however, is probably based more on intuition than consciously practiced.

Trends are the primary technical tool of almost all traders, trading indicators, and trading systems. As such, the concept of trend is embedded in almost all technical trading literature, thought, and practice. "The trend is your friend" is an often-repeated aphorism. The desire to both identify and follow trend is practiced with an almost religious zealousness.

There exists a hodgepodge of technical tools designed specifically to recognize the creation and termination of trends. The use of moving averages is probably the oldest and most widely followed method to capture trend. Although a lagging indicator, the use of moving averages is widespread not only as a stand-alone tool (20-, 50-, and 200-period simple, weighted, and exponential moving averages are widely available and found in all charting packages) but also as the underlying trigger in a host of technical tools. For example, moving average convergence divergence

1

(MACD) is based solely on moving averages.[1] Bollinger bands are nothing more than +/– standard deviation bands arising from underlying moving averages.[2] The list goes on and on.

Equally widespread is the use of trend lines. A trend line is nothing more than a line drawn across three or more price point highs or lows on a chart. Once drawn, a trend line has a rising, horizontal, or declining slope, and the slope of the line is interpreted as the direction of the trend. Trend lines are used repeatedly as a visual aid in the recognition of trend. They appear throughout technical analysis literature and are commonplace in practice. The vast majority of the technical patterns a technician examines are based upon trend lines—even though few technicians are aware of this. For example, the neckline of a head and shoulders pattern or the upper or lower boundaries of a rectangle are both trend lines.[3] The entire concept of support and resistance is based on trend lines as well. A support or resistance line is nothing more than a trend line consisting of upward, downward, or horizontal slope.

The concept of momentum, another formidable technical crutch for technicians, is also rooted in the idea of trend. Momentum indicators attempt to address the "proclivity for prices to move in a general direction" part of the definition of trend. They are widely used by traders who follow a trend when trading and also by those attempting to anticipate a trend's demise. In the latter case, by measuring the rate of change inherent in a trend, momentum indicators attempt to predict an imminent trend change.

Finally, many of the most popular trading systems, both past and present, are based primarily on the concept of trend. The term trading systems refers to any systems approach to trading that is codified in some set of rules of when to enter and exit a position. They can be manually implemented or automatically traded (commonly referred to as program trading).

A famous and widely popularized manual trading system based solely on the concept of trend was the "Turtle Trading" trading system. Turtle Trading came about as an experiment conceived of and implemented by the legendary futures trader Richard Dennis[4] in 1983–1984. Dennis recruited and trained 23 individuals from all walks of life on the principles of trend based trading—principles that allowed many of the recruits to become successful traders in their own right.

Program trading systems (though the components of these systems are almost always proprietary and thus hidden from public view) are thought to universally have trend following as their key trigger for position entry and exit. Although each automated system varies to some degree, with respect to other factors such as reward-to-risk and drawdowns, the key component remains that of trend following.[5]

Given the importance of trend, one would think that this fundamental technical concept had been refined to perfection, with all ambiguities long since resolved. The reality is that trend is still not completely understood. Thus, this book focuses on a redefinition of trend through qualification, explores the implications of trend qualification, and examines the practical applications that flow from it. Trend qualification, like everything in technical analysis, offers no guarantees for predicting the future, as predictions are always fraught with error. Refining the definition of trend does, however, increase the probabilities of realizing an expected outcome.

Given its undeniable importance to all traders and its pervasive use in most trading tools, literature, and trading systems, the precision with which we define trend is critical to increased trading success. This statement rings true regardless of whether you are trading soybean futures in Chicago or a solar energy company in China. It holds true in South America, Asia, Europe, and the United States. Whether we look to currency, stock, futures, or even bond markets, trend is everywhere and so fundamental to technical analysis that the two are virtually inseparable. Sure, there are other components, but when you build a house, you don't start with the roof—you build from the foundation up.

It is for this reason that we embark on a redefinition of trend with the goal of solidifying our technical foundation. Our quest is for the treasure of increased predictive accuracy, and it is with the knowledge of trend qualification that we find a more perfect model: a methodology for evaluating the past and present in order to more accurately predict the future.

PART I

Trend Theory

Most literature on the subject of technical analysis focuses on application—how to apply some tool set to the market to magically make money. Very little of the available literature digs deeper into the mysteries of trading markets, asking the more philosophical and theoretical questions regarding what really makes the market do what it does.

Step back and consider the approach used in scientific inquiries. The common practice is to develop a hypothesis that attempts to explain the observed phenomenon. Next, studies are devised to test the hypothesis. After testing, the hypothesis is revised as needed, retested, and, as a result of this process, eventually a theory is created that explains most aspects of the phenomenon. Once understood, the theory can be utilized to create a simplified model of the reality.

In the field of study commonly referred to as technical analysis, the concept of trend is arguably the most fundamental of all technical building blocks. Without an accurate understanding of what trend is and how it can be reliably identified, technical analysis is crippled, at best.

Given the unquestioned importance of trend, there is an unparalleled need to create a theory of trend that utilizes the circular process of proposing and testing a hypothesis. In practice, this approach builds a solid foundation, a lasting foundation that isn't subject to the whims of the day.

The early work of Charles Dow and Thomas Hamilton is the most defining work on trend, and their trend model is studied intently. From that material, the objectives, inputs, definitions, and relationships of the currently practiced model of trend are exposed and analyzed. The Dow/Hamilton model can be referred to as the classical model of trend, given its ground-breaking work and application.

Although an excellent model, the Dow/Hamilton model's focus was rather narrow. Later practitioners, rather than extending the model in order to properly apply it to other phenomenon, chose to take the simple way out. Rather than do the legwork required to formulate a new theory and resultant model, these modern-day practitioners chose to simply distort and stretch the classical model to fit their needs. Such an approach is problematic.

Thus, Part I addresses theory and model. It begins with a presentation of the classical model of trend followed by the proposed neoclassical model. Both are presented in depth with an eye toward their objectives, internal assumptions, inputs, definitions, and the relationships among those moving parts.

The neoclassical model is comprehensively documented and its far-reaching implications are analyzed. Starting from a set of objectives that seek to explain how all trends are created, persist, and eventually meet their demise, observable phenomenon (market behavior) is utilized to validate the model. As such, the neoclassical model is essentially a replacement for the classical model, extending its scope and applicability—but it doesn't stop there.

The neoclassical model introduces another equally important, if not more important, concept. The model proposes that not all trends are equal in terms of their quality; that some trends are better than others. Initially that may not sound groundbreaking, but the implications are huge. If a trader can discern one trend as having an increased likelihood of continuance as compared to another, then naturally the trader would gravitate their efforts into trading the trend that had the most promise. The resulting yields should increase, and thus the model provides a valuable application in the "real world" of trading.

To summarize, not all trends are created equal and the neoclassical model provides the theoretical foundation for both the identification and qualification of trends. The model that springs forth yields abundant opportunities for practitioners in a very practical sense. In all human endeavors, applications without theories and resultant models typically end up on the trash heap of failed ideas. The currently practiced trend model is a failure not because of the model itself, but because the model has and is being applied in a manner it wasn't designed for. There is a better way. Through a painstaking examination of the existing model followed by the creation and exposition of a new, more comprehensive one, future generations of traders shall have the benefit of a theory that more closely matches the reality and objectives that they are most interested in.

CHAPTER 1

Redefining Trend

Trend, as it applies to securities trading, is loosely defined as the proclivity of prices to move in a general direction for some period of time. This definition appears to be a reasonable description, given the references made to *trend* throughout the technical literature. Note, however, that this definition neither indicates the direction of movement nor precisely defines the concept of time. Instead we are offered a broad picture of the inertia of prices moving along in one direction or another and continuing to do so for some unspecified period of time.

When you look for definitions of *trend* in the body of technical analysis work that has formed over the past century, there are few to be found. A general definition is contained in what has become known as the defining work for classical technical analysis, *Technical Analysis of Stock Trends* by Robert D. Edwards and John Magee.[1] Edwards and Magee explain how Charles Dow is believed to be the first person to make a thorough effort to express the notion of a general trend. Dow's research led to a series of editorials published in the *Wall Street Journal*. After Dow's death, the succeeding editor at the *Journal*, William P. Hamilton, continued to write about the market averages and trends. Eventually, Hamilton took Dow's work and organized it into a set of principles that later came to be known as the Dow Theory. That theory is heavily premised on the principle of identifying the general market trend.

Probably the most influential work on the Dow Theory is provided by Robert Rhea, who in 1932 published a book by the same title, *The Dow Theory*. Rhea recounts the work of Hamilton and provides what is probably

the most complete literary definition of trend, described in the context of
bull and bear markets.[2]

> *Successive rallies penetrating preceding high points, with ensuing
> declines terminating above preceding low points, offer a bullish in-
> dication. Conversely, failure of the rallies to penetrate previous high
> points, with ensuing declines carrying below former low points, is
> bearish.*

Outside of Hamilton's definition, *trend* is heavily referred to yet almost
universally lacking a definition. The notion of trend is widely accepted,
but other than in the early works of Dow and Hamilton, the absence of
a definitive definition is deafening.

Open almost any book on trading and you will see references to *trend*.
It doesn't matter if the subject matter addresses tape reading,[3] the psycho-
logical aspects of trading[4] or something as unique as explaining the market through chaos theory,[5] almost every trading book makes references to
trend, yet provides no definition. It's as if the definition is so widely known
that it need not be repeated. Clearly all these technicians view *trend* as
important—certainly important enough to take the time and trouble to use
the concept in their books and to utilize that concept to explain their trading systems and insights.

Given that *trend* is such a fundamental concept to the study of technical analysis, this absence of a precise definition is, in a word, baffling. Few
would argue about the definition of a price-to-earnings ratio (PE). There
is little disagreement in the world of finance about such concepts as PEG
ratios, profit margins, return on assets (ROA), or a whole host of financial
criteria used to evaluate a company's financial health. In fact, the less-than-
rigorous nature of technical analysis is what frustrates so many traders.
It is why fundamental traders (those who analyze the fundamentals of a
company and use that analysis to make investment decisions) mockingly
refer to technical traders as voodoo traders or worse. How can you use
the conclusions of a field of study when a most basic concept is—shall we
say—fuzzy?

The most complete definition of *trend* (as popularized by Rhea) has
held sway for more than a century now and has been used liberally by
all who have followed. It is based on the concept of price and direction
and was originally provided in the context of the general market trend,
a trend that is measured in years—not months, weeks, or, heaven for-
bid, days. Over the years, though, the notion of trend has increasingly
been applied to price movements within shorter and shorter time frames.
Given the criticality of the concept of trend to all technical traders and to
technical trading in general, it is necessary to ask if this definition,

postulated over a century ago and directed at major market movements, is applicable in shorter time frames. Is the generalized and widespread practical application of *trend* meaningful, and has the liberalization of the applicable rules surrounding this most basic concept rendered the term useless? I'm afraid it has.

The concept of trend is as basic as financial theory gets, and the application of the concept reaches to the very heart of technical analysis. Billions, if not trillions, of dollars are wagered on the direction of currencies, bonds, commodities, and stocks on a daily basis. The willingness of traders and investors to put their money at risk on the pure faith in the proclivity of prices to continue to move in a general direction for some period of time is self-evident. It happens on a daily basis all around the world. What if the daily actions of the stock market participants could be distilled and utilized in such a way as to increase the predictive accuracy of future price movements? What if a trend model could be defined, refined, and directed to address the need for trend identification on a more granular level, in terms of time, widespread applicability, and probabilities? This is the objective of trend qualification, and the pages that follow seek to address these desires.

The concept we construe as *trend* is, simply put, a model. Models consist of inputs, definitions, and relationships usually expressed as methodological rules or equations. They are nothing more than a mechanism to artificially impose structure on some part of a more complicated reality. The models we humans construct attempt to simplify yet capture the essence of the reality we are modeling. The ultimate model is the one that utilizes the smallest number of inputs yet reflects reality perfectly. The performance of most models is, however, always something less than ideal.

Models can be extremely complicated or relatively simple. Econometric models are well known for comprising hundreds, if not thousands of inputs, variables, and equations in their attempts to reflect all or some part of the economy. The model developed by Charles Dow to measure primary stock market direction (trend) was much simpler, consisting of only three variables—the instrument being measured, its price, and time.

The trend model conceived of by Dow over a century ago (as documented by and expanded upon by Hamilton) was purposefully developed to forecast major cycle changes in the market. Hamilton wrote of major bull and bear market cycles that consisted of three trends: the primary, secondary, and minor trends. In Hamilton's opinion, it wasn't worth examining minor trends, as they represented brief fluctuations that had no real effect on the larger trend of the market. Hamilton's real concern was to identify primary trends: those that would last for longer than a year and potentially for many years.

To this end, Dow and Hamilton originally began to monitor a critical group of stocks that they thought could provide a reliable indication of the general economy's health. If the group of stocks was strong and certain strength characteristics were met, then the economy would be strong and a primary bull market trend would likely ensue. The first group of stocks measured the industrial base of the country. Although the components have changed over time, the index remains and is called the Dow Jones Industrial Average. The second group of stocks concentrated on the movement of goods throughout the country. At the turn of the century, that was limited to railroad stocks. Like the industrial average, this second group of stocks has changed over the years, as well, yet it remains with us today. It is called the Dow Jones Transportation Index.

Assuming that one could determine the stock market's primary trend in a reasonably reliable manner, what value does it provide? The answer to that question is rather obvious. An accurate predictive model of trend is indeed a gem to behold. As the trend model suggests, trend is the proclivity for prices to continue in the direction of the trend. Thus, once identified, a trend can be followed until it ends, which brings us to the second major component of the trend model: identifying the trend's demise. Hamilton's trend model addressed this need as well.

Since it is generally accepted that, once established, there are greater odds that a trend will continue, the logical trading axiom is that you should always trade with the trend. Almost all trend-based trading systems (technical analysis tools and methodologies) generally accept this notion and attempt to trade with the trend. Equally important is the identification of a trend's end and there is another distinct set of tools and methods that attempt to determine this. Both trend-following and trend-exhaustion tools and methodologies are all loosely centered on the notion of trend as first described by Dow and Hamilton.

For example, an old mainstay and still popular model for trend determination is the moving average. There are simple moving averages, exponential moving averages, and even triangular moving averages. The rules governing their use are varied and easily outnumber the variations in moving average types. The crossover theory, for example, purports to indicate when to buy and sell. This theory is based on the use of two moving averages, each consisting of a different time period. When the faster of the two moving averages (shorter time span) crosses over the slower moving average line, then a buy or sell indicator is triggered.

Every popular charting package has a multitude of technical analysis tools available for use. The vast majority of these indicators are related to trend in one way or another. For example, a popular trading package from Investools.com offers more than 160 tools in their premier charting package. The proliferation of tools, many of which are related to trend, is overwhelming. In trading, what is needed is simplicity. The entire point of developing a model is to capture reality in the simplest possible manner.

A trading model is a very serious tool. It needs to capture the reality of the market because your money is at stake. There are literally thousands of inputs at work in the stock market. To distill that down to a minimal set of core inputs with a reasonably simple set of rules is what the astute trader strives for. To accomplish this, the model must account for the ultimate price determinant—supply and demand. It needs to be applicable to any time frame. It has to work the same for a stock as it does for a stock sector or an index, and on any market anywhere in the world. The model should apply equally to other markets including bonds, currencies, and commodities. It needs to be generic enough to do all these things yet still yield specific recommendations based on price direction: on trend initiation, continuation, and the potential for reversal.

That is a lot to ask of a model. Naturally, such a model will not always be right, but few models are. The goal is to get it right most of the time. Is such a system possible? Not only is it possible, it exists. The model is called trend qualification.

CHAPTER 2

Classical Trend Model

The existing and widely followed model of trend—a model that has held sway for more than a century—consists of three inputs and a number of rules governing their relationships. Although deficiencies exist, this trend model has been and continues to be used throughout the technical analysis literature and practice. For convenience, we refer to this model as the "classical trend model" or "classical trend theory."

1 - OBJECTIVE 2 - INPUTS 3 - DEFINITIONS 4 - RULES

1 -
OBJECTIVE OF THE MODEL

Probably the most important knowledge a trader can strive to attain is to identify the primary objective of any tool he or she may choose to utilize. With the classical trend model, Hamilton specifically discussed the model's objective in numerous references. That objective focused on making every possible effort to discern the primary movement of the market. Rhea described this succinctly in the following manner:

> *It must always be remembered, however, that there is a main current in the stock market, with innumerable cross currents, eddies, and backwaters, any one of which may be mistaken for a day, a week, or even a longer period for the main stream. The market is a barometer. There is no movement in it which has not meaning. That meaning*

*is sometimes not disclosed until long after the movement takes place,
and is still oftener never known at all; but it may truly be said that
every movement is reasonable if only the knowledge of its sources is
complete.[1]*

The knowledge that a model provides is only applicable to that which
it was intended for and is only as good as the construct of the model itself and the inputs provided to it. The trend model developed by Dow, and
perfected by Hamilton, was and remains exceptionally good at recognizing
the primary movements of the market—those long periods of time where
the general movement of the price action is climbing or falling—which are
called bullish or bearish markets. It is when Dow's model is applied to the
micro level of the markets rather than the macro level that it has serious
limitations, primarily because it was not designed for that task.

INPUTS

Although Hamilton's classical trend theory was written with an eye toward
identifying primary broad market movements, that objective was achieved
by examining the movement and interaction between two more narrow
components of the overall market, the Dow Jones Industrial and Transportation Averages. The inputs to the model were,

- The instrument being measured
- Price
- Time

By monitoring the price direction of these two averages, Hamilton's
trend model was able to provide predictive capabilities for the majority of
the stocks that constituted the general market, and to do so for the long-
term time frame,

MODEL DEFINITION

To paraphrase and generalize Hamilton's writings, the definition of an up
or a down trend is:

- *Uptrend (bull market).* A series of higher highs and higher lows over a
  given time frame.

- *Downtrend (bear market)*. A series of lower lows and lower highs over a given time frame.

Hamilton went on to say that the intervening period between a high and a low needed to consist of a minimum of a 3 percent price change from top to bottom.

For the purpose of this discussion, a rally or a decline is defined as one or more daily movements resulting in a net reversal of direction exceeding 3 percent of the price of either average.

4 — RULES FOR THE MODEL

For a model to achieve its objectives it must combine the model defini-tion with the input variables through a set of rules; rules that govern the model's relationships. Those rules form the heart of the model and, in the case of the classical trend model, the rules were reasonably small in num-ber. Those rules are presented in the following paragraphs. *A - C*

A — Both Averages Must Confirm

Although Dow and Hamilton's studies represent the original work on the concept of trend, their primary goal was reasonably narrow: to determine the primary and secondary trends as they relate explicitly to the general market. In that vein, they created and tracked the trend of the industrial and transportation indexes. Hamilton explicitly wrote about the need for both indexes to confirm one another in order to trust the observed trend for the general market: *correlation (sympathy), S. Dev*

> The movements of both the railroad and industrial stock aver-ages should always be considered together. The movement of one price average must be confirmed by the other before reliable in-ferences may be drawn. Conclusions based upon the movement of one average, unconfirmed by the other, are almost certain to prove misleading.[2]

Since the relationship between these two averages applies specif-ically to the trend of the broad market average, the applicability of the general trend model as practiced by countless technicians in today's world is fraught with error. The convenient omission of this relation-ship calls into question the applicability of the trend model as currently practiced by most technicians and its widespread adoption into countless technical tools. Essentially, today's practice of the trend model has cast aside one of the original key relationships because it no longer describes the landscape that modern technicians wish to model. Perhaps this occurred because it was convenient—or perhaps the relationship of two averages was abandoned out of ignorance. Whatever the case may be, the trend model used excessively today wasn't designed for what it is being applied to.

B Time Frames

Most technical literature has paraphrased Hamilton's original definition of trend in an isolated fashion. Specifically, when technicians speak of trend they usually say the trend for a stock or even a sector is up or down or sometimes sideways, irrespective of the time frame. The lack of clarity regarding the time frame is starkly apparent and leads to both confusion and disappointment on a regular basis.

Hamilton's writings, however, clearly spoke of time frames. His precise words, as related by Rhea, are "There are three movements of the averages, all of which may be in progress at one and the same time."[3]

In this one sentence, Hamilton clearly and concisely states that there are multiple trends (movements) at work at the same time. In the same quotation, he goes further to say that:

> *The first, and most important, is the primary trend: the broad upward or downward movements known as bull or bear markets, which may be of several years' duration. The second, and most deceptive movement, is the secondary reaction: an important decline in a primary bull market or a rally in a primary bear market. These reactions usually last from three weeks to as many months. The third, and usually unimportant, movement is the daily fluctuation.*[4]

Rhea goes on to give further explanations but Hamilton's thinking can be summarized as:

- Primary trends are defined as the broad, overall up and down movements, which usually last for more than a year and could run for several years.
- Secondary trends are defined as important reactions that interrupt the progress of prices in the primary direction (i.e., corrections to the primary trend).
- Minor trends are defined as brief fluctuations in price that rarely last as long as three weeks and usually less than six days and are unimportant—essentially they are "noise."

As was obvious to Hamilton, any model of trend must account for the fact that multiple trends are apparent at all times for a given instrument. They may be the same or they may be quite different. The notion that there is more than one is both critical and must be accounted for.

The classical trend model also recognizes that, although the trend of individual stocks is highly correlated to the general trend, they may be different.

> *All active and well distributed stocks of great American corporations generally rally and decline with the averages, but any individual stock may reflect conditions not applicable to the average price of any diversified list of stocks.*[5]

The implication of this relationship is once more tied to the objective of Hamilton's work. Since Hamilton's interest was in determining the broad market's direction (trend), he had to account for the fact that not all stocks would move in that same direction. Thus, in a strongly bullish market there would be stocks that were weak and, conversely, in an extremely weak market, there would remain stocks that were strong.

The implication of this acknowledgment is that there are separate trends for separate instruments that, although influenced by the broad market's movement, would not necessarily be moving in the same direction as the general market. Hamilton did not, however, integrate this notion into a workable set of rules and relationships that could be used to determine a trend for the separate instrument. The extent of his work was simply to acknowledge the disparity.

Identifying a Change of Trend

The identification of a trend change is explained in the context of the primary and secondary trend. As Hamilton related, the only trends you should have interest in are the primary and secondary. Knowing when a trend ends or begins is fraught with error though.

> *For the purposes of this discussion, a secondary reaction is considered to be an important decline in a bull market or advance in a bear market, usually lasting from three weeks to as many months, during which interval the price movement generally retraces from 33 percent to 66 percent of the primary price change since the termination of the last preceding secondary reaction.*[6] *[Emphasis added]*

This rule indicates that as much as two-thirds of the advance or decline could evaporate yet the trend could still be in place. In practice, few technicians are willing to sit by and watch such a significant portion of their gains evaporate (assuming their purchases occurred early enough to have accumulated gains). The proliferation of modern-day technical tools directed toward discovering a change in trend specifically attempts to reduce this onerous wait period. Hamilton indicated that there wasn't a better way.

APPLYING THE MODEL

Perhaps the best way to comprehend the classical trend model is to see it. As with every model, there is the theoretical and the practical. As we now know, the trend model was originally developed in order to determine the direction of the broad markets. To aid in that determination, the industrial and transportation averages were developed and tracked.

Figures 2.1 and 2.2 visually demonstrate an uptrend as defined by the classical trend model set forth by Dow and Hamilton.

FIGURE 2.1   Primary Bull Market—Dow Jones Industrial Index, January 30, 2003 to April 11, 2006

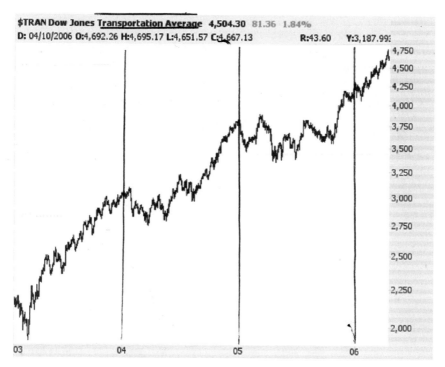

$TRAN Dow Jones Transportation Average 4,504.30 81.36 1.84%
D: 04/10/2006 **O:**4,692.26 **H:**4,695.17 **L:**4,651.57 **C:**4,667.13   **R:**43.60   **Y:**3,187.99

FIGURE 2.2 Primary Bull Market—Dow Jones Transportation Index, January 30, 2003 to April 11, 2006

In these two charts, all of the characteristics enumerated by Hamilton are present. The instruments observed are the Dow Jones Industrial Average (Figure 2.1) and the Dow Jones Transportation Average (Figure 2.2). Time is designated on the X-axis and price on the Y-axis. On each chart, there are a series (two or more) of higher price highs and higher price lows. The distance between the highs and lows exceeds the minimum of 3 percent.

Both the industrials and the transports are confirming the uptrend, and the time frame being confirmed is the primary trend. In all respects, these charts accurately reflect each of Hamilton's rules and relationships with respect to the trend model.

For a bearish primary trend, the charts are reversed, as shown in Figures 2.3 and 2.4.

Again, in each of these charts, the inputs, definitions, and relationships are quite evident.

Since the classical trend model is presently widely applied without regard to each of the basic tenets specified by Hamilton, the following charts

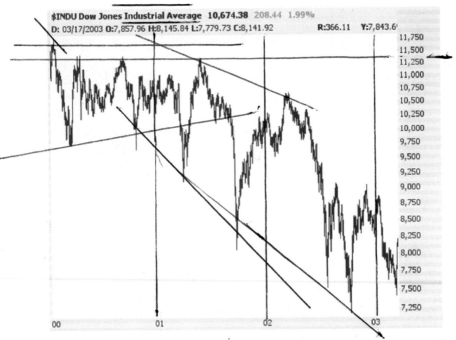

FIGURE 2.3 Primary Bear Market—Dow Jones Industrial Index, January 3, 2000 to March 17, 2003

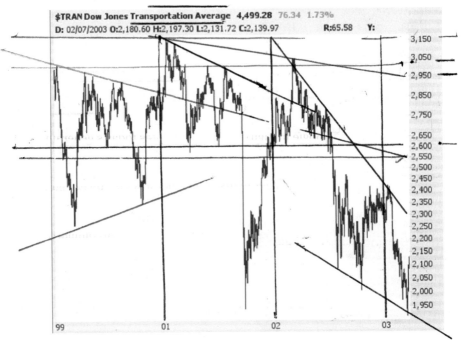

FIGURE 2.4 Primary Bear Market—Dow Jones Transportation Index, January 3, 2000 to March 17, 2003

GOOG Google Inc.(NQ NM) **492.28** 7.43 1.53%
D: 06/08/2009 O:439.50 H:440.92 L:434.12 C:438.77   R:6.80   Y:415.9679

Higher Price Highs

Higher Price Lows

FIGURE 2.5 Classical Chart of Uptrend—Google (GOOG), April 14, 2009 to June 12, 2009

demonstrate the practical modern-day application of the trend model and its pitfalls. Figure 2.5 displays today's generally accepted definition of an uptrend in Google stock over a two-month time frame. As required by the currently practiced notion of trend, a series of higher highs and higher lows are evident.

The same chart of Google in Figure 2.6 demonstrates today's generally accepted notion of a downtrend as well—just over a different time slice or time frame.

In both charts, a series of higher highs and higher lows or lower highs and lower lows are the primary determinants of a trend. Once two or more highs are created along with two or more higher lows, an uptrend is declared and remains in effect until two or more lower lows occur. Similarly, the end of a downtrend would contain the same characteristics, only in reverse order.

Expanding and combining these two charts, the end of an uptrend and beginning of a downtrend become apparent when viewed through the lens of the modern application of the classical trend model.

FIGURE 2.6 Classical Chart of Downtrend—Google (GOOG), May 6, 2009 to July 8, 2009

At this point, one must ask if this loosely defined notion of a trend is beneficial to traders. Based on the information in Figure 2.7, should you sell your stake in Google because the uptrend has evidently come to an end, as evidenced by two lower lows? Most traders would say "Yes!" More astute traders might qualify the answer saying "Yes, on this time frame." Both would be wrong. They would be wrong because they are using a trend model that no longer reflects the original relationships by Hamilton and never was designed to forecast trend for an individual instrument nor for a time frame other than the primary trend.

SUMMARY

In summary, the classical model of trend expressed the following basic rules and relationships:

- A trend is evident when two consecutive sets of higher highs and higher lows (uptrend) or lower highs and lower lows (downtrend)

2.6 NOT SAME 'TIME' FRAMES AS 2.7

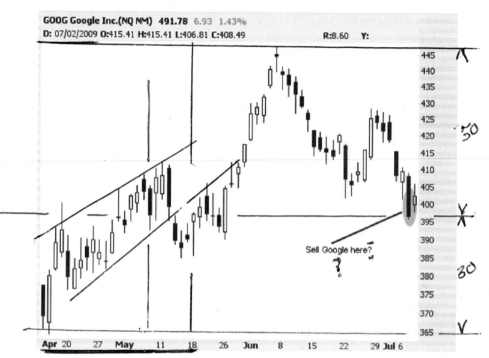

FIGURE 2.7 The End of an Uptrend—Google (GOOG), May 6, 2009 to July 8, 2009

occur. The intervening period between higher highs and higher lows requires a minimum of a 3 percent difference in prices.

- Both averages (industrials and transports) must confirm a trend change.
- Multiple time frames are always in existence, leading many market technicians to mistakenly believe that a primary trend change has occurred when in reality it hasn't. Again, a trend change requires two consecutive higher highs and higher lows or lower highs and lower lows confirmed by both averages.
- Not all instruments will necessarily follow the general market trend. This fact should be taken into account when identifying and following the general market trend.

In contrast, the trend model practiced today has been distilled to the following: A trend is evident when two consecutive sets of higher highs and higher lows (uptrend) or lower highs and lower lows (downtrend) occur within any given time frame. This practice is problematic, as discussed in the next chapter.

Also, Compare these with same data in Fig 3.2

Also, Read lead-in page 25

CHAPTER 3

Neoclassical Trend Model

With a reasonable understanding of how the classical trend model was originally constructed, it is easy to see how it has morphed into something far less desirable. Traders currently employ the model in a way that it was never intended to be used.

Refer back to Figure 2.7 to see an example of an apparent end to an uptrend in Google that would lead shorter-term traders to abandon their trading. The lower close creates a series of lower highs and lower lows—the very definition of a downtrend or, in this case, the termination of the uptrend. It is unambiguous based on the classical trend model as currently practiced, yet it is *absolutely the wrong time to sell*. If you had sold your Google shares on the notion that the uptrend had concluded, which would have been justified given the currently practiced model of trend, you would have done absolutely nothing wrong. Of course, this provides little solace to the ego and the pocketbook. Traders and investors buy and sell stocks, commodities, and other financial instruments to make money.

As can be seen from Figure 3.1, selling Google based on the currently practiced view of the classical trend model would have taken the trader out of a trade while the uptrend was far from being over. In fact, Google was really just getting started, as it would climb another $230, all the way to almost $630, before the uptrend ended.

If a trend model is a tool that traders use, it needs to be a tool that fits the environment that they are trading and consistently leads to profitable results. It is required to be *right* most of the time. Thus, one might ask the obvious: "Is such a desired outcome possible, and if so, how might that model work?"

FIGURE 3.1 A Mistaken End of an Uptrend—Google (GOOG), April 14, 2009 to January 11, 2010

The answer is, of course, the subject matter of this book. Such a tool does exist. It is referred to as the neoclassical trend model and it contains an additional input, a modified definition, and a new set of rules and relationships. The neoclassical trend model no longer consists of black and white—up or down and nothing in between. It displays varying shades of trend. It qualifies trend on a more granular level; a level that allows the trader to make intelligent decisions based more on probability than supposed absolutes.

OBJECTIVE OF THE MODEL

The objective of the neoclassical trend model is to extend the range of trend modeling as compared to the classical model in terms of instruments that are capable of being modeled and in terms of the time frames modeled. Both of these objectives must be met with a model that has a reasonably high predictive capability. If this can be done, then the acute deficiencies of the modern application of the classical model can be overcome.

The neoclassical trend model looks and behaves significantly different from the classical model; the simplest way to begin to get a feel for it is through the examination of a few charts. The most significant advantage to this new and improved model is that it is constructed with the objective of measuring trend in varying instruments across all time frames, which is, after all, how traders want to use it. It doesn't hurt that it also qualifies the trend *as it unfolds*.

In Figure 3.2, the same Google chart presented previously is revisited. In this chart, the additional input to the model is highlighted (volume) along with its effects. Volume is compared along with price when determining trend and it is done at a particular time—at the swing points.

In this chart it is evident that, as prices declined, volume likewise declined. The critical question that the neoclassical model always asks is "What was the comparative volume at the previous swing point as the current price violated that area?"

FIGURE 3.2 Neoclassical Trend Model—Google (GOOG), May 2009 to August 2009

In the case of Google, when the lower price low occurred, volume decreased as compared to volume at the previous swing point low. Think about that for a second. The number of sellers actually decreased as prices moved lower. There was neither the desire nor the urgency to sell the shares by the vast majority of the shareholders. The actual volume statistics in this example were approximately 4.1 million shares at the first low and 3.3 million shares at the second—almost 25 percent fewer shares traded at the lower price. Clearly the bulk of the potential sellers chose not to sell their shares at the lower prices.

If the holders of Google stock were unwilling to sell their shares *as the price continued to decline,* then doesn't that call into question the notion that the trend is actually changing? Does it seem reasonable to assume that a bearish trend has begun to unfold? Isn't this purported trend change a bit suspicious?

Suspect Trend

When the current price trades lower (downtrend) or higher (uptrend) than the previous swing point price and volume contracts, the trend is suspect.

Suspicion and confirmation are the two qualifiers used in the neoclassical trend model. If, in the above example, volume had expanded as the swing point broke, then the trend qualifier would be *confirmed.*

Confirmed Trend

When the current price trades lower (downtrend) or higher (uptrend) than the previous swing point price and volume expands, the trend is confirmed.

In general, and in the particular case of the Google trade, if you had a position in Google when a suspect trend change occurred, you should be less likely to sell because the potential trend change is *suspect.* As we shall see, a suspect trend change doesn't mean that prices can't continue in the direction of the suspect trend—it's just that the probability of doing so decreases. A suspect trend is just that: suspicious. It is dangerous to simply trust it without reservation. A suspect trend change should temper your anxiousness to participate. It adds color to the notion of a trend.

With suspect and confirmed qualifiers, the notion that not all trends are created equal begins to resonate. Qualifying trends is the art of separating the
trends you can trust from those that you cannot. As we shall see further
on, the degree of trust is not performed in a vacuum but instead results
from a blending of time frames, other technical constructs, and the varying instruments being observed. Much more about those ideas is presented
throughout this book.

This notion of trend qualification applies equally to both up- and down-
trends. For confirmation, there needs to be enthusiasm in buying or selling a stock, and that enthusiasm needs to be exhibited at the critical
moment—whenever a swing point is crossed. There are sound reasons for
the notion that swing points hold extremely high significance when determining trend. After all, typically it is at the swing points where new price
discovery occurs. In the vast majority of cases, swing points are found at
the edge of the existing price range—usually forming the boundary that
separates existing and accepted price points from undiscovered higher or
lower ones. To commit to buying or selling a stock at a new high or a new
low requires conviction and it is at the swing points that conviction is most
visible. It is a time where the buyer or seller of a stock can no longer hide
in the crowd of bids and asks for the stock. The pressure to step away and
discontinue the buys or sells at new highs or lows is great. It takes a lot of
resolve to persevere. If prices breach a prior swing point high or low and
there are a greater number of buyers or sellers, then information regarding
the significance of the move is transmitted to all who are willing to listen.
It is at the swing points where the market speaks in an unmistakable and
forceful manner. It is at the swing points where trends are born and die.

INPUTS

Trend qualification takes four inputs; an additional input is added to the
original model created by Dow. The inputs Dow used—the instrument being measured, its price, and time—are joined by volume. For the neoclassical trend model, volume becomes a significant qualifying factor when a
swing point is tested.

Although in the narrowest sense volume characteristics are significant
at the swing points, there are additional areas of applicability for volume
characteristics outside the confines of the trend model. The significance of
this statement shall become more visibly apparent further on, as we wade
through the actual application of the model.

❷ MODEL DEFINITION

In the neoclassical trend model, there remain three trend directions, although each of the three is qualified. Trend is no longer just bullish (up), bearish (down), or sideways. It's no longer all or nothing. Trend now has qualification. Before defining trend, however, a few preliminary definitions that add clarity to the definition of trend are discussed.

Bars

Every equity chart consists, at a minimum, of three items. On the Y-axis is price, while on the X-axis is time. Within the confines of the space demarcated by price and time, there are bars representing the opening and closing prices as well as the extreme high and low price for the bar. We use the commonly known bar to represent a span of time. To show the flexible extremes of this graphic, consider a chart that spans four hours of trading where each bar represents a five-minute interval compared to a 10-year chart where each bar represents three months. Bars allow for the abstract concept of time to be represented on charts.

Note that all popular charting packages offer bar graphs using either high-low bars or "candlesticks." The charts you see in this book are all candlestick charts, simply because they reveal more information at a glance once you grow accustomed to reading them. Either bar charts or candlestick charts are acceptable for trend modeling and both represent the following data points for each and every bar:

- High price
- Low price
- Opening price
- Closing price

In addition, every charting package also associates two other critical data points with each bar. One is the notation for the bar itself, indicating the time that each bar represents, whether it be one-minute, one-year, or any other increment that can be conceived in between these two extremes.

The second critical item is a volume bar that correlates to the price bar. This can be represented in any quantitative increment as supplied by any reliable provider. The only critical item is that, for swing-point comparisons, you should always compare volume and price bars from the same data provider. You do this to make certain that you are comparing apples to apples and not to oranges.

Another item relating to volume is the question of what volume one uses, given the proliferation of before- and after-hours trading. Ideally, the volume used should reflect all volume that occurred for the instrument being examined during the period of time reflected in the bar's high, low, opening, and closing prices. For comparison purposes, you can compare only to a similar bar. For example, it would not be valid to compare a volume/price bar in after-hours trading to a volume/price bar in normal-hours trading.

○ Swing Points

In most cases, swing points are a common term used to signify a high or low bar on a chart where prices once traded to but turned away from. As implied, swing points consist of two types; swing point highs and swing point lows. Swing points rest at the core of trend qualification. Without them, qualification would be impossible. But how does a particular bar become a swing point? What actualizes a swing point? What moves a swing point from potential to actual?

When observing a chart with the desire of identifying swing points, the first step is to note the high and low of the current bar and to compare that to the preceding bar. If the high of the current bar is higher than the preceding bar, then the currently examined bar has the potential to be a swing point high. Conversely, if the low is lower than the previous bar, then it has the potential to be a swing point low. Note that if the bar being examined has both a higher high and a lower low than the preceding bar, then it has the potential to be either a swing point high or low. In rare cases, it can actually end up being both.

Potential swing points become actual swing points based solely on time and price action. For a potential swing point to actualize, the swing point must remain the highest high or the lowest low for a specified period of time. The time element can be optimized for differing markets and equities, but my research has shown that six bars tends to represent the optimal "wait time" across most equities, sectors, and general market indexes. Five to seven bars seems to harmonize the best with most markets and individual stocks. Whether it is five to seven days, five to seven weeks, or five to seven months, the market has a way of usually backing and filling after that period of time once a move begins. As we shall see later, the desire is to always gain the earliest possible recognition that a trend no longer exists but to be alerted to that only in those cases where the trend truly has changed. The fewer bars it takes to signify a trend change, the faster the notification of the change. The tradeoff is that the earlier the notification, the greater the number of false reads.

Specifically stated, whenever a potential swing point has remained the highest high (potential swing point high) or the lowest low (potential swing point low) for six successive bars, then the potential swing point becomes actualized. Programmatically, a counter for successive highs and successive lows would be maintained and the coding snippet might look something like the following:

↓ **Potential and Actualized Swing Low Coding Snippet**

```
For each successive bar read ...
If the SuccessiveLows counter is greater than 6
Then the PotentialSwingLow becomes an ActualizedSwingLow.
Reset the SuccessiveLows counter to 1 and record the
ActualizedSwingLow. Mark the current bar as the "new"
PotentialSwingLow.
Else If the low of the new bar yields a lower low than the
PotentialSwingLow
Then that bar replaces the PotentialSwingLow. Reset the
SuccessiveLows counter to one.
Else if the low of the new bar yields a higher low than the
previous low bar
Then increment the SuccessiveLows counter by one
```

The same coding snippet would apply to swing highs as well.

↓ **Potential and Actualized Swing High Algorithm Snippet**

```
For each successive bar read ...
If the SuccessiveHighs counter is greater than 6
Then the PotentialSwingHigh becomes an ActualizedSwingHigh.
Reset the SuccessiveHighs counter to 1 and record the
ActualizedSwingHigh. Mark the current bar as the "new"
PotentialSwingHigh.
Else If the high of the new bar yields a higher high than
the PotentialSwingHigh
Then that bar replaces the PotentialSwingHigh. Reset the
SuccessiveHighs counter to one.
Else if the high of the new bar yields a lower high than
the previous high bar
Then increment the SuccessiveHighs counter by one
```

FIGURE 3.3 Actualized Swing Point Highs and Lows—SPY SPDR S&P 500 ETF, March 1, 2002 to August 1, 2006

When actualizing a swing point, the information that needs to be recorded and referred to again and again for future swing point tests is the high or low that the swing point defines as well as the volume associated with the actualized swing point.

Figure 3.3 shows multiple actualized swing point highs and lows on a long time frame (over four years of data) for a very bullish time period. Although some of the actualized swing points may seem unnatural and arbitrary, the methodology for how to determine them is presented shortly. [For the sake of brevity, throughout the book, actualized swing point highs and lows are simply referred to as "swing point high" or "swing point low." When speaking generically (referring to either a low or high), the terminology utilized is simply "swing points." When speaking of potential swing points rather than actualized swing points, then the explicit term *potential swing points* is used. Furthermore, in the figures the following notation is used for brevity: SPL (actualized swing point low), SPH (actualized swing point high), PSPL (potential swing point low), PSPH (potential swing point high).

Note that one characteristic of the neoclassical model is that in a strongly trending market (up or down), swing points are naturally created as prices move higher and higher. This serves a very useful purpose, as shall be demonstrated later.

Testing Swing Points

Swing point tests are the mechanism for qualifying trend. Trends are necessarily transitory states, always transitioning from one trend state to another and doing so as a result of swing point tests. Swing point tests not only assist in the identification of trend transitions but also in the reaffirmation of existing trends.

Swing point tests necessarily consist of one of two types: a swing point high test or a swing point low test. The definitions, as you would expect, are similar.

Swing Point High Test
A swing point high test occurs when the current bar's high exceeds the previous and nearest (nearest in terms of a higher price) swing point high.

Swing Point Low Test
A swing point low test occurs when the current bar's low exceeds the previous and nearest (nearest in terms of a lower price) swing point low.

Defining a swing point test is reasonably simple when compared to defining the success or failure of such a test. It is much too easy to confuse the meaning of a successful test as opposed to a failed test because the conveyance of success or failure is necessarily tied to the existing trend in which the test occurs as well as the type of test that is being conducted (a test in the direction of the prevailing trend or against it).

As an example, if the trend is currently bullish and a test occurs that attempts to capture and exceed a prior swing point high (in the direction of the prevailing trend), then, to be successful, it would need to actually capture and exceed the previous swing point high's price. A failure would be where price pushed higher but closed lower than the high price of the prior swing point high. It is a failure because the trend wasn't extended.

It is worth noting that even in this circumstance a new potential swing point high is established.

If, on the other hand, the trend is currently bullish and a test of a swing point low occurs (against the prevailing trend), then a successful test would result if the price traded lower than the low of the swing point low but closed higher than that same low. It is successful because the prevailing trend is maintained. A failure would create a trend transition (from bullish to sideways in this case).

When qualifying trends, there are two trend designators for each of the three trends, making a total of six trends that require labeling. A bullish trend can be either "confirmed bullish" or "suspect bullish." The same is true for a sideways trend, which can be "confirmed sideways" or "suspect sideways." Finally, a bearish trend also appears in the two forms, "confirmed bearish" or "suspect bearish." The only addition to this notation is for a sideways trend where sometimes no qualifier exists at all. In that case, the sideways trend is deemed ambivalent.

The formal definitions for each of the qualified trends are:

Bullish Trend

- *Confirmed bullish trend.* As part of the same directional move, a series of higher price highs and higher price lows (not necessarily sequential), where price trades above and closes higher than the most recent previous swing point high, while volume expands as compared to volume at the previous swing point high.
- *Suspect bullish trend.* As part of the same directional move, a series of higher price highs and higher price lows (not necessarily sequential), where price trades above and closes higher than the most recent previous swing point high, while volume contracts as compared to volume at the previous swing point high.

Bearish Trend

- *Confirmed bearish trend.* As part of the same directional move, a series of lower price highs and lower price lows (not necessarily sequential), where price trades below and closes lower than the most recent previous swing point low, while volume expands as compared to volume at the previous swing point low.
- *Suspect bearish trend.* As part of the same directional move, a series of lower price highs and lower price lows (not necessarily sequential), where price trades below and closes lower than the most recent previous swing point low, while volume contracts as compared to volume at the previous swing point low.

Sideways Trend

- *Confirmed sideways trend.* The interruption of a bullish or bearish trend where sequential swing points interrupt the existing trend of higher highs and higher lows, or lower highs and lower lows, while volume expands on that interruption.
- *Suspect sideways trend.* The interruption of a bullish or bearish trend where sequential swing points interrupt the existing trend of higher highs and higher lows, or lower highs and lower lows, while volume contracts on that interruption.
- *Ambivalent sideways trend.* A sideways trend that is the result of ambivalence. An ambivalent sideways trend does not result from a swing point test but instead comes about without a test as additional swing points are created. An ambivalent sideways trend occurs when there exists a series of swing points where no swing point test is involved, resulting in the actualization of two lower swing point highs and two higher swing point lows, or two higher swing point highs and two lower swing point lows.

Each of these definitions includes qualifications in the two conditional statements contained within the definition. Trend is qualified based on the behavior of *volume* and the *closing price* as compared to the previous swing point. To reaffirm a trend or to confirm a trend transition, price and volume are examined in tandem, not in isolation.

Another notation that has illustrative value is the use of color when referring to trend. A suspect trend would be noted as red, denoting caution and concern, while a confirmed trend is usually denoted as green, which is commonly thought of as a positive direction in which all systems are "go." In using color, trends can be easily identified instantaneously in the same way candlestick charts use color to provide instant information regarding the positive or negative associated with each candle bar.

Upon reflection, by combining these two qualifiers (price and volume) we have, in a way, come full circle to the original definition of trend put forth by Dow and Hamilton more than a century ago. In their model, the recognition of a primary trend required the two indexes they created (industrials and the transports) and tracked to *confirm* one another. In a similar vein, in the neoclassical model we track volume and price at the swing points and suggest that these two characteristics need to confirm one another for trend to be wholeheartedly believed. If confirmation isn't present, then that gives rise to suspicion and distrust, much in the same way that nonconfirmation between the industrial and transportation indexes in the Dow Theory could not be trusted.

RULES FOR THE MODEL

The input variables and definitions are governed by and bound together by the rules and relationships. Those rules and relationships are the glue that binds the model together. In the neoclassical model of trend, there aren't an excessive number of rules. The rule specifications of the neoclassical definition of trend are presented in the following paragraphs, but the framework of their application and nuances inherent in that framework are fleshed out in the remainder of the book.

Every market, market sector, and security is always trending. The trend may be bullish (up), bearish (down), or sideways, but a trend is always in effect. From the prior definitions, we know that there are three basic trends leading to a total of six qualified trends (seven if you include the ambivalent sideways trend).

The labeling of a trend as confirmed or suspect is dependent on what the market reveals at the swing points. It is volume at the swing points that provides the information needed to qualify trends. Over time most stocks, stock sectors, and general market indexes travel full circle, passing through all these trends as the business cycle plays out. This isn't always the case but is generally true. Thus, the charts that follow all depict the SPDR S&P 500 ETF (SPY) at various points in time, each of which captures each of the possible six trend types.[1] Each chart is a one-year weekly chart. Annotations clarifying the trend example are included along with a paragraph or two clarifying and reiterating the trend's characteristics.

Confirmed Bullish Trend

Figure 3.4 displays a confirmed bullish trend. A confirmed bullish trend requires a series of higher price highs and higher price lows (a minimum of two highs and lows),where each successive price high closes higher than the previous swing point high and volume expands to confirm the break when compared to the previous swing point high.

Note that as price rises and closes above the previous swing point high, a new swing point high is guaranteed to be created (even though it is not actualized just yet). That part creates the bullish trend. The other part is for volume to expand and it did—505 million shares compared to the prior swing point high of 271 million.

Suspect Bullish Trend

Figure 3.5 continues the chart from the previous figure, showing the ETF a couple months later in 2006. In this figure, the final thrust higher takes

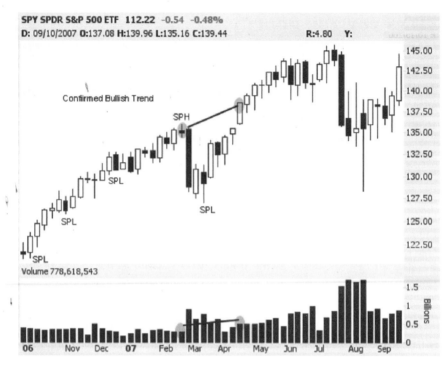

FIGURE 3.4 Confirmed Bullish Trend—SPY SPDR S&P 500 ETF, September 18, 2006 to September 17, 2007

price over the previous high and closes there, but volume diminishes. That creates a suspect bullish trend.

Similar to a confirmed bullish trend, a suspect bullish trend requires a series of higher price highs and higher price lows, although not necessarily sequentially. In this particular example, there is a lower swing point low just prior to the higher swing point high. As shown in examples further on, this sometimes occurs and is part and parcel of the model. The fact that a higher high registers is enough to change the trend back to bullish, but only suspect bullish, because volume is lacking. Many tops in stocks and the market are created in this manner.

Confirmed Bearish Trend

A confirmed bearish trend has essentially the opposite configuration of a confirmed bullish trend, as shown in Figure 3.6. In this chart, a series of lower price highs and lower price lows are needed but, most importantly, a test of a swing point low has to occur and succeed (the low is broken and

FIGURE 3.5 Suspect Bullish Trend—SPY SPDR S&P 500 ETF, November 6, 2006 to November 5, 2007

closed under) while volume expands. In almost all cases[2] it also needs to occur where the existing trend is sideways—not bullish. A sideways trend is the normal buffer between bullish and bearish trends.

In this particular chart, the suspect sideways trend transitions to confirmed bearish when not one but two swing point lows are knocked out in one fatal swoop on expanding volume.

Suspect Bearish Trend

A suspect bearish trend mirrors a confirmed bearish trend except that volume does not confirm. Figure 3.7 displays such a configuration although it is murky because the transition from a suspect bullish trend all the way to a suspect bearish trend takes place on one single bar.

The first swing point low that is removed is the rightmost swing point low shown in the Figure. The test of that swing point low was successful in that it traded and closed under the low on increased volume. The result was a transition from suspect bullish to confirmed sideways trend.

FIGURE 3.6 Confirmed Bearish Trend—SPY SPDR S&P 500 ETF, July 9, 2007 to July 7, 2008

On the exact same bar, price also traded below the next prior swing point low (leftmost shaded bar), and again it closed under that bar as well. In this case, however, volume on the testing bar was less than volume at the prior swing point low. The result in this case was another trend transition, this time from the confirmed sideways trend just registered to a suspect bearish trend.

Confirmed Sideways Trend

Figure 3.5 includes an interesting formation that is highlighted in Figure 3.8. The formation was higher volume lows and lower volume highs that were indicative of the fact that the SPY ETF was beginning to show signs of wear and tear after having been in a bull market since 2003. By the end of 2006, the price declines were creating lower swing point lows, yet the price of the SPY ETF would nevertheless climb to higher highs, reestablishing the bullish trend. Each time swing point lows were tested and broken, volume expanded and price closed below the previous swing point low.

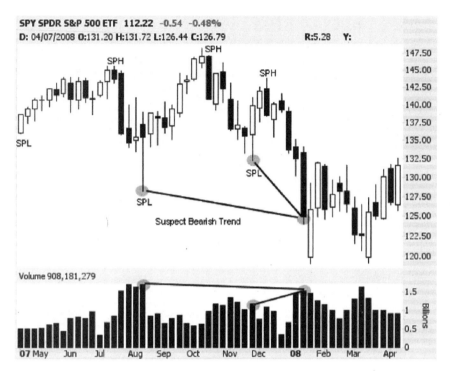

SPY SPDR S&P 500 ETF **112.22** **-0.54** **-0.48%**
D: 04/07/2008 O:131.20 H:131.72 L:126.44 C:126.79   R:5.28   Y:

FIGURE 3.7 Suspect Bearish Trend—SPY SPDR S&P 500 ETF, April 16, 2007 to April 14, 2008

The fact that volume expanded was the market's way of confirming that the strength of the trend had indeed changed. Because sideways trends are often referred to as consolidation periods or range trades in the technical literature, they are often looked upon as indecision states. The neoclassical model really doesn't change this concept other than recognizing that a sideways trend can be strong or weak. The model also reflects the idea that trend transitions from bullish to bearish or bearish to bullish pass through the sideways trend state as part of that transition. As shown in Figure 3.8, sometimes that transition is rather brief though and practically unnoticeable.

A confirmed sideways trend can occur in either direction. One method is to transition from a bullish trend to a sideways one. Another possibility is to transition to a sideways trend from a previously bearish trend. The example shown in Figure 3.8 is the transition from a bullish to a sideways trend. A confirmed sideways trend implies that the previous trend is probably complete on this time frame with decreased odds of an immediate

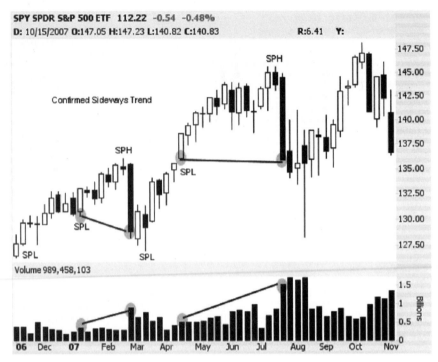

FIGURE 3.8 Confirmed Sideways Trend—SPY SPDR S&P 500 ETF, November 6, 2006 to November 5, 2007

restart. Clearly, in the case of the SPY ETF in Figure 3.8, those odds were beaten, not once but twice.

Suspect Sideways Trend

In Figure 3.9, a suspect sideways trend occurs when prices bounce in early April 2008, overtaking the bounce that occurs immediately after the extreme selling that took place from the end of December 2007 through the first two weeks of January 2008. As prices moved higher and higher, eventually the swing point high was overrun, but volume did not expand. The lack of volume made the transition to a sideways trend suspect.

Ambivalent Sideways Trend

Ambivalent sideways trends are reasonably rare occurrences but they do happen and, for completeness, have to be accounted for. Figure 3.10 is an example of the creation of an ambivalent sideways trend. Note that no

FIGURE 3.9 Suspect Sideways Trend—SPY SPDR S&P 500 ETF, July 9, 2007 to Jully 7, 2008

swing point test occurs as part of the trend's creation. The fact that a higher low (once actualized) creates a series of higher lows with a series of lower highs leads to a sideways trend and ambivalence.

Trends Are a Cyclical Smorgasbord

The markets are cyclical. The same patterns occur again and again, and the three trends and six resultant qualified trend designations, as shown in the SPY ETF charts, are just one of many possible examples. Figure 3.11 spans the entire time frame for the six individual charts (Figures 3.4 to 3.9) and drives home the notion that trends come into existence and eventually disappear with the sideways trend serving as the conduit from bullish to bearish and vice versa.

What is quite fascinating about this chart and the markets in general is that stocks and markets often come full circle. Looking at Figure 3.11, you can see just how true that aphorism is. From a confirmed bullish trend all the way to the opposite confirmed bearish trend, the stock market

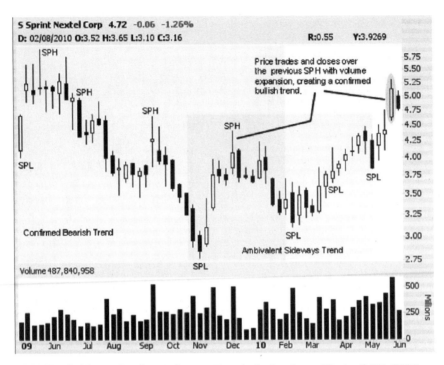

S Sprint Nextel Corp 4.72 -0.06 -1.26%
D: 02/08/2010 O:3.52 H:3.65 L:3.10 C:3.16   R:0.55   Y:3.9269

SPH

SPH

SPH

SPH

SPL

Price trades and closes over the previous SPH with volume expansion, creating a confirmed bullish trend.

SPL

Confirmed Bearish Trend

Ambivalent Sideways Trend

SPL

SPL

SPL

Volume 487,840,958

SPL

09 Jun Jul Aug Sep Oct Nov Dec 10 Feb Mar Apr May Jun

FIGURE 3.10 Ambivalent Sideways Trend—Sprint Corp. (S), April 27, 2009 to June 1, 2010

as measured through the SPY SPDR S&P 500 ETF completed the business cycle of boom and bust, traveling all the way up to new highs then all the way back down again. Along the way, the qualified trends were identified and provided early warning signs for those traders who were listening and looking—warnings to get into the market and warnings to get out.

Time Frames

Time frames are arbitrarily chosen periods of time during which the analysis of trend occurs. The vast majority of technicians have standardized their charts with bar widths of daily, weekly, and monthly durations, although there isn't an agreed-upon period in which to display those bars. For example, should a technician typically set the time period at three, six, or even nine months when examining daily bars? What is the appropriate length of time to use when examining the short-term time frame?

In Hamilton's writings, the long-term trend (primary trend) was spoken of as lasting as many as several years in duration, while the

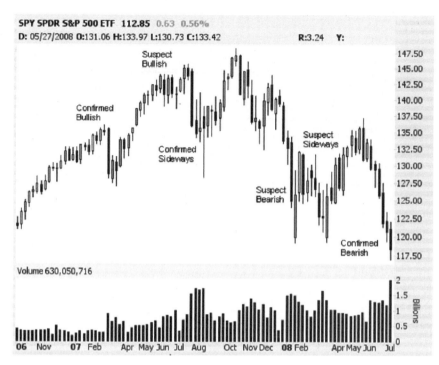

SPY SPDR S&P 500 ETF 112.85 0.63 0.56%
D: 05/27/2008 O:131.06 H:133.97 L:130.73 C:133.42   R:3.24   Y:

FIGURE 3.11 Cyclical Nature of the Market and Trend Transition—SPY SPDR S&P 500 ETF, September 18, 2006 to July 7, 2008

intermediate-term trend (secondary trend) was suggested as lasting from three weeks to many months. Again, there is no agreed-upon time frame.

Rather than struggling with the absence of an agreed-upon time frame for analyzing each of the three trends, it seems more appropriate to approach the problem in a different manner. This time-frame problem actually has two characteristics: the width of the bar and the length of time examined.

Given that it takes six consecutive bars of higher or lower prices to create a swing point, clearly the time frame needs to be long enough to allow sufficient time for swing points to spring into existence. Examining a chart with only 15 price bars, for example, is unlikely to yield any swing points. Conversely, a chart with 200 price bars is probably excessive, as far too many swing points will occur.

As for the width of the bar, it seems logical to use the generally agreed-upon bar widths of daily, weekly, and monthly changes across the three time frames of short, intermediate, and long term.

Ideally, it is advantageous to consider roughly the same number of bars across all three time frames. When constructing a daily chart, three months of data results in roughly 60 bars. The same is true when analyzing the intermediate-term time frames using a year's worth of data consisting of weekly bars. Finally, a five-year chart using monthly bars likewise provides a roughly equal number of bars for the long-term analysis. Algorithmically, use of these numbers as standards for time-frame analysis results in a reasonable consistency across all time frames and removes the need to treat the analysis of differing time frames differently.

The significance of time-frame analysis shall be considered in greater depth in the following chapters, but, naturally, differing trends may exist on differing time frames for the same instrument. When broadening the instruments being studied to include market sectors and the general broad market indexes, then differences between the trend of the instruments across the same and differing time frames are almost guaranteed. By marrying time-frame analysis across varying instruments using qualified trends, trading decisions can be vastly improved.

SUMMARY

History is replete with examples of improvements to existing systems. Whether physical or theoretical, improvements typically result from the synthesis of prior knowledge with new thoughts and methods. Eventually, through trial and error, a new workable knowledge springs forth with increased or improved capabilities expressed through a more complete understanding.

In the world of trend analysis, Charles Dow and William Hamilton set out over a century ago to create a methodology to forecast the future movement of stocks. They settled upon the notion of trend, while creating and tracking a couple of indexes, and then proceeded to document what they found.

As often happens in the name of progress, their work has evolved over the years and the concepts as presented have been bent and twisted into a set of tools and procedures that neither Dow nor Hamilton would likely recognize. Such is the nature of progress sometimes.

Now, in the twenty-first century, we reevaluate the ideas of these two giants of finance. We reconsider their ideas with an eye toward uncovering their true meaning. With an understanding of the initial assumptions, we use that knowledge to consider how a more perfect trend model could be constructed.

Based on years of trading and study, this book is the culmination of that endeavor. It keeps trend as the centerpiece of an approach to determine price direction, just as Dow and Hamilton sought to over a hundred years ago. It seeks to improve upon their work by creating a model that allows a practitioner to both determine trend and forecast the likelihood of its continuation across all instruments and over varying time frames. The model is the neoclassical model, and it entails the qualification of trend as measured by volume at the swing points. These swing point tests properly confirm or draw suspicion to the trend created. The singular notion of trend is replaced with dual values: confirmed or suspect. Trends are no longer treated as one and the same but as consisting of two flavors.

Trends continually come into existence and eventually end. This happens over time, and given the cyclical nature of the business cycle trend, transitions throughout the business cycle repeat as well. The transitions follow a pattern just as the business cycles that drive them. The examination of trend across a multiplicity of time frames reveals their interrelationships, thus shedding light on the transitions that have occurred and are likely to occur. The complex can be made simple. Qualified trends, their transitions, and the relationships between the market, sectors, and stocks all can be examined for predictive capabilities. It may sound like a daunting task, and at times it feels like one, but the complexities are within reason and the value gained can be immeasurable.

Chapter 4 lifts the hood on the neoclassical model and studies its internal workings more carefully. Elaborations on such notions as the swing point logic and how to identify swing points are performed. Various swing point formations are considered along with a more in-depth discussion of how to determine and qualify trends. The related concept of "retest and regenerate" is also introduced. The objective is to provide a solid understanding of the theory and intricacies of the model with sufficient detail so that the application of the model can begin. It is with a thorough inspection of the model that *true trend* can be understood, and Chapter 4 seeks to provide that deeper understanding.

True Trend

True trend, as it applies to securities trading, is the result of trend qualification: the act of qualifying trends as suspect or confirmed on each of the time frames.

CHAPTER 4

Determining Trends

Traders constantly attempt to determine both the direction and the directional conviction of the instrument they are trading. For the sake of simplicity and illustration, I shall assume that the instrument being traded is a stock. If a trader wished to either purchase (go long) or short sell (go short) a stock, it is important that they have a good sense of the trend for that stock on the time frame that they wish to trade. As we will see, a superior strategy is not only to have this information readily available but also to know the sector trend for the stock as well as the general market trend. This will be discussed in more depth further on, but for now, I will concentrate on describing a stock's trend—its true trend—the strength of that trend and the likelihood of that trend continuing. In later chapters I will expand this notion to include other factors that influence the stock, rather than examining it in isolation.

FUNDAMENTALS FOR THE LONG TERM

"In the long run," John Maynard Keynes once said, "we are all dead."[1] His reference, though made in a different context, is quite applicable to stock markets anywhere in the world. The point is that, although fundamentals ultimately are reflective of the *real* value of a stock, in the short run you can easily lose all your money betting on the fundamentals. Said another way, in the end stock prices do reflect the true fundamentals of the companies they represent because stock prices eventually are reflective of what a company earns and is expected to earn. As time passes, perception

49

becomes reality and prices adjust to reflect this reality. All the while, a new set of perceptions continues to be created because an abundance of additional influences that can and will affect a stock's price always come forth. Thus, although the fundamentals do matter, they usually matter most *in the long run*. Meantime, in the short run, you can go broke trading the long run using only fundamentals.

Making money trading stocks typically requires a trader to synchronize with price direction for the time frame being traded. When investing in a company on a two- or three-year horizon, then trading the fundamentals might represent a reasonable approach. Most investors and traders, however, are most likely unable to accurately assess a company's fundamentals for the long run. Worse, they probably will be unwilling or unable to sit tight in a stock that they believe has great long-term fundamentals if the price declines by some large percentage while they wait. That is why many traders are technical in their approach and tend to gravitate toward the use of trend when making both investing and trading decisions.

SWING POINT LOGIC

The neoclassical trend model has, as a fundamental assumption, the notion that the ideal place to measure the affirmation or dismissal of trend is at the swing points. Since the discovery of true trend is the objective, the notion that true trend can be discerned when a swing point test occurs is at the heart of the model. This necessitates some additional discussion.

Consider Figure 4.1. In this chart, it is quite obvious that the highlighted swing point is at the edge of the price boundary for the time frame displayed.

Now consider what it would take for prices to push over the edge of the annotated swing point high and trade higher. What would it take to engage a large enough number of buyers with sufficient firepower to become aggressive enough to bid prices higher than the $48.77 price point that, heretofore, has served as a cap on price? What would it take not only to see prices trade higher than $48.77 but to do so based on increased enthusiasm, as measured through increased volume? Wouldn't that suggest to all viewers that something significant has happened or is about to happen with Celgene? That is what the market does, after all: It discovers price. That discovery mechanism is the result of the constant bidding between buyers and sellers in a free market where all known news that affects the share price of Celgene is discounted immediately.

Consider for a moment the discounting process. Information is discounted immediately once widely known, through the discounting

FIGURE 4.1 Swing Point High—Celgene Corporation (CELG), May 11, 2009 July 22, 2009

mechanism, which works in one of two ways. One way is for a public announcement to be made, in which the information is disseminated simultaneously to all interested parties. Investors and traders either buy or sell the stock based on the disseminated news at the time that it is announced. In this arrangement, price moves *with the news*.

The other possibility is for price to *precede the news*. When price precedes news, it is usually because one or more of the large players in the stock has price-impacting information that has yet to be made public. This is a clear example of insider knowledge guiding some traders to buy or sell. The law enforcement side of the Securities and Exchange Commission (SEC) makes it amply clear that insider trading does occur, and for every prosecution that takes place it can be safely assumed that there are probably dozens if not hundreds of cases of insider trading that are never brought to justice.

Consider the situation. Assume that the traders with insider knowledge have significant resources at their disposal, either individually or as a group. Furthermore, assume that the information they are privy to has significant profit potential. If they act on this knowledge, they will begin to purchase the stock, and the increased buying pressure will force prices higher. Others will notice the movement and will join in, thinking that someone must know something. All of this occurs in the absence of news. It is, however, reflected in the charts.

The hypothetical situation just described occurs on a much more frequent basis than most would think. Where there are large sums of money to be made, there will be unscrupulous players trying to get it. Greed and money go hand-in-hand on Wall Street. This has been true ever since the New York Stock Exchange came into being. To think otherwise is to be naive. It will be the case until Wall Street is no more.

Regardless of the method by which news is disseminated, evidence of the news always finds its way to the charts. The chart impact is naturally dependent on the significance of the new information and how it affects the company's fortunes. Continuing with the Celgene chart, Figure 4.2 displays the effect of the simultaneous distribution of price-impacting news. In this particular case, Celgene's earnings and clinical trial data were released simultaneously and the positive potential growth of share price was great.[2]

FIGURE 4.2 Break of Swing Point High on Simultaneous News Distribution—Celgene Corporation (CELG), May 11, 2009 to August 3, 2009

The news release results in a gap up in price that quickly begins to reflect the newly released information. The market always attempts to immediately discount newly released information that has an impact on current and potential earnings. In this particular case, the news pushes prices over the previous swing point high and the event occurs with conviction, as evidenced by increased volume.

Consider what the chart pattern in Figure 4.2 really says about the mind-set of the buyers. The fact that prices gap higher *and over a swing point high* requires confidence on the part of the buyers. For buyers to pay a significantly greater price than had heretofore been paid, and to do so in increasing numbers, says a lot about the buyer's perception of the company's financial future. Rightly or wrongly, it clearly indicates that those buying believe that the new information carries a high probability that prices will continue to *trend higher.* Greater confidence means that buyers are willing to "pay up" to purchase the stock. The buyers become enthusiastic and aggressive. The result is that they overwhelm the sellers, forcing the price to increase. Volume rises in tandem with price. Given a greater demand for the stock, demand overcomes supply and the only way to balance the equation is for price to rise, to entice more sellers to sell. This is simple economic forces—supply versus demand—and these are most evident and carry tremendous significance at the swing points.

However, this example is not meant to imply that rising prices and increasing volume that do *not* intersect a swing point are any less significant—it's just that you cannot measure them as easily as you can measure changes at the swing point. Absent of a swing point, there is nothing to which you can compare the eagerness of buyers. To be able to state that buyers are willing to pay up only occurs when the term *pay up* means "pay higher prices than have printed since the last point of significance," and that moment occurs at the swing points—especially those that form price boundaries.

This notion of "paying up" also applies to "paying down." Imagine a situation in which bad news drives the price of a stock much lower than it has traded at previously. The exact same situation applies—only in reverse. Greed becomes fear and sellers will take lower and lower prices to escape from the stock that they hold.

To emphasize the need to measure a move against a swing point, Figure 4.3 is a chart of the same stock, Celgene, in which simultaneously released information is seen as positive for the company, yet this doesn't occur at a swing point.[3] Though all news is important to varying degrees, there is no way for a chart reader to ascertain the significance of the news and its impact on the company, because it doesn't show the same level of commitment that would be evident if prices were to contest a swing point.

Again, it is only at the swing points that one can measure how intense the desire to own or to get rid of a stock really is. It is at the swing points

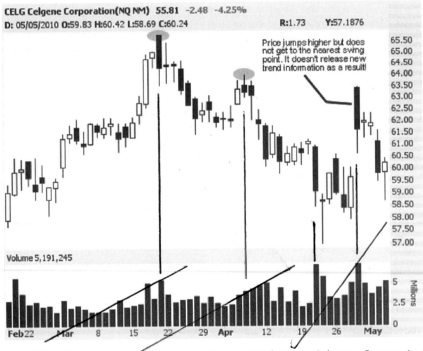

CELG Celgene Corporation(NQ NM) 55.81 -2.48 -4.25%
D: 05/05/2010 O:59.83 H:60.42 L:58.69 C:60.24   R:1.73   Y:57.1876

Price jumps higher but does not get to the nearest swing point. It doesn't release new trend information as a result!

Volume 5,191,245

FIGURE 4.3 Positive Simultaneous News Distribution—Celgene Corporation (CELG), February 17, 2010 to May 5, 2010

where desire becomes most apparent, because it is at the swing points that the buyer or seller *must* step into a new and unknown price zone. Buyers and sellers are comfortable within existing price zones, but it takes true belief to pay up with higher prices or to dump at lower prices. That is why swing points that demarcate price boundaries have special meaning. The enthusiasm to buy or sell stock is most apparent when that stock is either hitting new highs or new lows for the current move. That is why trend is best measured by observing the behavior exhibited at the swing points.

Identifying Swing Points

It's quite natural to think of a swing point as you would a sore thumb—they are unavoidably noticeable. Swing points, by their very definition, are typically thought of as a price point that is "at the edge" of all other prices points within the general time proximity. Consider Figure 4.4, which is annotated for each swing point high (SPH) and swing point low (SPL).

In this chart, notice how the vast majority of the labeled swing points appear visually to be the swing point high or swing point low price point

GOLD Randgold Resources Limited — American Depositary Shares Each Re(NQ NM) 81.32
D: 05/21/2010 O:78.98 H:82.57 L:78.69 C:81.32   R:3.88   Y:

FIGURE 4.4 Swing Points—Randgold Corp. (GOLD), February 22, 2010 to May 21, 2010

with respect to all prices that are reasonably near. This is typically what one finds when examining a chart for swing points—they more or less identify themselves.

There are swing points, however, that are not as obviously noticeable in the identification process. In Figure 4.4, the two darkened ovals identify less obvious swing points. Note that both of these price points are identified as swing points because they meet the identification criteria used to specify swing points. There are times where less than obvious bars end up being a swing point. These two bars are prime examples. In some cases these less obvious swing points end up being less valuable as well, and that is understandable because the price area that they identify isn't a price point that demarcates a price boundary. As I shall show a bit further on, they do have a purpose, but the purpose is almost always associated with stock exit rather than entry.

In some ways it is unfortunate that the swing point identification process identifies less obvious swing points but, as I have said, they do have value nevertheless, especially when price behavior is unidirectional (see the section titled "Unidirectional Price Points" in this chapter). Even in those cases where a nonboundary swing point ends up having absolutely no value, there is still value gained by having the ability to follow a single and simple identification process rather than a more complex process, riddled with rules and exceptions.

Getting back to the chart displayed in Figure 4.4, the fourth swing point high would probably not be an easily identified swing point to most observers. The same is true of the third swing point low. The general rules governing swing point identification would identify these additional swing points and, although they are reasonably straightforward, they are easily overlooked if the algorithmic method is not used uniformly. As such, it is worth a few minutes, along with a few words, to provide a detailed examination of the swing point identification process. Because swing points are at the heart of trend determination, it is important that swing point identification be consistently performed. What follows is the edification of the process buttressed by some examples that help to illustrate the identification of both simple and more complex swing points.

When examining a chart, it should be noted that all swing points start out as "potential" swing points. In fact, almost every bar on a chart represents a potential swing point high or a low (the notable exception is a bar where the high and the low are contained within the high or low of the preceding bar). As time progresses and bars are added to the chart, every so often a potential swing point "actualizes." Using the same chart (Figure 4.4) but with fewer bars for illustration purposes, the identification process begins with the leftmost bar on the time frame being examined. For the first bar, the high and low of the bar are noted. These two price points become the potential swing point high (PSPH) and potential swing point low (PSPL), and are labeled as such in Figure 4.5.

Moving from left to right, bar 2 has a lower low and a lower high than bar 1. The lower high implies that bar 1 remains the potential swing point high, while bar 2 becomes the new potential swing point low. Progressing forward, each new bar's high and low are examined with respect to the current potential swing point high and potential swing point low. If a higher high occurs, then the currently examined bar becomes the new potential swing point high. If a lower low occurs, the currently examined bar becomes the new potential swing point low.

In this particular chart, a new potential swing point low is registered for each of the first four bars (each low was lower than the previous bar). Bar 1 remains the potential swing point high, however, since the first four bars have lower highs. On bar 5, a higher low is registered and thus bar 4 remains the potential swing point low. Bar 1 remains the potential swing point high.

On bar 6, a higher high occurs and replaces the potential swing point high from bar 1. By the time bar 10 is reached, bar 8 is the potential swing

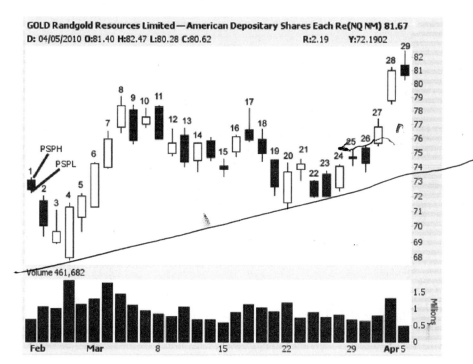

FIGURE 4.5 Potential Swing Points—Randgold Corporation (GOLD), February 22, 2010 to April 5, 2010

point high while bar 4 becomes an actualized swing point low because it is the lowest recorded low for six consecutive bars. The proper notation is to label bar 4 as a swing point low (SPL) and to register bar 10 as the new potential swing point low, as shown in Figure 4.6.

This process continues for each bar on the chart, resulting in six swing point highs and five swing point lows as shown previously in Figure 4.4. In fact, this process is applicable to any chart (stocks, commodities, Forex, or any other market for that matter), and is true for any time frame as long as each time frame consists of equal distant bars. Charts are a reflection of the sum total of all events (both physical and mental) that affect prices and that is true of all markets all around the world.

Swing Point Formations

The most common and prevalent swing-point formations are the easily identifiable swing points, as shown in Figure 4.6. There are others, however, that require a bit more attention.

FIGURE 4.6 Registering Actual Swing Points—Randgold Corporation (GOLD), February 22, 2010 to April 5, 2010

Cluster Swing Points There are occasions where one may question which bar to use when determining the swing point. One such question arises for cluster swing points—a group of bars with price lows or highs that are in close proximity both in price and time and end up becoming a turning point (swing point). The Randgold chart example shown previously contains one cluster formation that is examined in Figure 4.7.

On this chart, there are five consecutive bars with price points that are in very close proximity. Bar 1 has the highest volume while bar 5 has the lowest price. Which bar or combination of bars should be used?

After examining countless charts over the years, the conclusion reached is that a trader should simply listen to the market. The market speaks through volume and price over time, and the bar with the lowest low is the bar to be used. Exceptions could be made to the rule, but exceptions are just as prone to error. The ideal case would be to use the bar with the greatest amount of volume, but that creates its own problems. In doing so, there would be a need to require specific rules to dictate what a cluster is and when the rule applies. Rather than travel down the slippery

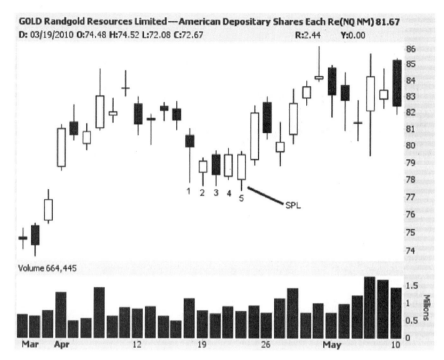

FIGURE 4.7 Registering an Actual Swing Point—Randgold Corporation (GOLD), March 29, 2010 to May 10, 2010

"exceptions" slope, the rule is to simply use the lowest low that the market leaves. In fact, the lowest low usually has meaning. In this particular case, what really occurred were five separate attempts to take prices lower, and none of them succeeded.

Bar 1 opened higher, traded much lower, then reversed and traded back near the opening price prior to closing. In other words, the buyers overwhelmed the sellers at the lower price point. Again, in bar 2, a lower low was reached but, by the end of the trading day, prices closed higher than they were when they opened. Bar 5 exhibits the same pattern where, after five consecutive attempts, the buyers once more overwhelmed the sellers after a lower low was made. Bar 5 is the lowest low. Bar 5 is the potential swing point and is actualized six bars later. The volume associated with bar 5 is the volume to compare to on any subsequent test of this swing point.

By using the swing point the market leaves, a desirable consequence occurs in the majority of subsequent swing-point tests. In this case, the preponderance of evidence suggests that the buyers are in command at this

FIGURE 4.8 Identically Priced Swing Points—SPDR S&P 500 SPY ETF, February 2, 1993 to April 19, 1993

price point. Any future test that witnesses volume expansion that is greater than volume at this swing point would indicate that the supply/demand equation has changed. Later, when the notion of differing time frames is considered, cluster swing points on one time frame usually end up as single swing points on a longer time frame, which many times adds more color to the interpretation of the charts.

Finally, in Figure 4.7, note that to get through the swing point, those buyers who stepped up in the previous four bars will either become turn-coats and sell out or will increase their holdings on the belief that further price appreciation is yet to come. This is a desirable consequence and, in a somewhat mysterious way, the market ends up doing what it needs to do with respect to providing informational tidbits that can be examined and deciphered.

Identically Priced Swing Points In rare cases, two price lows or two price highs that are within six bars of each other may end up having the same high or low. Figure 4.8 shows such an example.

In these rare cases, the bar that should always be used is the bar that has the greater amount of volume associated with it. I do this because it makes any subsequent test of the swing point a more difficult test. The determination of whether the potential swing point becomes actualized is to count six bars from the bar containing the greater volume, and if it remains the lowest/highest price, then that higher volume potential swing point bar becomes actualized.

Unidirectional Price Points   There are times when a market, market sector, or stock becomes unidirectional and advances or declines for an extended period of time without relief. In those situations in which bar after bar prints lower or higher (depending on the direction), the question becomes "Doesn't this type of behavior distort the ability to use swing points for trend discovery and qualification?" The answer unfortunately is sometimes "yes."

Figure 4.9 is an example of the inability to create a swing point high due to unidirectional price behavior. For the Powershares QQQQ Trust Series

FIGURE 4.9 Unidirectional Price Points—Powershares QQQ Trust Series ETF (QQQQ), February 5, 2010 to April 27, 2010

ETF shown in this chart, not a single swing point high is created for more than 11 weeks.

When a market doesn't ebb and flow but instead exhibits one-way price action, how are swing points designated? Actually, the real question is why is it necessary to have swing point designations on a given time frame? That question is best answered by first clarifying the importance of swing points.

In the neoclassical model, swing points serve two primary purposes:

1. To determine trend
2. To qualify trend

To determine trend, as we shall see, swing points are the basis for establishing and qualifying trend. If swing points are not created, as in Figure 4.9, then trend cannot be determined even though, in this case, trend is painfully obvious. This is a serious problem in those rare cases where a confluence of events denies us the ability to establish market direction for the time frame being examined. This rare case occurs only when the time frame being examined happens to line up with price action where no swing point high (bullish) or no swing point low (bearish) is identifiable. As I show later, it isn't necessary to locate two swing point highs in order to establish trend, but it is necessary to have at least one swing point established in the direction that the market is moving and on the time frame being examined. Without this minimal input, trend cannot theoretically be established even though the trend is obvious to anyone examining the chart.

If unidirectional price movement is to be adequately accounted for in the neoclassical trend model, then something has to be done. One option would be to relax the trend identification rules and to create a special case for this odd behavior. Unfortunately, rule-bending always has ramifications that are usually as unfavorable as the reason for bending the rules. Another possibility, and one that carries far less negative ramifications, is to simply extend the time frame far enough back to locate the last swing point high or low so that a comparison can be made. In fact, this is an elegant solution to an uncommon problem.

Again, using the same QQQQ ETF, if the time frame is extended to include earlier price points, then trend can be easily established using the same exact rules. Similarly, the idea of qualification is also assignable again using the same set of rules. Figure 4.10 provides an example of this time frame extension to include earlier swing points.

In this figure, by moving to a longer time frame that affords additional earlier price bars, a swing point high is revealed. That swing point, once identified, can be used. This provides a simple solution to the problem,

FIGURE 4.10 Time Frame Extension for Unidirectional Price Movement—Proshares Ultra S&P 500 (SSO), January 25, 2010 to April 27, 2010

allowing the trend model to work as designed. In this particular case, a suspect bullish trend is identified and remains in place until the final high is established toward the end of April. Keep in mind that unidirectional moves lasting for 50 or 60 bars are reasonably rare and seldom encountered. When they are, however, an extension of the time frame provides an elegant means to resolve the need to identify and assign trend.

Stacked Swing Points   Similar to unidirectional price points, stacked swing points are the opposite side of the same coin. Again, continuing with the QQQQ ETF example, Figure 4.11 shows how swing point lows would be labeled for this unique sort of price behavior.

In the case of stacked swing points, it might appear that the labeling of swing points adds little value. In fact, the earlier discussion regarding the apparent lack of value for swing points that are not located on a price boundary finds significant value when unidirectional price movement occurs.

FIGURE 4.11   Stacked Swing Points—Powershares QQQ Trust Series ETF (QQQQ), February 5, 2010 to May 10, 2010

Notice that the labeling of swing points for a unidirectional market is consistent with the general rules for swing point labeling where every sixth bar becomes an actualized swing point high if no other lower bar occurs in the intervening time. Once labeled, the value created is that the identified swing point ends up achieving the ultimate objective of trend analysis—the ability to provide a trader with a reasonably accurate read of the "true trend" as early as possible. To consider this further, imagine a trader having taken a long position in the QQQQ. Day after day he smiles and pinches himself because he can't believe his good fortune as the price continues to rise and his bankroll grows larger. Like all good traders, though, he knows that the trend will eventually end, so he continues to monitor the charts and the market behavior, anticipating an eventual turn.

As prices continue upward, the continued counting and labeling of each swing point low is religiously maintained. Finally, the trading becomes choppy and the last actualized swing point low is broken for the first time (see the highlighted bar). In this example, as the swing point is tested and broken, volume expands to confirm the trend change. That is the warning sign to the trader. Two days later, price collapses and all the gains since February are jeopardized as six weeks of gains are removed in a day.

Like an early warning system, the violation of a swing point is never something to simply ignore. The break of a swing point (high or low) on increasing volume, if recognized and respected, can allow an astute trader to take full or partial profits and/or avoid losses, while the great majority of traders remain unaware of the potential consequences that are likely to soon materialize.

Swing Point Validity across Time Frames

When labeling swing points, if a technician begins by labeling the longer time frame, then the swing points labeled on that time frame will, in many cases, continue to have significance on the shorter-term time frames. Not every swing point will have validity, though, because swing point identification is dependent upon the starting reference point in terms of time.

The inverse case will almost be guaranteed to have little applicability across varying time frames. When labeling a short-term time frame, for example, then pulling back the chart to an intermediate-term time frame, only a small subset, if any, of the labeled swing points will have validity.

There's really nothing invalid or inconsistent as a result of this labeling process; instead, it is simply the result of the inherent property associated with how much time is represented in each bar and the starting reference point of the chart itself. On the differing time frames, neither is identical.

IDENTIFYING AND LABELING TRENDS

Although the quality of a trend is determined at the swing points, the establishment of trend itself requires more than a single swing point test. What is meant by this statement is that although the creation and destruction of all trends result from a swing point test, it is the establishment of prior swing points that, taken in context with the current swing point test, determines whether a trend is established, continues, or is destroyed.

Although subtle in distinction, qualification of trend is always based on a singular event—the volume comparison of a prior swing point to the volume of the bar testing the previous swing point. To determine a trend's direction, however, requires the interpretation of the prior trend (as expressed through prior swing point tests) in addition to the currently tested swing point. Although triggered by a single event (a swing point test), it is not the result of an isolated event but instead the interpretation of a number of previously established events in addition to the current one. Much more is said about this throughout the remainder of the book, with many charting examples used to illustrate the concept.

Bullish and Bearish Trends

A confirmed bullish trend was defined as a series of higher price highs and higher price lows (not necessarily sequential), where price trades above and closes higher than the most recent previous swing point high, while volume expands as compared to volume at the previous swing point high.

Confirmed Bullish Trend
As part of the same directional move, a series of higher price highs and higher price lows (not necessarily sequential) where price trades above and closes higher than the most recent previous swing point high while volume expands as compared to volume at the previous swing point high.

If the qualitative part of the definition is removed, then a bullish trend is defined as a series of higher price highs and higher price lows (not necessarily sequential) where price trades above and closes higher than the most recent previous swing point high. This is equivalent to the classic definition of a bullish trend.

Bullish Trend
As part of the same directional move, a series of higher price highs and higher price lows (not necessarily sequential) where price trades above and closes higher than the most recent previous swing point high.

Thus, for a bullish trend to exist there must be a series of higher price highs and higher price lows. For every chart, the initial analysis starts by picking the time frame to analyze, then working from the left to the right side of the chart, identifying the potential and actualized swing point highs and lows. Once this part of the analysis is done, the current trend can be established. Figure 4.12 is a review of the process, revealing the distinction between trend creation and trend qualification. The establishment of trend is a process. It requires a series of events that, when put together, creates a complete picture. The qualification of trend, however, is a single event: "What was the result of a swing point test? Did volume expand or contract as a swing point was overrun?"

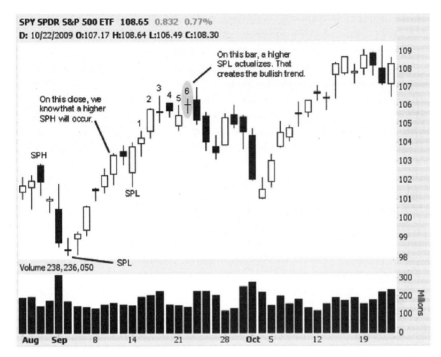

SPY SPDR S&P 500 ETF 108.65 0.832 0.77%
D: 10/22/2009 **O:**107.17 **H:**108.64 **L:**106.49 **C:**108.30

On this bar, a higher
SPL actualizes. That
creates the bullish trend.

On this close, we
know that a higher
SPH will occur.

SPH

SPL

SPL

Volume 238,236,050

FIGURE 4.12 Minimum Number of Swing Points Needed to Define a Bullish Trend, SPDR S&P 500 SPY ETF, August 26, 2009 to October 22, 2009

In Figure 4.12, the minimum number of swing point highs and lows needed to create a trend is apparent. The chart starts with a swing point high followed by a swing point low. The second swing point low creates "a series of higher lows" and the actualization of the second swing point low occurs on the sixth higher low bar, as indicated on the chart. While this is unfolding, a series of higher highs is also occurring. The close above the initial swing point high (noted on the chart) necessarily guarantees that a higher swing point high will eventually occur. It is necessarily a higher high because the high of this bar is higher than the previous swing point high. Regardless of what happens to the next six bars, this highlighted bar (or some subsequent bar) will necessarily end up being a higher swing point high. Thus, once the second potential swing point low actualizes, a bullish trend is created, and it is created without the potential swing point high actualizing.[4]

Once a trend is established, then it needs to be qualified. The qualification, as is evident by now, is centered on how volume and price act at the time of a swing point break. In Figure 4.12, volume expanded on the day that the prior swing point high was overrun. When volume expands and price closes higher, then the bullish trend can be qualified as *confirmed*.

Confirmation is an important concept, although, like anything in trading, it offers no guarantees. Nonetheless, there is a significantly increased likelihood that the trend will continue if the trend is confirmed. That knowledge provides the trader with an edge. In trading, an edge can be the difference between making money and losing it.

Another item of note in Figure 4.12 is that it is not always the case that the swing point highs are realized before swing point lows. The majority of the charts encountered will see the swing point highs realized prior to swing point lows, and the opposite is true for bearish trends, but it need not be. The difference between bullish and bearish trend identification lies only in the direction of the swing points on the chart. This bullish trend is bullish because there is a series of higher highs and higher lows. Likewise, a bearish trend results from a series of lower highs and lower lows.

Bearish trends are essentially defined as the exact opposite of bullish trends. Rather than going higher, price is moving lower. The behavior at the swing points defines the quality of the bearish trend, and a series of lower highs and lows defines the bearishness.

Numerous examples of bullish and bearish trends are provided in the next chapter, with differing qualifications.

Sideways Trends

Unlike bullish and bearish trends, sideways trends result from either conflicting consecutive swing point highs or lows, or from a transition from a prevailing bullish or bearish trend. Looking back at the definition from Chapter 3, a sideways trend is predicated upon the notion that the trend is no longer bullish or bearish, but instead is conflicting.

Confirmed Sideways Trend
The interruption of a bullish or bearish trend where consecutive swing points interrupt the existing trend of higher highs and higher lows or lower highs and lower lows, while volume expands on that interruption.

Suspect Sideways Trend
The interruption of a bullish or bearish trend where consecutive swing points interrupt the existing trend of higher highs and higher lows or lower highs and lower lows, while volume contracts on that interruption.

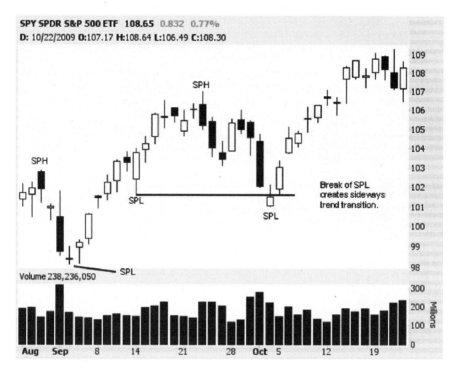

FIGURE 4.13 Transition to a Sideways Trend—SPDR S&P 500 SPY ETF, August 26, 2009 to October 22, 2009

Consider Figure 4.13 as an example of a sideways trend as a transition from a previously bullish trend. In this chart, the bullish trend is interrupted and a transition to a sideways trend occurs.

Sideways trends, once transitioned to, may persist for an extended period of time and develop into a series of conflicting highs and lows. In Figure 4.14, the existence of a lower low for the swing point low followed by a higher high for the swing point high conveys a confused state of affairs. A sideways trend, once established, is typically a state of confusion, a tug-of-war between two roughly equal and opposing forces attempting to move price in their desired direction.

In this chart, there is clearly no up or down direction, only a horizontal one. Horizontal price action is what defines a sideways trend.

The opposite configuration would also delineate a sideways trend—a series of swing points with two or more higher swing point lows in conjunction with two or more lower swing point highs (as seen in Figure 4.13).

In all these cases, once transitioned to, a sideways trend implies the absence of a bullish or bearish trend. It indicates that neither the bullish nor

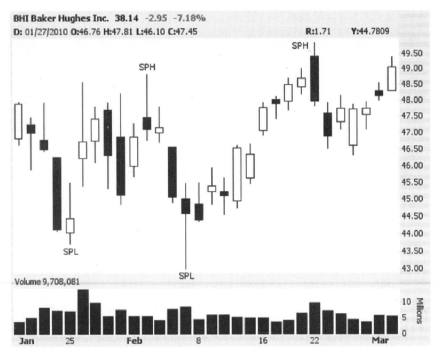

FIGURE 4.14 A Sideways Trend—Baker Hughes, Inc. (BHI), January 19, 2010 to March 2, 2010

the bearish forces have a significant enough following to make headway in their desired direction. Until one side or the other convincingly wins the battle, the trend remains murky and prices continue to drift with no linear direction.

SUMMARY

Although fundamentals eventually drive price, in the short run, perception can move prices contrary to the longer-term target. A trader can go broke waiting on the market to realize how cheap or expensive (if short) a company really is.

Rather than to solely trade the fundamentals, an alternative is to determine and trade trend. Proper identification and qualification of trend provides a trader with a greater likelihood of trading success—not a guarantee of one.

At this juncture, the concept of trend determination and qualification are probably reasonably well understood. What is needed now is to present examples of each of the possible trend transitions and continuations to crystallize the ideas. The final chapter of this first section focuses on just that, while introducing some peripheral ideas that complement the practical usage of qualified trend.

CHAPTER 5

Qualifying Trends

Every time frame necessarily has trend. This is true of all markets and all instruments. Trend is always with us and always apparent on the charts. The absence of trend only appears to be true at the beginning of a chart (leftmost edge) where the identification of a sufficient number of swing points has yet to occur. Pull the chart back 20 or 30 bars and trend suddenly appears where it previously was absent. The absence of trend is simply the result of where charts start and stop, and nothing more, and that is arbitrarily chosen each time a chart is drawn.

Many bars on a chart have the potential to start, stop, or to continue an existing trend, and all analysts factor into that their conceptual decision-making process. The market is nothing more than a gigantic and continuous voting machine, on a market, sector, and individual stock level. Votes are cast in the form of prices paid. The trend is nothing more than a reflection of that voting process across all time frames, whether the votes occur each minute, hour, day, week, year, or at even longer intervals.

As discussed previously, the votes take on added significance *at the swing points*. It is at the swing points that trends are born, reaffirmed, or die. It is at the swing points that qualification can and does occur.

USING SWING POINT TESTS

In Chapter 3, the notion of swing point tests was introduced in conjunction with the idea of qualification. As discussed there, the neoclassical definition of trend expands the definition of the three basic trends in order to qualify them. The result is the six qualified trends previously enumerated and defined.

But what are the rules for transitioning from one trend to another? How is a trend reaffirmed? What makes a trend strong or weak? Does a swing point test occur at the top or the bottom of the bar being tested? Can a trend change from weak to strong, and what are the rules surrounding such a transition? All of these questions, as well as many others, are pertinent to successfully navigating the markets and being able to stay ahead of the pack. Each of them has significance no matter what time frame you are trading on. In a way, swing point tests are the gateway to trends.

Now that we know how to determine a swing point and to use it to determine trend, exactly how are swing points utilized to qualify trend? Swing points always contain two critical informational components—the price high (if a swing point high) or price low (if a swing point low) that occurred at the swing point, and the volume associated with it. Those two informational data points are the key to comparisons. The comparison occurs each time a swing point is tested. Additionally, for a trend to change, a swing point test must necessarily trade beyond and close over (bullish trend) or under (bearish trend) the swing point being tested.

Another informational item that presents itself when a swing point test occurs is the direction of the existing trend. In all cases, the result on trend of a swing point test is dependent on the prevailing trend when the test occurs.

All trends are either *confirmed* or *suspect* or, in the case of a sideways trend where no swing point test occurs, *ambivalent*. The terms *confirmed*, *suspect*, and *ambivalent* were consciously chosen to instantaneously convey the certainty associated with the trend.

Confirmed implies certainty and, although nothing is certain in the stock market, confirmation is the next closest thing. Confirmation occurs only when a swing point is broken and *volume expands*. The fact that volume expands as prices trade at levels not traded at for a reasonably significant period of time (if at all) tells us that the buyers (bullish trend) or the sellers (bearish trend) are quite intent in their actions. The result of such significant behavior usually does not disappear immediately, and that is why confirmation of a trend is a critical event that carries considerable significance.

Suspect trends present a problem to the trader because, although the trend is established, the conviction associated with it either is waning or has never reached the level of seriousness seen with confirmed trends. A suspect trend, though it can continue for an extended period of time, has to be viewed with a cautionary note. A trader necessarily must be more careful when trading in the direction of the trend when the trend is qualified as suspect.

To both reinforce and elucidate these ideas, the remainder of this chapter examines numerous charts with annotations and considerable discussion. The emphasis is placed on crystallizing the concepts through visualization and repetition. None of the material is complex but there are nuances that require additional explanation here and there. It is through practice that perfection is found, and with trends and trend qualification something close to perfection is attainable.

TREND CONTINUATION AND TRANSITIONS

Each time a swing point test occurs, either a trend continues or a new trend is initiated. Those are the only two outcomes. The decision criterion takes into account:

- The prevailing trend when the test occurs.
- A comparison of the price and volume of two items.
  1. The swing point being tested.
  2. The bar that is performing the test.

A trend change can occur only when the testing bar breaks through an existing swing point. To break through means that the bar being tested is surpassed and the closing price surpasses the bar's high or low (bullish or bearish) of the bar being tested. If the test is in opposition to the prevailing trend and a break occurs, then a trend change likewise occurs. If the test is in the same direction of the prevailing trend, then the trend continues although a trend continuation may serve to alter the strength or weakness of the prevailing trend. The quality of a trend change or continuation reflects the strength or weakness of the trend as measured through volume at the time of the test.

Table 5.1 summarizes the possible scenarios and outcomes when a swing point high is tested.

Irrespective of the prevailing trend, when a swing point high is tested, prices can either close over the swing point high or fail to do so. Additionally, how volume expands or contracts into that test is all-important. When these two criteria are combined, there are four possible outcomes. Adding in the notion of the prevailing trend at the time of the test yields the matrix depicted in Table 5.1, which details the outcome possibilities involving swing point high tests.

Table 5.2 contains the same set of scenarios and outcomes as Table 5.1, except that the test involves a swing point low. When combined, these two

TABLE 5.1 Swing Point High Test Outcomes and Implications

Prevailing Trend	Price	Volume	Trend Implication
Bullish (see Figure 5.1—DGIT)	Price closes over the SPH being tested	Volume expands	Confirmed bullish trend continuation
Sideways (see Figure 5.9—RBY)	Price closes over the SPH being tested	Volume expands	Confirmed bullish trend transition
Bearish (see Figure 5.10—RBY)	Price closes over the SPH being tested	Volume expands	Confirmed sideways trend transition
Bullish (see Figure 5.2—DGIT)	Prices close over the SPH being tested	Volume contracts	Suspect bullish trend continuation
Sideways (see Figure 5.4—DELL)	Prices close over the SPH being tested	Volume contracts	Suspect bullish trend transition
Bearish	Prices close over the SPH being tested	Volume contracts	Suspect sideways trend transition
Bullish, Sideways, and Bearish (see Figure 5.11—NE)	Price surpasses SPH but price closes under the SPH	Volume expands	Existing trend continuation. Expect a retest as a result.
Bullish, Sideways, and Bearish (see Figure 5.12—RBY)	Price surpasses the SPH but price closes under the SPH	Volume contracts	Existing trend continuation. Less likely to retest and break the swing point.

tables represent an exhaustive list of the test types and outcomes that are possible when analyzing trend.

To repeat, each and every time a swing point test occurs, one of two possible outcomes occur; either the trend continues or it doesn't. When you think of a test, you normally think of it in terms of success or failure, and it is possible to assign such an attribute to swing point tests, but unfortunately it turns out to be counterproductive. The variety of terms associated with *success* and *failure* is just too great. Rather than cluttering the vocabulary associated with trend qualification, it is much simpler to think of a test as either continuing the trend or changing it.

Therefore, to be clear, a trend change requires a change in the primary trend type (bullish, bearish, or sideways). A change in the qualification of an existing trend (suspect or confirmed) does not imply a trend change but instead should be considered a continuation of the existing trend. A change in the qualification of trend means simply that the prevailing trend is the same, getting stronger, or becoming weaker. That is, after all, what qualification means.

For example, for a suspect bearish trend to get stronger, price needs to weaken further while volume escalates. Said another way, the strength

TABLE 5.2 Swing Point Low Test Outcomes and Implications

Prevailing Trend	Price	Volume	Trend Implication
Bullish (see Figure 5.7—BEC)	Price closes under the SPL being tested	Volume expands	Confirmed sideways trend transition
Sideways (see Figure 5.15—DELL)	Price closes under the SPL being tested	Volume expands	Confirmed bearish trend transition
Bearish (see Figure 5.13—DELL)	Price closes under the SPL being tested	Volume expands	Confirmed bearish trend continuation
Bullish (see Figure 5.8—DVN)	Prices close under the SPL being tested	Volume contracts	Suspect sideways trend transition
Sideways (see Figure 5.14—MON)	Prices close under the SPL being tested	Volume contracts	Suspect bearish trend transition
Bearish (see Figure 5.14—MON)	Prices close under the SPL being tested	Volume contracts	Suspect bearish trend continuation
Bullish, Sideways, and Bearish	Price surpasses SPL but closes over SPL	Volume expands	Existing trend continuation. Expect a retest as a result.
Bullish, Sideways, and Bearish	Price surpasses the SPL but closes over the SPL	Volume contracts	Existing trend continuation. Less likely to retest and break the swing point.

of a bearish trend increases if prices push through a swing point low on increased volume.

The same volume behavior would be true for a suspect bullish trend. For a bullish trend to get stronger; the price would need to appreciate further on increased volume as it crosses a swing point high.

To further describe all of the possible outcomes and ideas embodied in Tables 5.1 and 5.2, a number of charts are shown here (see Figures 5.1 through 5.15). In all cases, the chart formations are presented along with annotations and discussions to crystallize the ideas.

Bullish Trends

A bullish trend continuation is just what it sounds like: The trend is bullish (prices are increasing) when a swing point test occurs. The result of the test

FIGURE 5.1   Confirmed Bullish Trend Continuation—DG FastChannel, Inc. (DGIT),
September 2, 2009 to November 13, 2009

is that the bullish trend continues. The strength of the trend may remain the
same, increase, or weaken, but it does continue.

A trend transition implies that the trend changes as a result of a swing
point test. How the trend changes and how strong or weak the newly created trend is depends on the result of the test that occurred when the trend
changed.

The following few paragraphs display examples of trend continuations
and transitions for prevailing bullish trends.

Continuations   Figure 5.1 is an example of a bullish trend continuation.
In this example, the prevailing trend was suspect bullish; at the conclusion
of the test, the trend remains bullish, although stronger.

Since a bullish trend has two possible qualifiers (suspect and
confirmed), there are four continuation possibilities. Two of the four
continuations result in a trend that is equally strong or weak. The other
two continuation formations result in a trend that is either stronger or

weaker than before. The four combinations and their strengthening or weakening characteristics are:

1. Suspect bullish continuation to suspect bullish (result is an equally weak trend).
2. Confirmed bullish continuation to confirmed bullish (result is an equally strong trend).
3. Suspect bullish continuation to confirmed bullish (result is a stronger trend than the prevailing trend).
4. Confirmed bullish continuation to suspect bullish (result is a weaker trend than the prevailing trend).

In Figure 5.1 the trend strengthens as a result of the final swing point test displayed on the chart. Originally the prevailing trend was suspect bullish, as annotated. At the conclusion of the swing point test, though, the trend strengthens to a confirmed bullish trend. It does this because when the swing point high is tested, two events occur. First, the closing price for the testing bar is higher than the high of the bar being tested. Secondly, volume expands as the test completes.

Measuring the demand for a stock at the swing points is what trend qualification is really all about. Common sense tells us that when comparative volume expands, there is increased interest in either buying or selling the stock at that price point. In this particular example, the interest is in buying the stock, and that interest has grown irrespective of higher prices. When demand for a stock is greater as price increases, that becomes an excellent indicator of the future price direction. If enthusiasm is increasing (as measured by volume comparisons) along with an increase in price, then the rational thought is to assume that there are increased odds that higher prices should prevail in the future.

The ramification of the price and volume action in Figure 5.1 is to alert both the buyers and sellers of DG FastChannel that the future price of this stock now has a much higher probability of trading even higher on the time frame being examined. In essence, the trend has become stronger, and the stronger the trend, the higher the probability that the trend continues.

The DG FastChannel chart also displays another bullish continuation that occurred prior to the one just exhibited. In this case, the trend continuation did not serve to strengthen or weaken the trend; instead, it remained the same. The annotations in Figure 5.2 highlight a prevailing trend of suspect bullish and a swing point high test and break that continue the bullish trend with a suspect qualifier.

FIGURE 5.2 Suspect Bullish Trend Continuation—DG FastChannel, Inc. (DGIT), September 2, 2009 to November 13, 2009

In this chart, the added annotations clearly indicate the conditions that need to be present for a suspect bullish trend to exist and in this case, to continue with the same qualifications. They are:

- A suspect trend occurs with a test of a previous swing point high where price closes over the previous high but volume contracts as compared to the bar being tested.
- A series of higher highs and higher lows on the time frame examined.[1]

By widening the time frame slightly more for this stock, as is shown in Figure 5.3, a number of additional and important trend characteristics are revealed.

At the left of the chart, the increase in price in September that led to the first swing point high (originally annotated in Figures 5.1 and 5.2) was suspect bullish. It was suspect bullish because the swing point high—September 1, 2009—had 409 million shares traded while the break of that swing point on September 15, 2009, had only 245.7 million shares

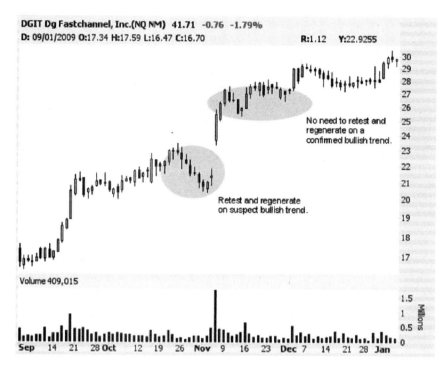

DGIT Dg Fastchannel, Inc.(NQ NM) 41.71 -0.76 -1.79%
D: 09/01/2009 O:17.34 H:17.59 L:16.47 C:16.70   R:1.12   Y:22.9255

No need to retest and regenerate on a confirmed bullish trend.

Retest and regenerate on suspect bullish trend.

Volume 409,015

FIGURE 5.3 Significance of Suspect Versus Confirmed Bullish Trends—DG FastChannel, Inc. (DGIT), September 1, 2009 to January 7, 2010

traded. The importance of the fact that it was qualified as suspect, yet still enjoyed a reasonably large price increase, should not be taken lightly.

Despite being suspect bullish in terms of trend qualification, a significant lesson is witnessed with respect to suspicious trends in this chart. Suspicious trends do not necessarily imply the end of a trend. In fact, the trend is always presumed to have the ability to continue *because it is the prevailing trend!* A suspicious trend has to be viewed through the veil of suspicion, but not necessarily ignored. Suspicious trends can continue far longer than ever imagined and produce fantastic gains. The implications of this statement are broad and in Part 2 there are numerous discussions and examples of staying with a suspect trend when trading. Clearly, selling your entire stake in a company because the trend has turned suspect on a short-term time frame is not a reasonable exercise of caution.

The next item of interest in Figure 5.3 is to note the more common behavior of a suspect trend. Typically a suspect trend creation or continuation results in a few bars that continue in the direction of the prevailing trend and are eventually followed by a "retest and regenerate" sequence as described later in this chapter in the section titled "Retest and Regenerate." For the sake of brevity, the creation or continuation of a suspect trend usually results in price retracing back to the price point where the suspect breakout occurred and either regenerating (proving that the prevailing trend is sustainable) or degenerating (the prevailing trend is not sustainable). This retest and regenerate phase is highlighted in the first of the two darkened ovals.

The third and most important concept embodied in Figure 5.3 is to observe the significant difference in price behavior as displayed in the continuation of the suspect trend as compared to the transition to a confirmed bullish trend. In this chart, the buyers of DIGT were quite lackadaisical in their willingness to "pay up" to own DIGT at higher prices when the trend was merely suspect. In fact, the price for DIGT at the end of October was roughly equal to what it was in early October when DIGT reconfirmed its suspect bullish trend.

Now, compare that behavior to what happens after the transition to a confirmed bullish trend, which occurred as a result of the gap up in price on November 5, 2009. In the gap-up situation, prices not only moved higher once the trend became confirmed bullish, but continued to move higher and higher for another two months before any kind of substantive decline occurred. There was no need to retrace and retest, as in the case with the suspect bullish trend reconfirmation, nor was there any intention of doing so. The buyers were clamoring to establish positions at higher and higher price points for a full two months after the trend qualification became confirmed.

Transitions A transition to a bullish trend always is the result of a move from an existing sideways trend to a bullish trend (either suspect or confirmed). There are cases where a bearish trend appears to transition directly to a bullish trend without an intervening sideways trend, but that is an uncommon occurrence. In reality, it actually passes through the sideways transition, but does so on a single bar so it "appears" to have sidestepped it. Although uncommon, this type of transition is rarely witnessed and usually the result of a one-time news event such as a buyout offer, or the unexpected approval of a drug application, or possibly a huge judgment in a legal case. Other than some sort of large, bottom line-affecting, one-time event, transitions from a bearish to a bullish trend or vice versa almost always move to and eventually through the sideways trend phase before reaching their ultimate destination.

An example of a transition from sideways to bullish is shown in Figure 5.4. In this chart, the large shaded area identifies the prevailing sideways trend for Dell Corporation. The trend is sideways due to the higher swing point lows in conjunction with the lower swing point highs.

DELL Dell Inc.(NQ NM) 14.04 -0.16 -1.13%
D: 06/07/2010 O:13.23 H:13.34 L:12.42 C:13.15   R:0.92 Y:12.1948

FIGURE 5.4 Transitioning from a Suspect Sideways to Suspect Bullish Trend—Dell Corp. (DELL), June 15, 2009 to June 14, 2010

The darkened oval area is the point where the previous swing point high is surpassed on a closing basis. The result is that the trend changes from suspect sideways to suspect bullish. Volume on the breakout bar was a little over 127 million shares while the bar that was being tested had 134.5 million shares.

Also exhibited in this chart is the notion of a bar that ends up being both a swing point high and a swing point low. When a bar has a huge price spread, there is always the possibility that this can occur, and the mid-August bar created such an occurrence, as prices for the next six bars were unable to penetrate either the top or bottom of that bar. Bars that define both a swing point high and a low are profitable bars to trade once price breaks above or below the bar. The result of such a break almost always carries price as much as a half to a full extension of the size of the bar that possessed both a swing high and low characteristics, and it usually happens in a straight-line fashion once the break occurs. In the case where the bar has wide price spread and high volume, it is even more appealing, because the typical case is for both sides to be tested. Thus, as is the case here, if prices break lower first, a trader can trade that direction with the idea of flipping the position around at some point to see a test of the high-volume high that was left on the chart.

Another item of interest in Figure 5.4 is that this chart is a weekly chart; each bar on the chart represents one week of price action rather than one day. All charts examined up until this one were based on daily bars. As previously stated, trend determination and qualification are independent of the time frame. The principles apply equally to any time frame, as long as the bars examined are equidistant.

Although it is probably already apparent, a trend transition to or from a sideways trend could manifest itself in one of seven ways, when taking all of the possible trend qualification possibilities into consideration (this includes the ambivalent sideways trend).

From a charting perspective, each of these transitions would appear essentially the same as the one displayed in Figure 5.4. The primary difference would simply be the direction of the prevailing trend and the trend transitioned to, in addition to the trend's relative strength. Naturally the trading implications are different and discussions on this topic are scattered throughout Part II, but the general appearance of the chart formation is strikingly similar.

Sideways Trends

Unlike bullish and bearish trends, sideways trends rest squarely in the middle of both the bulls and the bears. Sideways trends are created in one of three ways:

1. A bullish trend terminates, resulting in a sideways trend. The sideways trend qualifier may be confirmed or suspect, depending on how volume behaved at the swing point test.

2. A bearish trend terminates, resulting in a sideways trend. The sideways trend qualifier may be confirmed or suspect, depending on how volume behaved at the swing point test.

3. A sideways trend may also occur naturally with the absence of a swing point test. For example, a bearish trend may simply fade away with a higher swing point low occurring without a test. Similarly, a bullish trend may record a lower swing point high than the previous. In both cases, the sideways trend doesn't obtain a qualifier of "bullish" or "bearish," because no test has transpired. It is instead "ambivalent." Trend qualifiers only occur as the result of swing point tests. Without them, you cannot qualify.

DELL Dell Inc.(NQ NM) 13.09 -0.24 -1.80%
D: 09/08/2009 O:15.74 H:16.75 L:15.64 C:16.60   R:1.11   Y:8,791,337.307

On this bar, a higher SPL actualizes and the trend transitions from bearish to sideways.

Volume 114,987,431

FIGURE 5.5 Ambivalent Sideways Trend—No Qualifier—Dell Computer (DELL), August 31, 2009 to April 5, 2010

Transitions   Figure 5.5 provides an example of a sideways trend created without a swing point test. This is not a common case, but an outlier. In this weekly chart, Dell Computer starts out with a bearish trend that transitions to a sideways trend. It does this without a swing point test. In the absence of a swing point test, the ability to assign qualification to the new trend is impossible because there is nothing to compare it with, to determine strength or weakness. If no comparison exists, there is nothing to qualify.

The more common transition to a sideways trend occurs when a bullish trend is no longer bullish or a bearish trend is no longer bearish. In both cases, the existing trend terminates and a sideways trend comes into being. In these cases, qualification is applicable because a swing point test occurs as part of the transition. Unlike a confirmed bullish or bearish trend, the true meaning of a confirmed sideways trend is more of a negation than an affirmation. The implication of this is subtle but valuable to consider.

When a trend changes from a sideways or suspect bullish trend to a confirmed bullish trend, the interpretation of the trend change is in the affirmative—the buyers have taken control and the future expectations are that prices will likely move even higher.

When a bullish trend (confirmed or suspect) changes to a confirmed sideways trend, however, the interpretation should be viewed in a slightly different light. On the one hand, it is somewhat similar in that the interpretation of the trend change is also in the affirmative—the sellers have taken control and the future expectations are that the prices will likely move sideways at best or lower at worst for the time frame under examination. On a more basic level, though, it means that the odds of the trend changing back to bullish are less likely. In this sense it is more of a negation than an affirmation. It renders the likelihood of the trend changing back to the prior trend as unlikely, instead endorsing the idea that prices should move further in the direction of the newly established trend or even opposite to the previous trend.

Sideways trends typically tend to be transitory. The market is a constant battle for higher or lower prices. It's just that there are times where the buying and selling forces are reasonably equal and the result is a sideways trend. As you would expect, the relatively equal strength of the bullish and bearish forces exhibited during a sideways trend usually doesn't last

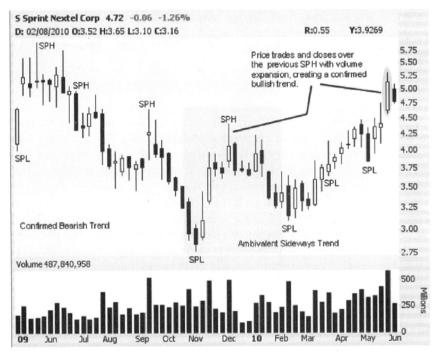

FIGURE 5.6 Transition from Bearish to a Sideways Trend—Sprint Corp. (S), April 27, 2009 to June 1, 2010

BEC Beckman Coulter, Inc. 56.29 -1.72 -2.97%
D: 10/12/2009 O:68.06 H:68.11 L:66.46 C:67.57

Test and break of the prior SPL creates a change in trend from suspect bullish to a confirmed sideways trend, since volume expands on the test and break of the prior SPL.

Volume 2,098,327

FIGURE 5.7 Transition from Suspect Bullish to a Confirmed Sideways Trend— Beckman Coulter, Inc. (BEC), February 2, 2009 to December 14, 2009

an exorbitant period of time. Stocks are constantly being exchanged between buyers and sellers, resulting in fluctuating prices. As soon as one side begins to dominate once more, the sideways trend ceases to exist.

Another example of a transition from a bearish to a sideways trend in which the sideways trend cannot be qualified is shown in Figure 5.6. Notice the overlap between the confirmed bearish trend (left side of the chart) and the ambivalent sideways trend. This is a normal occurrence because, with ambivalence, there isn't a swing point test bar that demarcates the transition.

The annotated oval at the very right-hand side of the chart demarcates the point where Sprint Corporation transitions once more. In this particular case it transitions from the ambivalent sideways trend to a confirmed bullish trend. It does so because multiple higher swing point lows are evident and now a higher swing point high is guaranteed.

For an example of a qualified sideways trend, take a look at Figure 5.7. In this chart, the prevailing trend was bullish until the previous swing point low was tested and broken. In this example, broken implies that the close of the testing bar was lower than the low of the swing point low that was tested.

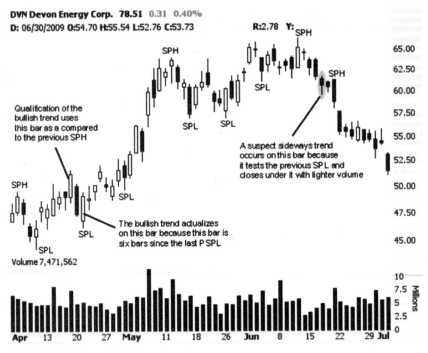

FIGURE 5.8 Transition from Confirmed Bullish to a Suspect Sideways Trend— Devon Energy Corp., March 23, 2009 to June 22, 2009

In Figure 5.7, the suspect bullish trend extended from April of 2009 until late October of the same year. This once more underscores just how long a suspect trend can exist as "suspect." The termination of the suspect bullish trend finally occurred as a result of the swing point test against the previous swing point low. The fact that volume expands as prices break lower creates the confirmed sideways trend.

Figure 5.8 displays both a confirmed bullish trend and the transition of that trend to a suspect sideways trend a couple of months later. Recognize that this is simply the result of where the examination of the chart begins, but interesting nonetheless. On the left-hand side of the chart, the exact point when the bullish trend actualizes is indicated in the annotations. Interestingly enough, many times a trend is created or is transitioned to yet a new swing point and doesn't actualize until much later. This is a common occurrence. The actualization of a trend always beckons the chart reader to qualify it. In this case, the higher price bar is compared to the previous swing point high and determined to have greater volume. That creates the confirmed bullish trend, providing the trader with a buy signal.

As for the creation of the suspect sideways trend, in this particular case, the prior trend was bullish and had been since late April. Notice how the break of the previous swing point low (as annotated by the oval farthest to the right on the chart) necessarily creates a lower swing point low, although actualization has yet to occur. Trend always results from the configuration of existing swing points when a swing point break occurs. When such an event happens, it behooves the observer to examine the chart to determine if the trend has transitioned or is a continuation. A swing point test that results in a new swing point low may or may not change trend. Likewise, it may or may not result in a differing quality of trend, as well.

In Figure 5.8, the trend does change and the appropriate qualifier to attach to the new trend is suspect sideways because volume diminished as compared to the prior swing point low that was tested and broken. That tells the chart reader that although prices can continue lower, the more probable outcome is that they will return to this area where price broke down in order to retest. Although it took another six weeks before it happened, that is what eventually took place in Devon Energy (not shown in this chart).

When trading, having the knowledge of what is likely to happen is the sort of edge that can lead to consistent profitability. Whether a trader trades on a fundamental or a technical basis, the need to have an edge is a well-understood fact. The edge could be the risk and money management tools and methodology that a trader employs. It might be the ability to read the true trend of a stock better than others. It could be insider information (even though that carries a stiff penalty if a trader is caught). It could be many things or even a combination of things, but at least one viable and consistent edge is required. Without it, trading is no better than flipping coins. Las Vegas provides better odds than the market for a trader without an edge. At least in Las Vegas there are plenty of pleasurable distractions in addition to losing all your money!

Another very interesting trend transition is the one shown in Figure 5.9. It is interesting because it yields a counterintuitive result. What's even more interesting is that the read of the chart works despite that seemingly awkward transition. This Figure displays a transition from a bearish trend (left-hand side of the chart) to a sideways trend, as denoted by the shaded rectangular area on the chart.

The highlighted oval area shows a swing point test of the previous swing point high. The test occurs on increasing volume and the close of the testing bar is greater than the high of the tested bar. That signals a trend transition, and since the prevailing trend was sideways, the transition is necessarily bullish. Almost any technician looking at this chart would not consider it in a bullish trend, let alone with a qualification of confirmed; but using the rules supplied for the neoclassical definition of trend, it does

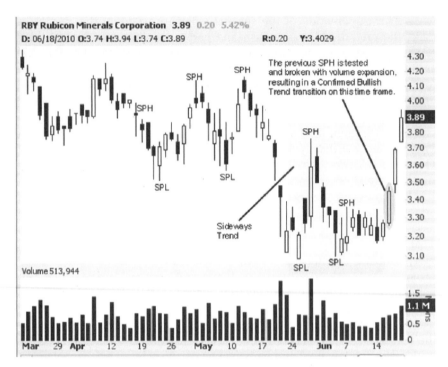

RBY Rubicon Minerals Corporation 3.89 0.20 5.42%
D: 06/18/2010 O:3.74 H:3.94 L:3.74 C:3.89   R:0.20   Y:3.4029

FIGURE 5.9 Transition from Sideways to Confirmed Bullish—Rubicon Minerals, March 19, 2010 to June 18, 2010

indeed meet the criteria of confirmed bullish. The result is that a trader trading true trend would be able to pick this stock up a lot sooner than most, and being quick to jump on a stock that is about to move is ideal.

Another example of a trend transition is seen in Figure 5.10, again using Rubicon Minerals. In the same general time frame as the previously examined Rubicon chart, the prevailing trend was bearish until a prior swing point high was tested and broken. The break of the swing point created a sequence of lower swing point lows but higher swing point highs. As discussed earlier, that defines a sideways configuration. Since volume expanded in this case, it was a confirmed sideways trend transition suggesting that, on this time frame, prices should continue to work in a sideways fashion, and that it was unlikely prices would resume the previously defined trend, which was bearish. Although this chart is far from a textbook example, price did generally work sideways once the test occurred, but the end result was a return to a bearish trend. As suggested before, nothing is for sure and when examining just one time frame, failures are more common. Part II looks at how to increase the probability of a correct chart read by examining multiple time frames as well as multiple instruments.

FIGURE 5.10 Transition from Confirmed Bearish to Confirmed Sideways—Rubicon Minerals Corp. (RBY), March 1, 2010 to May 19, 2010

Continuations Like bullish and bearish trend continuations, sideways trends can continue as well, although only through test failures. Figure 5.11 is an example of a sideways trend continuation. The company is Noble Corporation and the shaded oval area identifies the attempt to break a swing point high. The result was that price traded over, then closed under, the high of the prior swing point. That is what happens in a sideways trend continuation; the attempt to change trend fails and thus the prevailing trend continues.

Note that in this example, despite the lower closing price, volume expanded on the breakout attempt. For an astute trader, that nugget of information is rather useful. When volume expands on a swing point test, it signals traders that this area of the chart is hotly contested. Every point on a chart is a potential battleground and the significance or insignificance of each price area is communicated through volume expansion and contraction.

The problem is that most market technicians and commentators are unable or unwilling to correlate current price and volume actions with

FIGURE 5.11 Sideways Trend Continuation—Noble Corp. (NE), November 13, 2009 to January 21, 2010

previous ones. It is only when you compare what happened on this same battleground with what is currently happening that you are able to get a sense of what it really means. In the case where volume expands, yet price fails to close higher (this case), the story being told is that this battle for higher price is not over yet. Sure enough, after a few bars of consolidation, price does push higher once more, to contest the area yet again.

Now, contrast the price and volume action in Figure 5.11 with that in Figure 5.12, where volume contracts on a swing point breakout attempt. After being in a bearish trend, Rubicon Minerals Corporation had already transitioned to a sideways trend at the time when the highlighted swing point test took place. Volume contracted, indicating that fewer troops showed up to fight the battle.

When a swing point is tested but there is an inability to break through, the prevailing trend continues. Unlike Figure 5.11, volume contracted in this example, and in doing so, the chart was telegraphing that the price area where the test occurred is no longer a hotly tested area on this time frame and that the need to retest again is less likely to occur. It could

RBY Rubicon Minerals Corporation 3.64 0.37 11.31%
D: 04/27/2010 **O:**3.74 **H:**3.79 **L:**3.63 **C:**3.67   **R:**0.16   **Y:**4.0216

The prior swing point high is tested, but the close is under the previous high and volume contracts. The exsiting trend continues.

FIGURE 5.12 Sideways Trend Continuation—Rubicon Minerals Corp. (RBY), March 1, 2010 to May 19, 2010

happen, but unlike the case where volume expands, there is nothing to indicate a higher probability that this will happen. Although not shown on this chart (see Figure 5.9 for subsequent price action), prices did indeed fall further—below $3.50 on the very next bar—and spent the next four weeks attempting to work their way higher once more.

Bearish Trends

Bearish trends, like the bullish or sideways trends already examined, can also be either *confirmed* or *suspect*. Likewise, the concept of trend continuations and transitions is also applicable. Moving to a bearish trend involves the examination of swing point tests involving swing point lows.

The following few paragraphs examine bearish trend continuations and transitions.

Continuations   There isn't anything special about bearish trend continuations. All the rules that apply to a bullish trend continuation are exactly

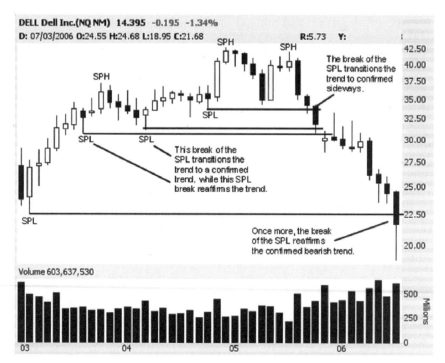

DELL Dell Inc.(NQ NM) 14.395 -0.195 -1.34%
D: 07/03/2006 O:24.55 H:24.68 L:18.95 C:21.68

The break of the SPL transitions the trend to confirmed sideways.

This break of the SPL transitions the trend to a confirmed trend, while this SPL break reaffirms the trend.

Once more, the break of the SPL reaffirms the confirmed bearish trend.

Volume 603,637,530

FIGURE 5.13 Continuation of a Confirmed Bearish Trend—Dell Corp. (DELL), January 2, 2003 to July 3, 2006

the same for a bearish continuation with the one difference being the direction of the trend.

An example of a bearish trend continuation is shown in Figure 5.13. In this monthly bar chart (each bar represents one month of trading), a trend continuation occurs on volume expansion.

In 2003, Dell's trend was bullish. By the end of 2004 and through the first part of 2005, that trend came to a grinding halt. In October 2005, the highest swing point low on the chart was crossed and the trend changed from bullish to confirmed sideways. That was the signal that something was seriously wrong, since this chart reflects the long-term time frame; the most important of all trends. Before the year was out, two more swing point lows were simultaneously broken with one monthly bar. The first of the two breaks resulted in the transition to a confirmed bearish trend while the second, technically speaking, reaffirmed that transition. Finally, at the end of this chart, another swing point low was broken and the trend was again reaffirmed as confirmed bearish.

When a trend continues, the trading ramifications are typically twofold. One implication is that a trader must recognize that the trend is truly entrenched. Juxtaposed to this is the fact that the longer the trend continues, the closer it comes to the time where it exhausts itself, since nothing goes up or goes down forever. While a downtrend may cause a trader to want to undertake protective measures, it should by no means cause him to fight the trend by trading against it. The trend really is your friend, especially if it is confirmed.

Figure 5.14 provides an example of a suspect bearish continuation. This chart happens to be a five-day, 30-minute bar chart of Monsanto, illustrating once more that these principles are for all markets and across all time frames. In this chart, Monsanto had carved out a sideways trend in the left-hand side of the chart. The first oval demonstrates the transition from the prevailing sideways trend and the resumption of a suspect bearish trend. The second oval highlights the trend continuation. Since volume once more was suspect, the trend qualifier remains suspect, and rightly so.

FIGURE 5.14 Continuation of a Suspect Bearish Trend—Monsanto Corp. (MON), June 14, 2010 to June 18, 2010

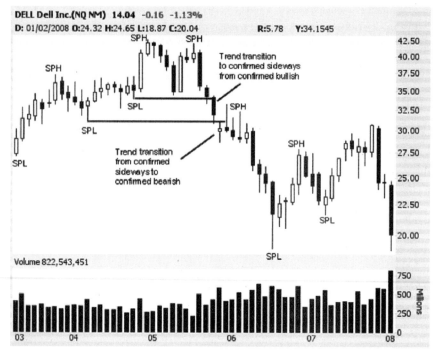

FIGURE 5.15 Transitioning from a Confirmed Sideways to Confirmed Bearish Trend—Dell Corp. (DELL), April 1, 2003 to January 2, 2008

Immediately afterward, prices reversed and began climbing again as the buyers flexed their muscles.

Transitions A bearish trend transition, like a bullish one, emanates from a prevailing sideways trend. In the previous chart of Dell Corporation (see Figure 5.13), the transition from a sideways trend to a confirmed bearish trend was visible. Figure 5.15 is a repeat of that chart with a small twist; the start of the chart begins three months later than the chart previously shown. Note how that alters the recognition of swing point lows at the beginning of the chart. If there is an Achilles heel of any chart interpretation methodology, it is the choice of where to begin the analysis. With a longer period of time, these anomalies work themselves out. That might not be true if too few bars are examined, which is why you should view charts with a minimum of roughly 60 bars.

As before, in this chart, Dell Corporation had enjoyed a bullish trend for the first half of the chart. The break of the initial swing point low necessarily creates a lower swing point low and thus guarantees a trend change.

The break to lower lows comes on increasing volume, and therefore the transition to a sideways trend is confirmed. The very next bar breaks the next swing point low and once more results in a trend change, this time to a confirmed bearish trend.

Summary

The most important takeaway from the entire concept of swing point tests is that the markets are constantly attempting to discount the future. The discounting mechanism is always at work and involves constant testing of price boundaries. Since swing points are typically at the price boundaries, it is at swing points where the market releases the greatest amount of information and it does so repeatedly.

The information released may confirm existing assumptions about the prevailing trend (continuation) or may instead call those assumptions into question (transition). It is the job of the trader and/or investor to observe and decipher the message being released, interpret it, and act upon it.

As with anything that involves the future, the information released will neither always be correct nor will it necessarily be free of ambiguity. In the latter situation, a trader should avoid trading the stock when clarity simply isn't there. In the case of the former, a trader should utilize sound risk and money management principles to prosper, even with a less than certain view of the future. The only certainty about the future is that there is no certainty, and the only item that a trader can truly control is risk. These are the truths of the market, and to prosper you must both recognize them and incorporate into your trading endeavors.

RETEST AND REGENERATE

Although not discussed in any depth, Figure 5.3 provided an example of a retest and regenerate sequence. Essentially, a retest and regenerate sequence is predicated on the need to retest a swing point area where price did succeed in both surpassing and closing beyond the previous swing point, but, in doing so, created a suspect trend. This can be true of both suspect bullish and suspect bearish trends. The need to retest occurs as a result of the suspicion created during the trend transition or continuation. To put it another way, anytime a suspect trend transition or continuation occurs, to remove the cloud of suspicion surrounding the price action, a retest is required and typically takes place on the time frame in which it occurred.

To say a retest is required when a suspect swing point break occurs is quite different from saying that it will happen. In the vast majority of the cases it does happen, and happens on the time frame on which it occurred, but it isn't 100 percent. Required, in this context, means that without a retest the suspicion will remain, and where there is suspicion there is difficulty in gaining confidence. Trading is mostly about confidence. The greater the confidence, the greater the ability to make money, as the size of the trades can be increased while maintaining reasonable risk.

When a trend transition occurs as the result of a swing point break and yet volume does not expand, the move is suspect. Suspect trends almost always result in an eventual retest on the time frame that the suspicion is created. Sometimes the retest occurs within a few bars. Other times the retest may not take place until many bars have passed. The idea of a retest is to confirm that the break was real and that the quality of the trend should shift from a suspect state to a confirmed one. It is the market's way of making certain that the swing point break was not a fluke, which is what a suspect break can imply. Until the retest and regenerate sequence takes place, confidence is lacking.

Figure 5.16 is an example of a retest and regenerate sequence that confirms the break was for real. In this chart, the exact point of suspicion was

FIGURE 5.16   Retest and Regenerate Sequence—United States Natural Gas Fund ETF (UNG), June 15, 2009 to June 14, 2010

created when price traded to and closed under the leftmost swing point low (shaded oval) and volume did not expand when compared to volume at that low. The swing point low that created the suspicion when broken is the bar that requires retest. The primary determinant in what gets tested is dependent on how soon the retest occurs.

If a retest occurs relatively quickly (within five or six bars), then the test is likely to involve either

1. The opposite side of the broken swing point bar or
2. The prior and opposite directional swing point (in this case the previous swing point high, since the trend is bearish).

To decide which of these is most likely depends on the volume of the testing bar as compared to the broken swing point bar. That decision criteria is as follows:

1. If volume on the testing bar is reasonably close to the amount of volume on the swing point bar that was tested, then a full or partial retrace to the opposite side of the broken swing point bar is all that can be expected if trend is intent on regenerating and continuing.
2. If the volume was instead quite light as compared to the swing point bar that was tested, then a retrace even further can be expected. That retrace can take prices all the way back to the next significant anchor bar (to be explained in Chapter 7) or the prior and opposite directional swing point. In this example that would have been the prior swing point high (the third denoted SPH) on the chart.

If the retest comes seven bars or more later, then most of the time a successful retest and regenerate sequence is limited to a test of the breakout area and not much more. The reason for this is because time has importance as well; if a swing point remains broken for more than five or six bars without a reactionary move by traders to move price back to where it previously traded, then the move is stronger than it appears.

Applying these principles to the UNG example displayed in Figure 5.16, once the bearish trend turned suspect bearish, the retest and regenerate sequence began immediately, starting on the very next bar. Since volume was reasonably equal on the testing bar as compared to the broken SPL bar, that suggested that the farthest-most price point to test was the high of the swing point low bar, which caused the trend to turn suspect to begin with.

Unlike all other tests discussed so far, in which the high or the low of the bar being tested must be surpassed, the idea of a retest and regenerate sequence is to determine the real strength of the trend that was created—nothing more. Since the trend was tagged as suspect, the desire is to determine if the side that was initially defeated at the swing point (buyers if a bearish trend or sellers if a bullish trend) truly is beaten and has thrown in the towel. If they have indeed given up, then the retest will indeed regenerate and the suspiciousness of the trend then has the possibility of having doubt removed. If, on the other hand, those traders on the losing side of the trade have more firepower and have yet to give up, then the retest has a real possibility of failing and degenerating and the suspicious trend was indeed justified and is likely to be reversed.

A successful retest and regenerate sequence would see the price push back to the retest area and "fail." Failure means that the attempt to reverse the established trend does not succeed. Failure implies success in that the suspiciousness of the trend is removed; that happens when the retest inches within a percentage point or two of the targeted test price and volume diminishes as compared to what is being tested.

Returning to Figure 5.16, because the retest and regenerate sequence begins immediately, the top horizontal line (as annotated on the chart) becomes the target price to be tested. In this example, the test was successful because price almost touched the top of the swing point low bar, and it did so with much lighter volume. The implication is that there were far fewer buyers willing to buy at that price point as compared to the number of sellers who were previously willing to sell at that price point. The result should be that prices will turn lower again and that is what happened. That is a successful retest and regenerate sequence.

Assume, for the sake of argument, that the target retest price point was surpassed and volume expanded. What would the market be saying? If the trend really were confirmed bearish, that simply should not happen. That would tell you that the suspiciousness was justified and that the trend is likely to reverse.

Notice what else takes place while this retest and regenerate sequence plays out. Turning to Figure 5.16 one last time to illustrate this idea, notice how the bar that broke the previous swing point low itself becomes a new swing point low (second shaded oval) as a result of the time that passes while the retest and regenerate sequence plays out. It is through this ebb and flow that the newly created swing point low will itself serve as the next test in the ongoing bearish trend and, once more, the bearish UNG traders will have to either prove or disprove that the suspect bearish trend is indeed to be trusted by confirming another swing point break.

Continuing with this particular example, the subsequent test of the newly created swing point low lacks volume once more on the break, which eventually leads to yet another retest and regenerate sequence, as

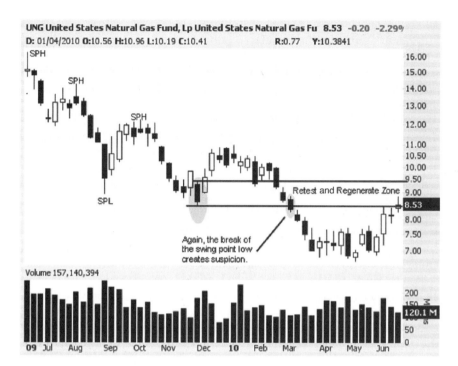

FIGURE 5.17 Retest and Regenerate Sequence—United States Natural Gas Fund ETF (UNG), June 15, 2010 to June 14, 2010

displayed in Figure 5.17. The difference between this particular retest and regenerate sequence compared to Figure 5.16 is that in this case the retest and regenerate sequence doesn't happen immediately (within five or six bars). Referring back to the retest and regenerate rules described previously, this implies that all that is needed is a test of the lows of the bar that was broken, which created suspicion.

As before, a lower swing point low is actualized in this scenario as well, providing the next test point in an ongoing series of tests as prices head lower. It is in this way that the market constantly provides input to the trader regarding the health and viability of the trend. When suspicion is raised, the market typically seeks to rectify it. When no suspicion exists, then the trend is much stronger and can run much farther before retracing.

Market Logic of Ebb and Flow

The stock market many times is referred to as ebbing and flowing. In some ways, the retest and regenerate sequence described above is part and parcel of this ebbing and flowing, but even without suspicion the ebb and flow occurs—just less frequently.

Sometimes it is a lot easier to crystallize a concept like ebb and flow when the reasoning behind the idea is considered. The backing and filling process that is referred to by ebb and flow is the market's way of building continued strength in a stock or an index. Strength is not synonymous with only a bull market. Strength exists in a bear market as well; it's just that prices are strongly heading lower, not higher. Backing and filling occurs in both bullish and bearish trends, although bearish trends typically move a lot faster than bullish ones because fear is a much stronger emotion than greed.

In both bullish and bearish situations, the process of moving in the direction of the trend, then retracing, then pushing farther once more in the direction of the prevailing trend makes the trend stronger, because the stock ends up transitioning from weak hands to stronger ones—hands that intend to continue holding the shares the next time it trades farther in that directional path. In a bullish market this process can be viewed as a slow accumulation by larger buyers. Typically larger buyers tend to slowly and discretely accumulate, given the opportunity. They have deep pockets and are the ones who tend to put a bid under a stock. Naturally they want to buy and accumulate at the best possible overall price and thus, as they build out a large line of the stock, they do so patiently so as to not goose the stock higher, which would be detrimental to their desires. They prefer to see the stock work back and forth—not run higher. If it did the latter, they would not be able to purchase the stock at reasonable price points.

The enthusiasm to buy is somewhat subdued and that is because the stock is probably under accumulation—not mark-up. The mark-up phase comes only after accumulation is mostly done, and that is when you see the large and fast gains. Even in the mark-up scenario there is ebb and flow, but it comes less frequently and retraces are minor compared to directional surges.

Once a large buyer or a group of buyers builds out a large line of stock, it is in their best interest to hold it and to see to it that good stories circulate; bullish stories about how this or that may happen. The old adage on Wall Street is that for every stock, there is a story, and that's quite true because Wall Street sells stories; they sell hope, hype, and the promise of future potential. As the stories circulate, the large buyers attempt to goose the stock higher, creating additional interest in the stock in an attempt to lure additional buyers. If they succeed, prices will move even higher, and possibly much higher. This period is the mark-up period in which price gains momentum and owning this or that stock is all the rage. Think greed and think back to stocks such as America Online and Enron.

These stocks had spectacular rises on suspect fundamentals. They also eventually crashed right back down from where they came. Huge money was there for the taking as long as you could read the chart properly and exit prior to a spectacular fall.

As prices get marked up, large holders of the stock begin to sell into the strength. In a similar way that accumulation happens, distribution begins to occur. This is the process of slowly selling the line of cheaply accumulated stock at much better prices, and to do so discretely and slowly so as to not arouse suspicion. This process was prevalent 90 years ago and there is no reason to believe that it no longer applies.[2] The price action supports the idea that this game of pushing the stock higher then discretely selling into the rise remains with us today. It is called distribution. During this period, the stock ebbs and flows exceedingly although the trend begins to change. Most of the time it is subtle and the distribution period remains for a reasonably long period of time. For most stocks, it usually coincides with a top in the market. Eventually a mark-down period ensues that breeds fear and, though the market continues to ebb and flow, retraces become less pronounced as the bearish trend intensifies.

That is the logic behind why stocks ebb and flow when under accumulation and distribution. It is only during the mark-up and mark-down phases that large and fast price moves occur. Visually, during the mark-up and -down phases, the chart looks much more like a bungee jump rather than a ski slope. It is during the accumulation and distribution that stocks push backward and forward, building strength (to move higher or lower) while seemingly treading water. When swing points are surpassed, but on suspect volume, the patient buyers stand aside, letting prices fall back before they begin to accumulate again. The opposite is true for distribution. There the larger operators attempt to prop up prices when they fall and then sell again into the rise. The patterns look the same, only in different directions. The easiest way to know which situation the market is in is to simply look at where prices have been. If they have had a sustained advance, it is more likely distribution. If a sustained decline, then it is likely to be accumulation.

Multiple Tests on a Single Bar

Many times, multiple swing points end up tested on a single bar. The rule is to take each swing point bar in sequence from the most recent to the oldest and to compare each with the bar performing the break. If any of the swing point breaks result in a suspect bullish or bearish trend, then a retest and regenerate sequence is required. Figures 5.13 and 5.15 illustrated this process previously.

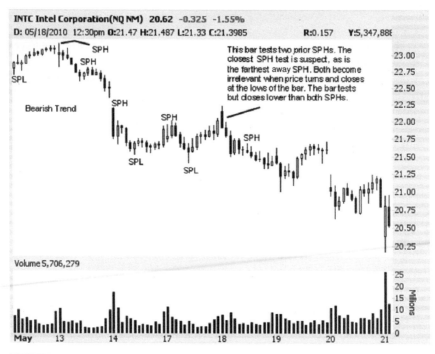

INTC Intel Corporation(NQ NM) 20.62 -0.325 -1.55%
D: 05/18/2010 12:30pm O:21.47 H:21.487 L:21.33 C:21.3985   R:0.157   Y:5,347,88€

SPH
SPH
SPL

Bearish Trend

SPH

SPH

SPH

SPL

SPL

SPH

This bar tests two prior SPHs. The
closest SPH test is suspect, as is
the farthest away SPH. Both become
irrelevant when price turns and closes
at the lows of the bar. The bar tests
but closes lower than both SPHs.

23.00
22.75
22.50
22.25
22.00
21.75
21.50
21.25
21.00
20.75
20.50
20.25

Volume 5,706,279

25
20
15 Millions
10
5
0

May   13   14   17   18   19   20   21

FIGURE 5.18 Multiple Simultaneous Swing Point Tests—Intel Corp. (INTC), May
12, 2010, 8:30 A.M., to May 21, 2010, 8:00 A.M.

As another example, consider Figure 5.18, which shows eight trading
days in Intel Corporation where each bar represents a 30-minute interval. In this chart, the trend is bearish. The annotated bar shows a spike
in price that tests the two preceding swing point highs but fails. The first
of the two is the more difficult comparison but, given the general rule, it
is the second bar that is compared to initially. In this case, the test failed
and prices moved lower once more, but had the test succeeded and prices
moved higher, breaking both swing point highs, the comparisons for each
would need to be accounted for. The initial test would be the nearest swing
point high and then the one prior to that. If either were broken with volume
contraction, then a suspect trend would occur. The first would be suspect
sideways, then the latter suspect bullish. The suspect bullish trend would
require a retest and regenerate sequence.

Replacing Suspect Trends

As already indicated, suspect trends can be made whole again, so to speak.
That can happen as a result of a retest and regenerate sequence, followed

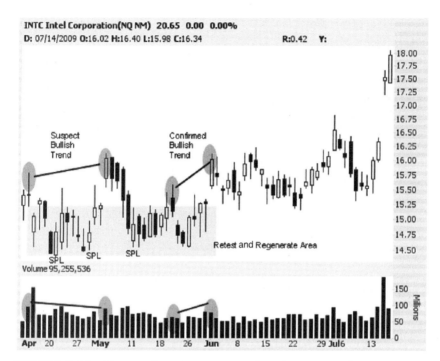

INTC Intel Corporation(NQ NM) 20.65 0.00 0.00%
D: 07/14/2009 O:16.02 H:16.40 L:15.98 C:16.34   R:0.42   Y:

FIGURE 5.19 Changing from Suspect to Confirmed Transition after a Retest and Regenerate Sequence—Intel Corp. (INTC), April 13, 2009 to July 6, 2009

by a subsequent push back in the original direction that once more tests the latest swing point that was created. If the test of the most recent swing point occurs on heavier volume, then the previously suspect trend returns to a confirmed trend state.

Figure 5.19 is a chart of Intel Corporation. The original break higher was suspect. Intel immediately turned and pushed lower to perform the retest and regenerate sequence. Because the disparity in volume on the suspect bullish break was tepid as compared to what was being broken, rather than stopping with a retest of the low of the swing point high bar that was broken, Intel pushed almost all the way back to the prior swing point of the opposite direction, which was, in this case, a swing point low. Once it was clear that volume was not expanding at this prior swing point, Intel turned and worked higher once more and eventually confirmed a bullish trend.

This particular chart is interesting because even though the bullish trend was confirmed, it would take another five weeks for price to really take off; the direction of the trend was higher and the confirmation of that trend eventually would bear fruit for traders who followed the signal and bought Intel shares.

SUMMARY

This brings the first section of the book to a close. The theoretical models were introduced and the weakness of the classical theory exposed with respect to how it is used in today's trading environment. A neoclassical theory was introduced and the framework considered in detail. That framework is centered upon the notion of identifying true trend and qualifying it. Considerable attention was paid to the proper identification of trend. To accomplish this, potential and actualized swing points were considered, and the various forms these take were examined. From there, the ideas of swing point tests and trend transitions were discussed.

Although the concept of time frames was introduced, these were presented in the context of examining swing points, not trading implications. That is discussed in the second section, where we consider application of the theory.

Essentially, at this juncture, you should have a good understanding of the neoclassical model—both what it entails and why it was needed. It is an improvement upon the existing model and provides practical reasons for adoption.

An exhaustive set of outcomes based on swing point tests was outlined. Those outcomes were dependent on the prevailing trend in addition to price and volume characteristics that are part and parcel of the swing point test evaluation process. Many examples were provided in an attempt to create a clear and concise picture of what each of the transitions look like, as well as the continuations of an existing trend where the qualifier may or may not change.

Thus far, the bulk of the material presented has concentrated on trend theory. What is the current thinking with respect to trend? From where did it emanate and how is it currently applied? Is there a better trend model, and if so, what is it?

For each of these questions an answer was sought and presented. With over a hundred years of technical analysis, the fact remains that the basic concept of trend has not been improved upon but instead has deteriorated. That deterioration has led to less value in the applicability of trend theory and all of its derivative indicators. This is the price one pays for lack of progress.

The thought that trend cannot only be identified with greater clarity but also qualified is an extremely powerful concept. When practiced, these ideas lead to an improved trade success rate and, equally important, the concepts lead to a plethora of higher quality trade management strategies.

Part II of this book shifts the focus from theory toward application, for it is the application of theory that leads to results. By applying the concepts of trend discovery, qualification, trend continuation, and transition, we can begin to see the concrete results that can be experienced in our everyday trading.

Application of Trend Theory

In Part I, both the classical and neoclassical views of trend theory were examined and explained. A significant amount of time was devoted to uncovering the underlying assumptions of the classical view and considering how currently practiced trend application seemingly ignores the basic tenets underlying that model.

Juxtaposed to the classical theory, a new age of trend theory was introduced—the neoclassical view. A rather in-depth discussion of the theory was considered, along with numerous charting examples and discussion. The concepts of trend creation and transition were examined, and the idea of trend qualification was introduced as a powerful alternative to the current practice, in which all trends are treated as being equal.

Now that a consistent and workable theory has been put forth, the final piece of the puzzle is to consider how to apply it. Although trend theory is a necessary condition to trading trends profitably, in itself it isn't sufficient. It is necessary to take the theory and integrate it into a workable and profitable trading system in order to achieve that ultimate goal. Thus, Part II of this book focuses on the application of the theory with respect to trading markets.

A trading system can be quite simple or complex, but whatever it ends up being, it must leverage the strengths of the model in a real-world setting. The strengths of the trend model are that it recognizes the creation and transition of trends while qualifying those same trends. This provides the trader with a bird's-eye view of the quality of a trend as it is created and continues to unfold. The ability to both recognize a trend and to measure the strength or weakness of the trend is what a trader should always seek to exploit. The implication is that a trader needs to time their entry and exit criteria based upon trend creation, continuation, and transitions.

To be fair and accurate, a successful trading system is a much broader concept than just entry and exit criteria. Entering and exiting trades are just a piece of the puzzle. A successful trading system must consider a much broader range of topics, such as risk management, proper size positioning, and portfolio management, to name a few. In *Trade Like the Little Guy*,[1] these broader concepts are covered in significant detail since the objective of that book centered around how to become a consistently profitable trader independent of the actual entry and exit methodology utilized. I am sure there are other books that seek to do the same.

Since the focus of this book is on trend theory and application, which is almost exclusively technical in nature, the concept of a "successful trading system" is necessarily narrowed to consider stock entry and exit criteria as it relates to trend. This doesn't imply that position sizing and the myriad other broader topics are completely ignored, but that they are considered ancillary to the main discussion of trade entry and exit. The result of this decision is to focus the majority of the effort on the application of trend theory as it relates to the technical decisions of entry and exit criteria, without cluttering the discussion with the broader concepts of a complete trading system.

CHAPTER 6

Preparing to Trade

Trends exist on every possible time frame that can or could be created. The trend may be either up or down; it may also be sideways, because a sideways trend is viable, as well. Once one or more arbitrarily agreed-upon time frames are established, then the possibility of identifying trends within a time frame is possible. The act of identifying a trend within a time frame implies the recognition of trend for each and every particular point in time encompassed by the time frame that is being analyzed.

It is quite apparent that there is less value in both identifying and analyzing a trend that was in effect during the early part of a time frame compared to a trend toward the end of the time frame, where end is defined as the present time. Unless research is being conducted, the true objective of integrating trend identification and qualification is to determine the trend and its qualities *for the current period of time.* It is the current period of time that is of greatest interest, because that is where tradable actions occur. There is little that can be done about what has happened—it is what is happening and is about to happen that is of interest to the trader.

In classical trend theory, Hamilton identified two time frames that were worthy of attention. In neoclassical trend theory, the tracking of three is proposed. These three proposed time frames consist of similar characteristics that complement each other. Although it is quite possible to analyze an even greater number of time frames for the same stock at the same time, such an analysis can quickly spiral into an incomprehensible mess. This is why few technicians choose to recognize and analyze more than two or three trends at a given time. The evidence suggests that little is to be gained in tracking a larger number of time frames, although tracking and trading multiple time frames offers significant benefits. With the trend theory as proposed here, in fact, three time frames is considered an optimum number; not too many to be overwhelming yet enough for a trader to be alerted to trend changes and to identify ideal entry and exit points. What one finds when studying various time frames is that, many times, one time frame will signal a change while others do not. In a similar vein, the divergence between time frames can many times lead a trader to a trading bias that they otherwise would not consider.

To introduce the concepts for trading true trends successfully, a few housekeeping items are in order. For example, trading always involves trading strategies. Fortunately, almost all strategies ultimately stem principally from only two methodologies, with respect to trade entry. Thus, a brief overview concerning trading strategies centered on trade entry is reviewed.

Another area that requires at least a brief mention is reward versus risk. It isn't possible to consistently trade successfully without some idea of the risk versus the reward of the potential trade. A brief discussion of this concept is provided but any trader who may need to brush up on his reward-to-risk skills is encouraged to read more about this important concept elsewhere, as the discussion here is quite brief and only scratches the surface.

The final section of this chapter deals with the important concept of time frames. Time frames are central to the neoclassical trend model, and thus a few more words to clarify what they are as well as some of the more important nuances of time frames seem worthwhile.

Like trading, introducing a broad model that changes the way traders approach trading is daunting. There are many pieces that constitute the art of trading and, although the model may boil down to a few simple concepts, the seemingly simple may end up being quite complex once the onion is peeled. The value provided, though, is tremendous, and a little more legwork to enable you to fully exploit the model is necessary, even for the trader who desires to push straight into application.

OVERVIEW OF TRADING STRATEGIES

Rather than diving straight into the pool of new-age trend trading, let's begin with a quick primer on the idea of trading strategies. In the world of trading, most trading strategies are centered upon one of two methodologies (although a few employ both). The competing methodologies focus on the question of when to enter a trade. Both methodologies work for strong or weak stocks, as long as they are trending up or down.

FIGURE 6.1 Buying the Breakout on Rural/Metro Corporation (RURL), April 9, 2010 to July 9, 2010

One methodology is to buy/sell a strong/weak stock *while it exhibits strength/weakness*, and is often referred to as momentum trading. The ultimate example of this methodology is to purchase a stock when it breaks out to higher highs on the time frame examined. Figure 6.1 is an example of this scenario.

The second methodology also attempts to exploit a strong or a weak stock, but the entry point in this methodology is to buy during the eventual and expected momentary weakness in a strong stock (or sell during momentary strength in a weak stock), in the context of an expected move higher/lower. Using the same chart, Figure 6.2 shows how the competing strategy issues a buy signal on Rural/Metro Corporation at a slightly later point in time, on a retest of the breakout rather than on the breakout itself.

In this book, almost every trade discussed is predicated on buying the retrace/retest rather than the breakout. The risk of not buying the breakout is that the stock may never retrace. Sometimes very strong/weak stocks do exactly that for a seemingly long period of time. That is possible but it is not the common case. Usually there is a second chance to get in and, from money- and risk-management perspectives, it is the better time to

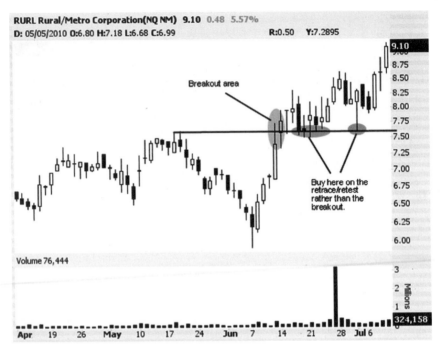

FIGURE 6.2 Buying the Retrace/Retest on Rural/Metro Corporation (RURL), April 9, 2010, to July 9, 2010

enter a position. The risk of buying the breakout is that the breakout fails and the stock comes right back down. Since buying the breakout means to purchase while a stock is making new highs, the cost of being wrong is rather extreme.

Although the difference between buying the breakout and buying the retrace may seem insignificant, the risk parameter is significant. When buying the retrace, rather than the breakout, there is a clear difference in the risk the trader takes. If the original push to higher highs was a true breakout, and at some point later prices retrace and retest the breakout area, the initial purchase is no longer executed when the stock is trading at the highs (presumably higher highs have already registered, as shown in Figure 6.2).

When buying a retrace, the initial purchase will occur at a "lower" price. This does two things. It provides the trader with an observable and objective measuring point for risk and reward. The second extremely important advantage is that it also lets the trader measure the conviction of the buyers versus the sellers as price retraces. Being able to objectively evaluate the conviction of the buyers or sellers as price retraces is a critical step, because in this scenario it comes before you make the purchase.

In Figure 6.2, the first bars that participated in the breakout showed 281,700 shares while the actual bar that broke the prior swing point high registered 113,800 shares. The volume on the prior swing point high (which is the bar to benchmark against) was just shy of 80,000 shares. Thus, the swing point was broken *with volume expansion* creating a confirmed bullish trend.

When prices retraced and retested the breakout bars three days later, they did so for five straight sessions with 137,000, 53,000, 183,000, 106,000, and 182,000 shares traded, respectively. Note that not one day came close to the 281,700 shares that RURL traded as it pushed into the new highs. Although the volume on the retrace was not as clear-cut a buy signal as one would prefer (remember that the bar that actually broke the swing point was 113,800 shares), it nevertheless was a fairly good indication that the breakout bar would hold because each attempt to trade lower could not close back inside the breakout area.[2] Finally, after a push higher, there was the final test about a week later and the volume that day came in at 143,000 shares—again, not nearly enough conviction on the sell side to take prices appreciably lower and keep them there, but still higher than an ideal buy scenario would have registered.

The point of this example is to illustrate how a strategy of buying a retrace can be implemented. In the above example, the purchase would be made on the retrace and a stop-loss order placed back below the breakout area (around $7.11 or so). In this way, by waiting to buy the retrace rather than buying the breakout, the market has had sufficient time to release additional information to the trader. That information provides the trader with parameters that can be used to create a trading plan centered on the idea of how much risk can be taken with respect to the potential reward that is available. It alleviates the need to "hope" the breakout is real and lasting, and instead allows the trader to measure the strength of the breakout once the retest of the breakout area occurs. It is at that particular point that a better indication of the lasting nature of the breakout can be discerned.

RISK VERSUS REWARD

No trading system or strategy would be complete without some discussion of risk and reward. In my book *Trade Like the Little Guy*,[3] almost 100 pages are devoted to risk and reward as it relates to trading. The building of a reward-to-risk spreadsheet matrix is presented to enable a trader to determine a reward-to-risk ratio *prior* to entering the trade. Money and risk management are a significant part of trading successfully. It's not only about finding great chart patterns to trade.

Although the focus of this book isn't centered on a complete discussion of risk and reward, any potential trade needs to be concerned with it and must have a minimum ratio of 2:1 reward-to-risk, and preferably a 3:1 ratio, or more.

So how does one compute reward-to-risk ratios? The simplest of models can be constructed by identifying just a few basic inputs. The minimal data points required are the potential entry and exit points (where the exit points encompass both winning and losing exits). The entry price is where the purchase or short sell occurs. The risk to the trade is where the stop-loss order is placed and the reward is the price point where the limit exit order is placed to capture profits. The ratio between the potential profit and the potential loss yields the reward-to-risk ratio. This somewhat simplistic but workable model is a way to compare one trade against another.

Now, quite naturally, there are ways to enhance this most simple of models. For example, not all trades have an equal probability of success or failure. That would be another important input that could be added to make the model more realistic.

The idea presented here suggests that a method of measuring reward and risk is necessary to successful trading, and to disregard the need is unadvisable. Ideal trades have reward-to-risk ratios of from 3:1 to 5:1. Anything much larger is probably not using realistic entry and exit criteria. Anything less is a questionable trade and should be avoided. With the idea of trade entry based on catching the retrace versus the breakout, along with at least a rudimentary understanding of reward versus risk, the next topic to consider is how to further enhance the probability of trade success. A method that does this and that comes as part and parcel of trend qualification is to broaden the trading perspective to include the examination of multiple time frames.

TIME FRAMES

Almost everything discussed in the remainder of this book is predicated upon properly reading and reacting to chart patterns for one or more time frames. For that reason, a quick review and further explanation of this important concept is presented.

As previously mentioned, time frames are arbitrarily chosen time slices represented as bars on a chart. Each bar on the chart represents one time period. The most commonly used "bar width" is the daily chart where each day's worth of trading is signified by one bar on a chart.

Recall that Hamilton asserted that there are three time frames: primary, secondary, and short-term (see Chapter 1). From those early beginnings, technicians almost universally embraced the notion of three distinct time periods or time frames. They do not agree upon the length of each time frame, nor do they agree upon the value of examining each of those time frames.

The neoclassical theory of trend suggests that all three be studied, and that they are actually quite complementary when constructed properly.

Duration

Although Hamilton ignored the shorter time frame because in his view it wasn't predictable, traders have always been drawn to it. Whether it is because it is more exciting, or simply because traders are impatient, trading the short-term time frame has been, is, and will likely always be part of the trading landscape. Since Dow and Hamilton's objective was to determine the long-term trend, the short-term time frame didn't prove to be valuable in achieving that objective. That doesn't mean that the short-term time frame cannot be traded profitably, nor does it mean that a profitable trading strategy that encompasses this time frame cannot be constructed. It simply means that for the purposes of Hamilton and Dow, it had little value. That is not the same thing as having no value in general.

Although trading the short-term time frame may, at times, seem difficult, that actually is true of trading any time frame. As long as the time frame duration is such that a perspective across three time frames can be developed, then any of the time frames can be traded both profitably and in a consistent manner. There are some who will argue quite vehemently that trading the shorter-term time frames is much easier than the long-term ones, and less risky. I have to agree that there is some merit in that thought. A significant advantage, for example, is that day traders totally eliminate overnight risk.

When speaking of time frames and how they are represented via the charts, back when Dow and Hamilton were researching and writing, they utilized daily bar durations across all time frames. In retrospect, using a daily chart for all time frames may have been the right choice then, but in today's computerized world there are many alternatives in terms of bar durations, and using those alternatives provides for a much less cluttered and confusing chart.

The longer the time frame, the greater the need for broader brushstrokes to create a comprehensive and understandable view of the stock. Too many brushstrokes in a picture create a cluttered view. In charting, less is more. When viewed with differing sizes (duration) of bars, the various time frames become more understandable. Trends across time frames are fractals; there are trends within trends that may or may not be the same. One time frame may complement or contradict another. In either case, valuable information is revealed that can be processed and considered. In trading, it isn't necessary to take every trade. A trader gets to pick and choose. A smart trader picks what she believes to be the best trades and leaves the marginal ones alone. It is the act of integrating the trends apparent on the various time frames that creates a more comprehensive picture of the stock. The ability to be more discerning when choosing a stock to trade is enhanced as a result. It is the interaction between the various time frames that many times leads to opportunities to enter into far more favorable trades than would have been possible without the multiple time frame perspective.

Varying Bar Widths

In Chapter 3, the idea of varying the width of the bar to accommodate varying time frames was introduced. The driving premise was to treat each chart as consisting of a roughly equal number of bars, irrespective of the "width of the bar." For example, a five-day chart where each bar represents 30 minutes of data would produce 65 bars on a chart. Similarly, three months of activity in which each bar represented a day would produce a chart with approximately the same number of bars. The same is true for a one-year weekly chart, as well as a five-year monthly chart.

The objective of creating a system where each chart has roughly an equal number of bars is twofold. First, it ensures some degree of predictability. By applying the same rules and procedures across the various time frames, the predictability of the outcome does not need to be second-guessed.

A second benefit is that it allows for standardization. If every chart has approximately 60 bars on it, then each chart can be treated as consisting of a maximum total of 10 swing point highs and lows, where an average number is more likely to be from three to six in most cases. Three to six swing point highs and lows on one time frame are more than sufficient to do the analysis that is needed. If more are present, it becomes somewhat burdensome to navigate. Too few would render the information less valuable, if not altogether worthless. If, for example, a chart yielded a total of two swing point highs and only one swing point low, it would likely be impossible to even assign trend with any confidence on that time frame.

Standardized Time Frames

In the neoclassical trend model, three time frames are recognized: short, intermediate, and long-term. These terms are specifically void of the concept of particular time durations, such as "day" or "hour" and that is done purposefully. The desire is to have time frames that are relevant to the activities of all traders, regardless of the actual length of time each trader may choose to trade. A short-term time frame chart for an intraday trader is guaranteed to have distinct and differing bar widths, as compared to the chart of a long-term trader, who typically buys and holds stock for months, if not years.

The key to a workable time frame is one that is applicable to all traders irrespective of their trading habits. The desire is for any time frame chosen to yield a reasonably accurate analysis of trend creation, transition, and quality for the time period analyzed. After examining numerous time frames of varying durations, the numbers of bars needed to best fulfill this objective across the majority of the markets and trading instruments is approximately 60. The preferred presentation style is to display using a logarithmic scale to give the percentages of price moves, which is more useful than absolute price moves. With the abundance of charting packages available to the average trader today, finding a package (either free or for a fee) can be easily accomplished and there simply isn't a reason not to do so.

Table 6.1 is an example of what differing types of traders might use for their respective time frames. A day trader, for example, will not be interested in a time frame of more than a few days, whereas a long-term investor will have little interest in a time frame that is less than a year, in most cases. How long one intends to be in a trade is usually the primary decision criterion when it comes to determining an appropriate time frame length—the shorter the expected trade length, the shorter the time frames examined.

TABLE 6.1　Time Frame Harmony for All Traders

Trading Style	Short-Term Time Frame	Intermediate-Term Time Frame	Long-Term Time Frame
Day Trader	One-day chart with five-minute bars = 78 bars per time frame	Five-day chart with 30-minute bars = 65 bars per time frame	20-day chart with 120-minute bars = 65 bars per time frame
Swing Trader	Three-month chart with one-day bars = approximately 67 bars per time frame	One-year chart with one-week bars = 52 bars per time frame	Five-year chart with one-month bars = 60 bars per time frame
Long-Term Investor	One-year chart with one-week bars = 52 bars per time frame	Five-year chart with one-month bars = 60 bars per time frame	15-year chart with three-month (quarterly) bars = 60 bars per time frame

Nevertheless, the utilization of three distinct time frames yields a valuable perspective when trading, irrespective of the expected or desired holding time.

Fixed Time Frames

As with most anything in life, to get something you typically have to give up something. It is seldom otherwise. As discussed at length already, the advantages of observing all time frames with a reasonably constant number of bars is paramount. The downside of arbitrarily establishing fixed time frames is that the interpretation of the time frame can sometimes lead to false conclusions. This is increasingly true when the number of bars being examined is decreased.

To alleviate this adverse effect, the suggested time frames and bar widths necessarily target the creation of each time frame with roughly 60 bars. Most charting packages place the time increment on the X-axis of the chart and price on the Y-axis. The time increment is further divided into time durations such as an hour, day, week, months, or even years, as well as a width for each bar displayed. The bar widths are correlated with the time duration. Common bar widths are minutes, hours, days, weeks, and months. Thus, it is not always possible for each time frame to have an exact number of bars represented. When you add in exchange holidays and early closings, then the charts become further distorted in terms of the number of bars presented.

The desire when analyzing a time frame is not to have an exact number of bars but to have a *sufficient number*. A sufficient number is something that approximates 60 bars. It could be as many as 70 or as few as 50, but nothing less. If less than 50, the odds increase substantially that an insufficient number of bars are present to provide a reasonably accurate read of the trend. When too many bars are present, the trend read isn't plagued by inaccuracy as much as by an increase in the complexity. It becomes more complex to read a busy chart with excess bars that, once identified, typically have little to no effect on the current trend. Thus, if a choice between too few bars and too many bars is required, it's best to choose too many—not too few. In this way, the potential weakness of fixed time frame lengths is overcome and only the complexity of the read is increased. Furthermore, the potential of reaching false conclusions is avoided.

Recognize that, in the end, unless each chart is examined uniquely with respect to the time frame duration, using any fixed number of bars will likely lead to some degree of misinterpretation from time to time. To avoid this by treating every chart uniquely would require the technician to relinquish the significant advantages of standardization, an advantage that isn't worth losing. Thus, standardizing on charts with roughly 60 bars offers significant advantages to the user while diminishing the potential of misinterpretations. In those rare cases where the standardized time frames are insufficient in duration to make a proper determination of trend, support, and/or resistance, then pulling the chart back another 20 or 30 bars is not only advisable, but valuable. Doing so will not yield an improper or incorrect reading, but instead enhances the probability of obtaining a proper reading. In essence, standardized time frames is a one-size-fits-all approach to reading charts for three distinct time frames and, in the vast majority of cases, it does an excellent job.

Insufficient Bars Available

When a company first goes public, there is no historical record. There are no previous price points where the stock has traded, no history of swing points, no way to compare today to yesterday, because few data points exist. It is only with time that a body of data is created and comparative analysis of current price and data can occur with respect to historical price and volume data.

As one can surmise, the shorter time frames will naturally become the first that can be analyzed while the longer-term time frames continue to suffer from a lack of comparative data points. With the passing of time, this issue will eventually be overcome for all time frames, but in the meantime, a trader may find opportunity even while the data is still sparse, at best.

In such a situation, it is possible to trade based on incomplete information with regard to each of the three time frames, but precautions need to be taken. For example, it would likely be wise not to trade with a position size that is equal to other positions being traded, since the uncertainty surrounding a chart without sufficient historical data is greater.

Another way to reduce risk would be to trade only on the time frame for which data is available. Initially that limits trades to intraday trading, but in three months' time, enough data is available to trade based on the short-term time frame that a swing trader would utilize.

Eventually the chart will fill out on all time frames and the problem of insufficient data will be alleviated. In the meantime, a trader must be respectful of that which he cannot know, given that there is insufficient data to draw conclusions upon. In the beginning, the interpretation of all but the shortest of time frames is beyond a technician's reach. Over time, that slowly expands to longer- and longer-term time frames.

Single Versus Multiple Time Frames

In Chapters 4 and 5, a number of charts highlighted the idea that the methods used to interpret a chart are independent of the time frames examined.

The ability to use the same rules when examining a short-term time frame or a long-term time frame is both powerful and valuable. It's powerful in that the same algorithms are applicable across all time frames. It's valuable because many opportunities that exist are discovered by comparing and contrasting various time frames for the same stock. Taking the idea a step farther, the stock can be examined in conjunction with the stock sector and/or the general market as well. And finally, all of these can be examined across all three time frames, as well. If you are trading a stock in isolation and based upon just one time frame, you are necessarily limiting your vision of the stock's potential and pitfalls.

As an example, take a look at the following two charts. Both charts are for the same trading instrument. The only difference is that in the first chart (Figure 6.3) the time frame is a five-day chart with 30-minute bars (intermediate-term time frame for a day trader), while in Figure 6.4 the time frame is a 20-day chart with two-hour bars (long-term time frame for a day trader). The time frames do overlap, with the longer one encompassing the shorter time frame.

FIGURE 6.3   Five-Day, 30-Minute Time Frame (QQQQ), July 2, 2010 to July 8, 2010

FIGURE 6.4 20-Day, Two-Hour Time Frame (QQQQ), June 12, 2010 to July 8, 2010

In Figure 6.3, the chart is bullish, but in Figure 6.4, the bullishness on one time frame turns into concern on another.

It is fairly clear that a distorted picture can be derived if only one time frame is observed. This isn't always the case, but many times it is. In general, a broad perspective utilizing all three time frames can increase the accuracy of the overall understanding of a stock's true trend. To not do this is like boxing with one hand tied behind your back. A key tenet to a consistently profitable trading system based on the neoclassical notions of trend theory is to exploit the opportunities and avoid the traps. Analysis of multiple time frames offers a clear advantage to the trader.

In a somewhat related concept, the vast majority of traders tend to trade a single time frame. Even if they examine multiple time frames, and many don't, they end up trading a single one. This isn't an indictment of the tendency, just an observation that there is a better way. Consider this: If multiple time frame analysis is an indispensable tool for profitable trading, then wouldn't it stand to reason that trading multiple time frames would offer additional opportunities that are lost if ignored?

A common trading technique used by many successful traders is to scale into and out of trading positions. The reason for doing so is to avoid one of the most common mistakes made by more novice traders: the thought that they have the ability to pick the top or bottom tick of a move.

The concept of "buying everything at once" or "selling everything simultaneously" is seriously flawed. It treats the market and prices as if they are black or white—discrete versus continuous. This mental obstacle is a key part of trading failure. Trading is not black or white—it is full of shades of gray. The market is not precise. There isn't some overriding equalization algorithm that takes prices to precisely where they should go and then reverses. The vast majority of the time, the price that a stock trades at is nothing more than a reflection of the perceived value of that company. Many times, it is more of a short-term reflection of the emotions of the traders trading the stock—not the stock's intrinsic value. To believe that the market will somehow trade to an exact and predetermined price level is naive. It is unlikely, and if you are basing your trading decisions on such an assumption, it is likely to be quite costly.

Moving back to the idea of multiple time frames, it is usually not the case that the "sell" or "buy" price on one time frame will be the same on multiple time frames. The charts usually do not line up that way. When they do, then the price area identified for a buy or a sell increases in importance, but that isn't the common occurrence. It is far more likely to see different buy and sell areas across differing time frames than in only one. Given this propensity for multiple entry and exit price zones, a far more practical method to practice is to consider buying and selling price zones when entering and exiting stocks, and to do this across multiple time frames.

Price Zones

Price zones are generally defined as a price area where price should trade to, but not beyond. The degree of confidence in the price zone is a reflection of how it is anchored, where anchoring is reflective of the expected supply of stock versus the demand for it.

Price zones offer a price area to use when trading technically. Contrast this with mainstream technical analysis literature that proposes price points and lines. The latter probably occurs because a zone seems quite inexact whereas a point or a line projects certainty, confidence, and knowledge. Unfortunately, what a trader uses to aid in his trading endeavors should be based upon practical results—not visual and mental impressions.

The fact is that there isn't a single indicator in the world that can pinpoint a turning point in a stock or a market with reproducible precision over time. It just does not exist. What does exist is the reality that a stock, a sector, and a market will trade to any of a number of price points while seeking its perceived value. It isn't necessary to know the exact place it will turn, but to be able to identify the general area. If that can be done with reasonable consistency, then a profitable trading system can be formed around it. In such a system, traders scale in and out of their positions, seeking an average price that meets their needs, and not necessarily an exact one.

SUMMARY

Trading trends requires preparation. Part of the preparation is the establishment of a trading strategy and a good understanding of reward and risk. Another element that has a significant effect on the success or failure of a trade is the timing, and reasonably accurate timing is predicated on the analysis of multiple time frames.

Not only is the timing of a trade one of the keys to successful trading, an understanding of which time frame it is that is being traded is just as important. A trader is unlikely to be successful if they look at a weekly chart to consider profit potential and a daily chart to consider loss potential.

The focus of Chapter 7 is on entry and exit as parts of the broad concepts of support and resistance. The idea is to clearly identify zones using some reasonably unique concepts that are an outgrowth of the ideas embodied in trend tests. As you might have guessed, volume is a key part of the process, since volume creates some of the constructs that allow a trader to anchor support and resistance zones in reality, and thus reduce the margin of error on entry and exit.

CHAPTER 7

Entering and Exiting Trades

A trader trades. To trade, he or she must enter a stock and eventually exit it—but when? What triggers an entry and, just as importantly, an exit? At this point in reading this book, a trader would hopefully attempt to trade in a congruent manner with the underlying trend of the stock. Even in that case, as shall be shown, a trader would not necessarily be trading in a congruent manner with the trend on each time frame, as all time frames are seldom in agreement. The simple and oft-repeated aphorism "trade with the trend" isn't as simple to follow as it sounds; what trend is it directed at and on what time frame?

Leaving aside the trend question (which the final chapters of the book are devoted to), this chapter instead focuses on timing. How can a trader time their entry and exit in the most productive manner possible? Anyone can look at a chart and point out two or three places where it made sense to purchase a stock. That is always easy in hindsight, but how does a trader do that in real time? The future is unknown and whether a trader's trading strategy is centered on buying momentum or retraces, the problem is the same: "How does a trader know when to enter a position so as to maximize their likelihood of trading success?"

As stated previously, in my opinion, purchasing retraces is preferable to momentum. The preference is rooted in the assumption that a methodology exists that allows a trader to determine, with a reasonable probability of success, when to purchase (or short sell) a retrace. If that assumption is met, then the mathematics of the reward-to-risk equation is necessarily in favor of the retrace trader, as opposed to the momentum trader. The same is true of the trade's probability of success. Both facts are rooted in another oft-repeated aphorism, "Buy low and sell high." The momentum trader translates that aphorism to resemble the motto of a Ponzi scheme: "Buy higher and sell higher." There's nothing to indicate that both methods can't be successful, but clearly it is less risky to buy low and sell high if low can be determined to actually be low.

So, is it possible to employ a higher probability methodology rooted in the notion of buying retraces? And, just as important, is it possible to determine when to make an exit in order to maximize the returns?

The answer to both questions is a resounding "Yes!" and it is centered on the idea of support and resistance.

SUPPORT AND RESISTANCE

Every technical trader has a reasonable understanding of support and resistance. A plethora of technical literature deals with support and resistance and all the various formations that are observable as part of these two concepts. Technical patterns such as downtrend and uptrend lines, horizontal support and resistance, flags, pennants, triangles, rectangles, and even channel lines are all based upon the idea of support and resistance.

The reason that support and resistance are critical to a trader is because every trader is faced with the same dilemma: when to get into a stock and when to get out. Although determining true trend and the quality of the trend will get a trader on the right side of the trade, entry and exit is the other half of that same trade, and it depends upon the ability to properly identify support and resistance.

Support
Support is generally defined as a price level below which price is less likely to continue to fall, due to the expected demand of stock versus the supply of it.

Support is an area on the chart where, for whatever reason, the expectation is that current prices will be supported. Resistance is essentially the opposite; an area of the chart where, for whatever reason, the expectations are for higher prices to be resisted. The reasons why the concepts of support and resistance exist are too numerous to be recounted here. The fact that books such as *Stock Market Logic*,[1] with an emphasis on the fundamentals of trading, discuss the concepts of support and resistance underlies the pervasive nature of these ideas. Even more technically inclined books, such as *Techniques of Tape Reading*,[2] with a focus on the mental rather than the technical aspects of trading, find it necessary to devote pages to the idea of support and resistance.

Almost without fail, however, almost every textbook example a trader finds presents support and resistance as an event: as a price point or as a line on a chart. That, unfortunately, is not an accurate reflection of what support and resistance are or how they operate.

Resistance
Resistance is generally defined as a price level above which price is less likely to continue to rise, due to the expected supply of stock versus demand for it.

Look at any chart and the majority of the price action that you witness is nothing like the textbook examples where prices decline exactly to some point or line and then turn around. The reality is that price usually overshoots or undershoots the expected price point, and it does so on a consistent basis.

Figure 7.1 is a three-month daily chart of Microsoft Corporation (MSFT), with two horizontal resistance lines and one downtrend resistance line drawn in.

FIGURE 7.1 Resistance Lines—Microsoft Corp. (MSFT), April 5, 2010 to July 2, 2010

FIGURE 7.2 Alternate Downtrend Resistance Line—MSFT, April 5, 2010 to July 2, 2010

Had a technician annotated the chart in early to mid-June, then the downtrend resistance line would mostly likely have appeared as shown in Figure 7.2.

Notice how the downtrend resistance line would have been broken and would thus have provided a false signal that the downtrend was over.

Now observe the horizontal resistance lines. With the resistance line as currently drawn, neither attempt to trade up to the line succeeds (see Figure 7.3). If a trader was attempting to sell Microsoft short as prices pushed to the resistance line, how would they determine at exactly what price point to initiate the short sell? In the same vein, suppose a trader owned Microsoft shares and decided that they needed to unload them. Naturally, the seller wishes to get the best price possible when selling as well. If a potential seller were to hold out, waiting to sell at the resistance line (as drawn on Figure 7.3), then they might still be holding the stock position. The problem is the same, regardless of whether the desire is to buy or to sell.

Fundamentally, the issue with support points and lines is that they are not reflective of reality when it comes to where support and resistance actually reside. Surely it is possible to trade using these somewhat archaic

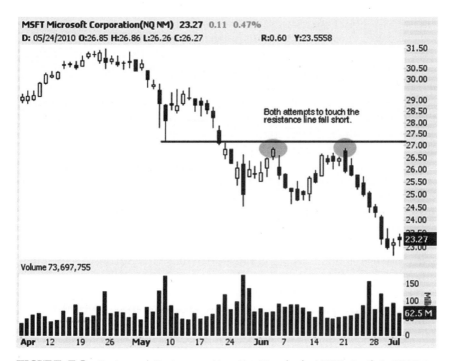

FIGURE 7.3 Horizontal Resistance Line Not Touched—MSFT, April 5, 2010 to July 2, 2010

methods, but why? Why not replace them with a construct that is more reflective of reality? Do away with lines and bring on the zone!

PRICE ZONES, NOT LINES

There is a fundamental problem with presenting support and resistance as points and lines. To the more naive technician, doing so suggests that a stock will trade to an exact line or price point, which is altogether untrue. This does not happen in the real world. In fact, it seldom occurs. It is unreasonable to assume that any technician can predict an exact price point where an advance or a decline will turn, yet when a line is drawn on a chart the implication is that this is in fact predictable.

A second and even more damaging issue is that when drawing lines and points on a chart signifying resistance and support, the mental tendency is to either purchase or sell at that price point—not at many price points. If a trader believes that a particular price point will be the turning point, then it would be inept to not wait for that exact price to print and do the selling.

Such action would not only be justified but unquestionable—assuming that the price point could really be identified. The problem is that *it can't*. The ability to pinpoint a price where a stock will trade to and then reverse is pure fantasy. It may happen on occasion but it is sheer lunacy to believe it will happen consistently.

To approach any reasonable semblance of consistency, a technician should always define zones—not price points. A zone is a price area on the chart where prices should trade to and have difficulty trading beyond. A price zone removes any notion of somehow knowing, *a priori*, an exact price point where a stock will trade to, and instead replaces it with a price area where prices should trade to. It also reinforces the idea that, because you can't really know the exact price point, you probably should buy or sell at differing price levels within the zone rather than at just one particular price point.

When assigning price zones, the typical desire of the novice is to assign a price area that is as tight (small price range) as can be. The common thought process is that the tighter the zone, the better. Although intuitively correct, the fact is that it really doesn't matter how wide the zone is, unless it is humongous. The zone should fit the chart and truly define the price region where prices should trade to but have a hard time trading beyond. That simple statement is what makes a zone valuable; the knowledge that prices should trade to it but probably not beyond it. If it really is possible to define a region where price should trade to, but not beyond, then a trading plan can be built around the zone, but if the zone doesn't truly reflect support/resistance, then the trading plan is much less valuable.

> **Price Zone**
> Price zone is generally defined as a price area where price should trade to, but not beyond. The degree of confidence in the price zone is a reflection of how it is anchored, where anchoring is reflective of the expected supply of stock versus the demand for it.

Figure 7.4 is the same chart previously shown of the downtrend resistance line for Microsoft (see Figure 7.2) with a $0.75 range superimposed on the downtrend line.

Naturally, one should wonder about the value of simply imposing a $0.75 range versus arbitrarily picking $1.00 or $2.00. Picking a range based on percentages would have more merit, as then it could be applied to all charts in an equal manner. Either way, though, one problem remains: "What width should the zone be?"

FIGURE 7.4 Downtrend Resistance Zone—MSFT, April 5, 2010, to July 2, 2010

Figure 7.5 shows the horizontal resistance line that was first displayed in Figure 7.3. Again, the width of the horizontal resistance zone is approximately $0.75, an amount that is simply pulled from thin air.

Again, the question remains. "What real value is added?" The answer is "very little." To be valuable, zones need to be anchored in some way. They need be bounded by something that is in fact important, something solid and unmoving. In the stock market, it is reasonably easy to tell what is of importance: It is the zone where either price and/or volume increases or decreases significantly on a comparative basis. It doesn't matter whether prices head higher or lower; when price and/or volume expand, there is almost always an underlying reason for this to occur. The reason may or may not be known, but it exists nevertheless. When there is a benchmark to compare the price or volume expansion to, then the relative value of the price area can be grasped.

Proper identification of support and resistance is very similar to proper identification and qualification of trend: Both depend on measuring conviction and desire at critical areas on the chart. Both derive their value from the trading action that they are centered on, and the ability to accurately identify both is what makes a trader successful. If a trader can determine

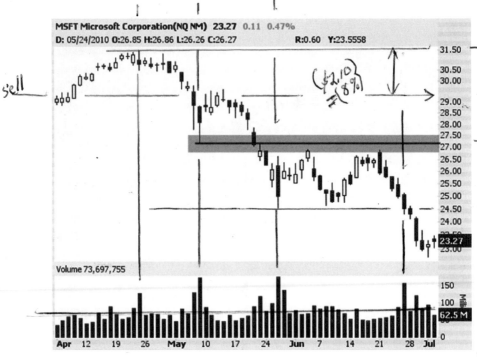

FIGURE 7.5 Horizontal Resistance Zone—MSFT, April 5, 2010 to July 2, 2010

the direction and then combine that knowledge with a reasonable timing methodology, then he or she has the essential technical ingredients to trade successfully.

Unfortunately, uptrend and downtrend lines do not lend themselves to this type of analysis because there simply isn't anything to which to anchor them. If you can't anchor a line to something of importance, then it has little value. The notion that a line rests upon three or four price points adds little value because the price points it rests on are viewed as somewhat equal in value. There is no evidence that this is true. Worse, drawing a support or resistance line provides a trader with the false confidence that the line is somehow a valid representation of support or resistance. Having three or more points on a line is great, but does a trader really derive increased confidence based on the fourth point on the line, or instead become increasingly worried?

The best work on uptrend and downtrend lines was by W. D. Gann. Gann spent a great deal of time developing the notion that the angle of the line has significance.[3] The degree of the angle was what his work was centered on, and it was directed toward addressing the issue of time and price. Steeper angles created less stable and more volatile price action, while flatter angled lines were less volatile. Gann pursued a unique idea that the angles also could measure time. Given that the trader's demise is usually the result of time combined with direction, Gann truly took his brand of technical research to new heights. If a trader wishes to use sloped resistance and support lines, Gann angles have the greatest potential for rewarding the trader, in my humble opinion.

But angular support and resistance are not critical to successful trading—they are useful if accurate, but not critical. Timing the entry and exit can be based solely upon swing point tests in addition to support and resistance zones constructed from horizontal lines or, more aptly, from zones.

Moving back to the discussion of horizontal support and resistance, Figure 7.6 is annotated to highlight those areas of the chart that have volume and price significance. Each of the circled bars exhibited significantly increased volume as compared to other bars on this particular time frame. In some cases, the price spread of the bar (the difference between high and low of the bar) was significant as compared to all other price spreads on this time frame. These price and volume patterns have

FIGURE 7.6 High-Volume and Wide-Price-Spread Bars—MSFT, April 5, 2010 to July 2, 2010

significance. They are not equal in importance to all other bars—they are more important. In this chart, the owners of Microsoft stock didn't sell or buy a significantly larger number of shares (as seen in the shaded ovals) at those annotated areas simply because they wanted to. Instead, they were compelled to.

In this particular example, something has made the owners fear that things might get worse and the price of the stock could go even lower. Something compelled them to sell their shares at lower and lower prices—at price levels that heretofore Microsoft had not traded at for a reasonably long time (in most of these cases).

There are a number of chart patterns that occur as a result of price and volume behavior that lead to the creation of support and resistance zones. The most valuable patterns are where both price *and* volume work in conjunction. The next few paragraphs look at the chart patterns that provide a technician with the ability to define support and resistance zones that have meaning and value.

DEFINING ENTRY AND EXIT POINTS

To identify support and resistance zones that have significance, the technical trader needs to find charting events that, in and of themselves, have significance. It has already been shown that swing points have significance. That importance is telegraphed to the trader as the collective set of market participants express their current view by attempting to stretch current price boundaries to either higher heights or lower depths. Conviction is measured through volume expansion as swing points were tested and broken. In this manner, the charts do provide signals of conviction and importance at swing points. As a result, swing points are excellent anchors for support and resistance zones, but they are not alone.

The charts also offer hints of conviction and importance at places other than the swing points. Those "other places" are indeed identifiable on a chart, just as swing points are. These other places are found on the following three identifiable events:

1. Volume escalation
2. Wide price spread
3. Gap formations

There is plenty in current technical literature that addresses volume escalation and gap formations, but not necessarily treating these as part of support and resistance identification. That is unfortunate because it is as part of support and resistance determination that these three gems shine at their brightest.

When one or more of the above attributes appear on a chart, they are referred to as *anchor bars*. Anchor bars many times appear in clusters or congruently. Additionally, swing points may contain anchor-bar characteristics as well, increasing their importance. When taken as a whole, swing points and anchor bars are useful chart events that, once related, permit a technician to construct support and resistance zones that have significance.

It is with this increased predictive ability to pinpoint price zones where prices should be supported and resisted that allows the technical trader to buy and sell retraces into support and resistance with greater confidence. When this skill is combined with qualified trend, a trader indeed has an edge.

Zones Anchored by Bars

Multiple anchor bars are created on almost all time frames and for all charts. An anchor bar is, for the time frame being examined, a bar where volume expands dramatically as compared to other volume, the price spread of the bar is large compared to all other bars, or the bar is the result of a gap up or down in price.

Anchor bars consist of one or more of these three defining attributes.

❅ Anchor
An anchor bar is, for the time frame being examined, a bar where volume expands dramatically as compared to all other bars, or the price spread of the bar is large compared to all other bars, or the bar is the result of a gap up or down in price or a combination of one or more of these characteristics.

❅ Anchor Top
An anchor top is the high price of an anchor bar.

❅ Anchor Bottom
An anchor bottom is the low price of an anchor bar.

Many times swing points also double as anchor bars. Anchors apply only to the time frame being examined, which tends to enhance their usefulness. Old anchors eventually slip off the left side of the chart as time progresses, leaving other anchors to take their place. Anchors on shorter-term time frames, if significant, can become anchors on longer-term time frames as well. This usually happens when a cluster of anchor bars forms, which magnifies their significance on longer-term time frames.

The value that an anchor bar brings to a stock chart is a reference point. Many times anchor bars involve swing points and price gap occurrences. In those cases where they don't, they remain extremely useful because they identify a point of contention—a place on the chart where an epic battle was fought between those wanting to buy and those wanting to sell. It is epic because a significant amount of force was brought to bear at that particular price point as represented on that particular bar. Epic battles are not soon forgotten.

From a trading perspective, the true value of an anchor bar is realized when they are utilized to "anchor" horizontal support and resistance zones.

Many times anchor bars are not isolated events. When envisioning the battle between buyers and sellers that occurs while an anchor bar is formed, it is not at all uncommon to see that battle continue on the very next bar. Battles are not always decided in one day. When this happens, an anchor bar cluster is created.

Similarly, sometimes the buy-and-sell troops take intervening periods of rest before resuming the battle. Almost invariably this occurs in close proximity to the original battle line. When this happens, congruent anchor bars are formed. Congruent anchor bars tend to reinforce the fact that this area of the chart has greater significance.

Other times, one side or the other fighting the buy and sell battle completely overruns the opposing force's battle line. The chart reflects this behavior as well. In this case, a price gap can occur or a high-volume anchor bar and/or an anchor bar having wide price spread is created. If the rout was complete, all these attributes can appear on the very same bar. Many times this type of action leads to the whoosh down or spike higher seen on the chart as the losing side turns tail and runs—for a bar.

Table 7.1 summarizes each of these five anchor bar types found on a chart, along with their essential characteristics. Essentially, there are three basic forms of anchor bars: those with high volume and/or those with wide price spread and/or those consisting of trading gaps. Congruent and cluster anchor bars are simply a combination of two or more of these three basic anchor bar types in a particular configuration that creates added significance. There is nothing to prevent gap anchor bars from sharing the attributes from other anchor bars.

TABLE 7.1 Anchor Bar Types and Characteristics

Type	Strength Characteristics
High-Volume Anchor Bar	When volume expands tremendously for an anchor bar as compared to all other anchor bars, then the greater the significance and strength of the anchor bar with respect to support and resistance.
Wide-Price-Spread Anchor Bars	The wider the price spread of the anchor bar, the greater the significance and strength of the anchor.
Gap Anchor Bars	Gaps are areas on the chart where price does not trade from one bar to the next. Gaps usually come in threes, and the first and third gaps have greater value when viewed as anchor bars.
Clustered Anchor Bars	Clustered anchor bars tend to reinforce each other; thus, when more than one anchor is located in close proximity to another, those anchors that are closely located act to support each other. The overlapping area is what provides strength to subsequent support and resistance tests.
Congruent Anchor Bars	Probably the strongest anchor bar attribute, when present, is the proximity of the anchor bar's top and bottom price points with respect to other anchors. When an anchor's top or bottom aligns with other anchor bars' tops or bottoms, then the significance of the price area where they come close or overlap is magnified; the greater the number of anchors that meet this condition, the higher the significance.

Each of these anchor bar types is considered in the following paragraphs.

High-Volume Anchor Bar   When volume expands tremendously for a bar as compared to all other bars on the time frame under examination, the result is a high-volume anchor bar.

> ***High-Volume Anchor Bar***
> In a high-volume anchor bar, volume expands dramatically as compared to all other bars on the time frame being examined.

High-volume anchor bars are just what they sound like, a place where price can be justifiably considered important as a result of volume expansion. To be a high-volume anchor simply requires that a bar exhibit a "significantly noticeable" volume increase as compared to all other bars on the time frame under examination. "Significantly noticeable" is not a mathematical designation, simply a visual one, and is thus necessarily imprecise. That doesn't, however, diminish its usefulness.

Looking back at Figure 7.6, it could be argued that the fourth from the last bar should be highlighted as well, and it would be a justifiable argument. Volume was easily over 100 million shares traded that day, while most days traded only 50 or 60 million shares. The limiting factor when identifying anchor bars is the number of bars identified. Since roughly 60 bars are present on a chart, a proliferation of anchor bars removes the value of identifying such a bar. Too much of anything usually isn't a good thing. If there are too many anchors, then the value diminishes. Value is derived from having just a few. Having more than five or six anchor bars is probably too many since, on most charts, there are roughly 60 bars. One out of every 10 is about as many as can be identified and still have value. As time passes, the chart may develop in such a way that a bar that was previously skipped over as an anchor ends up being identified as one because a sufficient number of previously identified bars have slipped off the left edge of the graph. The interpretation is fluid, as can be surmised, but the value is there.

With these anchor ideas in mind, revisiting the Microsoft chart from Figure 7.6 and annotating it using high-volume anchor bars results in an answer to the original question of where to draw the resistance zone (see Figure 7.7).

As shown in Figure 7.7, the width of a support or a resistance zone is completely dependent on the chart formation when incorporating the idea of anchor bars. There is no set percentage, and to believe that there is would be somewhat foolish. Every chart is an island unto itself. It has its own character, its own DNA. Although the application of neoclassical trend theory attempts to categorize and standardize all stocks, it does so gingerly and only in certain areas where the categorization is least obtrusive and most valuable to the technician and trader. In those areas where standardization cannot be achieved, then it isn't forced upon the charts. To do so would be counterproductive.

It is worth noting, that in spite of this nonstandardized approach to anchor bars defining support and resistance zones, the application of this process lends itself to automation, if so desired. At www.tatoday.com, qualified trends and entry/exit criteria are automatically generated to aid in trading endeavors. This approach to support and resistance is a bit more complicated, but certainly not terribly so.

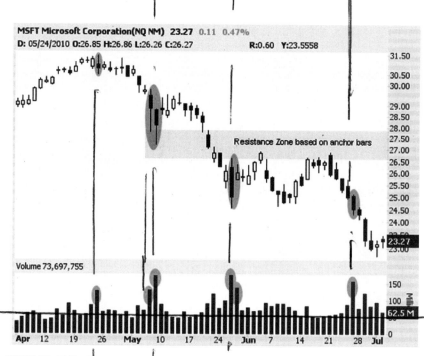

FIGURE 7.7 Resistance Zones Based on Anchor Bars—MSFT, April 5, 2010 to July 2, 2010

In Figure 7.7, notice how the use of a zone actually provides an entry or an exit in Microsoft's stock where none was offered previously when using a line. Stock entry would have been what a short-sell trader was attempting to gain, and the use of the zone based on high-volume anchors would have provided entry.

In the opposite situation, long shareholders of Microsoft who were inclined to sell would try to do so gracefully. Again the same anchored resistance zone would have provided two separate possibilities for exit. Without the zone concept, it would have been much more difficult and susceptible to greater guesswork.

Figure 7.8 provides another example of a high-volume anchor bar. In this chart, DG FastChannel, Inc., recorded more than 4 million shares on a weekly basis when compared to 2.5 million shares at the highest previous recording. When volume expands that much, that bar becomes a strong high-volume anchor bar.

For the purposes of support and resistance, when a high-volume anchor bar is created, the technician still must seek other bars of importance to combine with in order to create a solid resistance or support zone. That could be other anchor bars, gaps, or swing point highs or lows. In this

FIGURE 7.8 Resistance Zones Based on Anchor Bars—DG FastChannel, Inc. (DGIT), November 6, 2008 to November 2, 2009

particular chart, at the time that the high-volume anchor bar just described was created, there were two prior anchor bars with relatively larger-sized volume that are relatively close in price. Thus the technician can reach for these bars to create the support zone. As it turns out, the support zone does hold up reasonably well.

A quick word about support and resistance as it relates to a large volume bar as shown in Figure 7.8: The fact that volume expands dramatically relays two important items of information to the technician. First, it says that something of importance has occurred. It may or may not be in the news yet, but something significant has happened because, without significance, there would be no reason for that many shares to trade at a greater volume relative to its usual volume.

The second item is associated with the case where an abnormally high number of shares have traded. In that particular case, if the price spread is significant, then the highs and the lows of the large volume bar become natural magnets for price going forward. Magnets are covered as a later topic, but essentially they are price bars with huge volume either at the top or bottom of the chart. Magnets tend to draw prices toward them and, given their importance, they tend to be quite difficult to trade beyond the first time or two that the magnet bar is tested.

Given that support and resistance zones attempt to identify a price area that is difficult to trade beyond, a magnet bar is an excellent bar to choose when it comes to anchoring a support or resistance zone. Much more about magnet bars is presented later.

Wide-Price-Spread Anchor Bars   When a bar exhibits abnormally high price spread (the difference between the high and low of the bar) as compared to all other bars on the time frame being examined, then that is a wide-price-spread anchor bar. Such an event is usually an indication that one side or the other of the trade (buyers or sellers) were quite content when the bar began and reasonably certain that their view was correct. By the end of the trading bar, however, those same traders were quite uncertain and/or convinced that their initial outlook for price was just plain wrong. Essentially, as the bar was created, one or more huge reversals in sentiment took place. The result is a bar that has wide price spread as compared to all other bars that had previously traded on the same time frame. Such a bar becomes an anchor bar and has significance.

Wide-Price-Spread Anchor Bar
In a wide-price-spread anchor bar, the spread between the high and low of the bar expands dramatically as compared to the price spread on all other bars for the time frame being examined.

Wide price spread, like many technical constructs and concepts, is defined loosely. Wide price spread is rather noticeable when looking at a chart but isn't some fixed percentage across all charts since every chart trades with its own personality to some degree and that personality changes over time. Wide price spread is relative to all other bars for the observed chart. You will know it is wide price spread because when you look at the chart, you can't help but notice the wide disparity between the high and the low of the bar as compared to all other bars. A bar with wide price spread literally jumps off the chart!

When wide price spread occurs, many times it is accompanied by increased volume as the uncertainty creates heightened emotions, and elevated emotions are what create an increase in transactions. Examples of wide price spread are more common in individual stocks as compared to

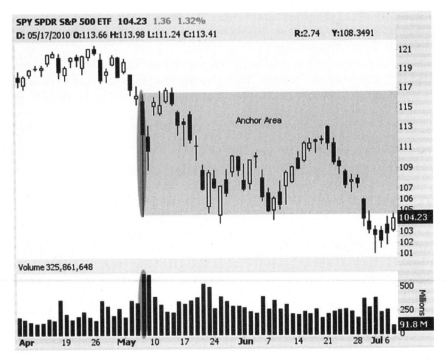

FIGURE 7.9 Wide-Price-Spread Spawning Anchor Bars—SPDR S&P 500 ETF (SPY), April 7, 2010 to July 7, 2010

the general market. When wide price spread does occur in the general market indexes, it has added significance.

Figure 7.9 is an example of a wide-price-spread anchor bar on a broad market index. In this case it was the SPDR S&P 500 ETF, which tracks the performance of the 500 large capitalization stocks on the New York Stock Exchange.

The trading that took place on the particular day highlighted in the chart was dubbed the "Flash Crash" because the majority of the decline occurred within a few minutes—thus the term *flash*. At the time, some market pundits suggested that the price action wasn't real and that it should be dismissed.[4] There is very little that happens in the markets that can be dismissed, especially when it ends up on the chart. The chart records all price and volume activity over some period of time. If errant trades don't truly occur, the exchange will bust the trades (undo the trade), and the highs and lows on the charts get corrected to reflect the "official" highs and lows once the trades are settled. In all other cases, because there is real money represented by the transactions that find their way onto the charts, you can rest assured that everything on the chart is real and has significance—even if it came in a flash!

Significantly wide price spread always creates an anchor bar. What is somewhat unique about some wide-price-spread anchor bars is that many times these bars end up anchoring both the top and bottom of price transactions for some time to come. Essentially they create a large "anchor area" where prices are trapped for an extended period of time. In the daily bar chart displayed in Figure 7.9, the highlighted wide-price-spread anchor bar traps prices for almost two months. Because this particular anchor bar had a downside bias (the bar was created as price decreased), the expectation would be that the bottom of the anchor bar is the side that should eventually break since the bias was bearish by virtue of the price decline that defined the anchor bar itself.

Gap Anchor Bars A gap is an area of the chart where prices simply do not trade. This could be on any time frame, but the shorter the time frame, the greater the potential for price gaps to exist. Finding a gap on a monthly chart is indeed much more difficult to accomplish since a month's worth of trading would need to occur without "covering" the gap area.

As with most general technical concepts, much has been written about gaps from a trading perspective.[5] Very little, however, has been written about how gaps factor into support and resistance. The significance of a price gap from a support or resistance perspective does have value and thus provides another tool to aid the trader in both entering and exiting trading positions. Like all support and resistance formations, the first time the gap is tested, it is usually at its pinnacle of strength. Each subsequent test has a greater likelihood of closing the gap.

As with almost any technical formation, there are variations of the technical patterns that define gaps. The most common gaps are islands, breakaway, continuation, and exhaustion gaps. Each gap has its own unique place as an anchor in the formation of support and resistance zones.

Figure 7.10 displays an island gap in a broad sector ETF, the SPDR AMEX Financial Select Index, which is a composite index for the financial stocks (XLF). The fact that the gap occurs in a sector makes it applicable to all financial stocks that trade in the sector. In other words, it has broader implications.

This particular type of gap is called an island gap. You can essentially think of an island gap as both a gap up and a gap down (or the inverse) that leaves the impression of an island when looking at the chart.

In this particular chart, once the island gap was created, it took almost five months to get back over the gap and to trade higher. Like everything else, the significance of the gap is influenced by the volume created as part of the gap creation. In the case of XLF, 112 million shares traded the day

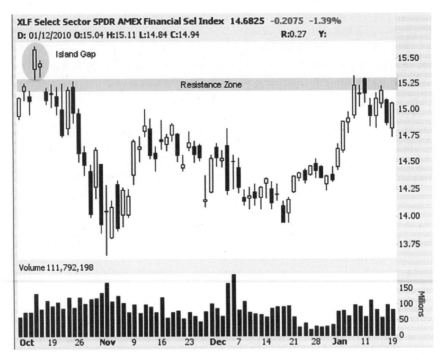

FIGURE 7.10 Island Gap Resistance Zone—SPDR AMEX Financial Select Index (XLF), October 9, 2009 to January 19, 2010

the island top was created. Each of the two attempts to trade back into the gap area saw fewer shares traded, and each failed. On the third try, the gap was filled, although volume was still lacking (see Figure 7.11).

One might wonder why this is the case—why, on the third try, were there enough buyers to push it over the top, although the number of buyers (as evidenced by volume) was fewer than the number of sellers when the gap resistance was created. That is best understood by considering the sequence of events. Assume that the number of natural sellers at the island gap resistance zone remained reasonably constant throughout the period where resistance held. These natural sellers are those shareholders who have, given the changing circumstances, now decided that their holdings are not worth keeping. An axiom in trading that expresses itself over and over is that the majority of shareholders stuck in a losing trade are not quick to take losses. In fact, the desire is to get out for even or as close to even as possible. These natural sellers create the supply of stock that is "naturally sold" as price approaches the area where the shareholders can escape their shares at breakeven or reasonable losses. Thus, the first attempt to trade higher consumes some number of those natural sellers. The fact that prices fell back lower is an indication that the number of buyers wasn't sufficient at that point to consume all of the offered shares. After trading lower, the number of buyers continued at a greater pace than sellers and eventually prices pushed back to the area where the natural sellers at the gap resistance zone were able to sell again for the price that they desired.

Once more, there were still more sellers than buyers, yet the pool of natural sellers at that particular price zone continued to decrease in number and size. Finally, on the third attempt, the ranks of natural sellers were sufficiently thinned such that even with fewer buyers than were originally registered when the island gap was created, the buyers ranks outstripped those of the sellers, resulting in prices moving higher and through the island gap resistance zone. It is in this way that prices can move higher on less volume, when compared to the volume of the prior price point. It is this sort of action that creates a suspect trend. It is suspect because conviction isn't shown; instead, the depletion of the natural sellers results in an increase of price. When conviction isn't on display, the trend transition is suspect and must be viewed as such. This is true of trend transitions that push through all types of support or resistance zones and on all time frames. This is true of all markets all around the world because human reactions to greed and fear are uniform across the globe.

When prices surge higher but volume doesn't expand, it tells the trader that technically this price area is quite vulnerable for a retest. In Figure 7.11, the effect of gap resistance failing to contain price despite lower volume is quite visible. The result was that the move eventually failed and prices traded back to and under the gap area once more.

What's more, when prices finally broke down after a suspect bullish trend had been established, they did so in exactly the same way—by leaving yet another island gap, as annotated on the chart.

There is a lot to learn in this particular chart. First, an island top gap is a formidable resistance zone if volume is reasonably significant on the formation of the island since many losing positions are left stranded. Second, a suspect bullish trend almost always makes it back to the scene of the crime to attempt a retest and regenerate sequence. If the retest occurs on lighter volume than the breakout, then the retest does its job and the original trend can regain precedence. If, as in the case of XLF in Figure 7.11, the volume coming back is heavier than that which occurred on the initial move higher (in this case higher than the volume that was registered on the formation of the original island gap resistance), then the breakout trend is confirmed as being inadequate and the trend transitions once more with confirmation. That is what happened to the XLF ETF on this time frame and the result was a confirmed trend change reflecting a weaker trend state.

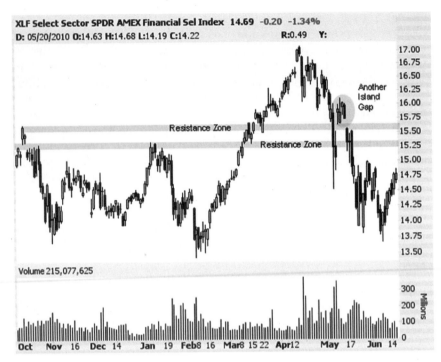

FIGURE 7.11   Island Gap Resistance Zone—XLF, October 9, 2009 to June 15, 2010

Finally, the last island gap created can now be combined with the high of the large anchor bar to create another resistance zone in addition to the original resistance zone. Both the anchor and the gap have merit and, when combined, make for an even stronger resistance zone for future prices to contend with.

The common three-gap sequence is a breakaway gap followed by a continuation gap that is eventually ended with an exhaustion gap. The sequencing is such that the breakaway gap starts a move (up or down) while the continuation gap (sometimes called a measuring gap) continues the move. Finally, an exhaustion gap is the last-gasp attempt to move farther in the same direction. The exhaustion gap almost always ends up being the final thrust of the move. Figure 7.12 is a chart of Interactive Brokers Group, Inc., and displays all three of these gaps.

Although gap formations are typically treated from a trade entry perspective in most technical literature, they do have additional value. That value is seen in support and resistance identification, which is why it is presented here.

FIGURE 7.12 Common Gaps—Interactive Brokers Group, Inc. (IBKR), July 20, 2009 to October 28, 2009

Each gap in the common three-gap sequence has certain characteristics that can aid in the formation of support and resistance zones. The first and the last gaps of the three-gap sequence can be quite useful in that identification process, while the continuation gap has minimum significance. All three are discussed below.

Breakaway gaps are so named because they tend to delineate between a previous price area and a new price area. A concept introduced later is the idea of floors and how, when moving between floors, quite often breakaway gaps are created. As such, breakaway gaps create strong areas of resistance or support in the direction of the breakaway and are by far the strongest of the three common gaps in that respect.

Figure 7.13 is a continuation of the Interactive Brokers chart previously displayed in Figure 7.12. In this chart, breakaway gaps are shown both on the way to higher prices and then eventually once again on the way to lower prices.

Breakaway gaps create strong support and resistance zones in their own right. In this chart, notice how the support zone created by the

FIGURE 7.13 Breakaway Gap: Support and Resistance—IBKR, June 15, 2009 to July 14, 2010

breakaway gap in the summer of 2009 held reasonably well as support for months and months into the future.

Flipping to the other side of the equation, the same is true of the huge breakaway gap from late October of 2009 when prices broke from $19 a share to a little over $18. That was a breakaway gap back the other way, leaving a resistance zone. It also, like the support zone, provided resistance for a significant period of time.

The continuation gap is the least useful of the three common gaps. Many technicians read a continuation gap as a halfway point of the entire move started by the breakaway gap. As a result, it is sometimes called a measuring gap.

From a support and resistance viewpoint, unless the continuation gap has a significant price spread on a percentage basis and does so with heavier volume, then it has little value and is best to ignore. In those cases where it does have a large gap area with volume, then the gap area becomes a support or resistance zone. Even in such a case, though, it is likely that the gap up or down would be picked up as an anchor bar anyway, so tracking continuation gaps for support and resistance is unlikely to yield

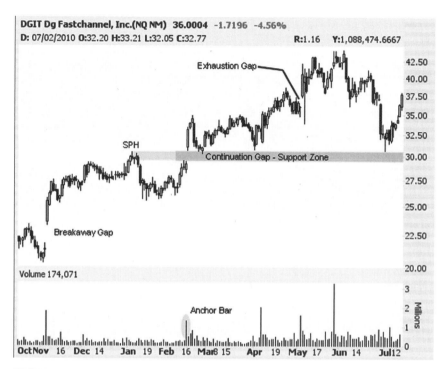

FIGURE 7.14   Continuation Gap—DGIT, October 16, 2009 to July 14, 2010

additional value—especially when compared to the effort of doing so. The limited value that can be gained is to use the gap area as a resistance or support zone when the above criteria are met. Figure 7.14 is an example of a continuation gap that also is a wide-price-spread anchor bar displaying increasing volume.

The problem is that, in most cases, the cost of tracking continuation gaps exceeds the benefit. In this particular example, using the anchor bar and the previous swing point high would have yielded almost an identical support zone (see the overlapping shaded support-zone area).

The real moral of the story regarding continuation gaps is to use them if they add value when attempting to create support or resistance zones to aid in trading; otherwise, they can be safely ignored.

Exhaustion gaps, like breakaway gaps, do have significance and can be used to identify support and resistance zones. Their use is slightly different than a breakaway, however, because the value becomes apparent once the exhaustion gap is filled.

Figure 7.15 shows the common gap sequence in a chart of Sprint Corporation. It takes more than a month to fill the exhaustion gap.

FIGURE 7.15 Exhaustion Gap—Sprint Corp. (S), February 5, 2009 to August 4, 2009

Once the gap is filled, then the exhaustion gap area becomes the resistance zone (or support zone, if the gaps occurred during a bearish trend). In the case of Sprint, it would be another 10 months before the resistance zone created by the exhaustion gap was exceeded again.

Clustered Anchor Bars   Clustered anchor bars refer to the situation in which multiple anchor bars are created in close proximity to each other and, as a result, they tend to reinforce one another.

Clustered Anchor Bars
Clustered anchor bars form a pattern of anchor bars consisting of two or more contiguous basic anchor bars.

Many times a double or triple cluster is created on a fast price rise or fall that involves two or three bars in succession. Figure 7.16 shows a clustered anchor bar setup.

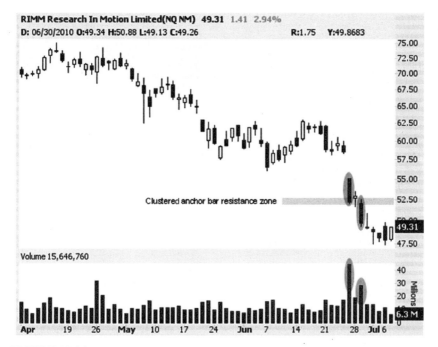

FIGURE 7.16 Clustered Anchor Bars—Research in Motion, Ltd. (RIMM), April 7, 2010 to July 7, 2010

In this chart, Research in Motion (RIMM) sold off in a fast and furious fashion. The two highlighted anchor bars are clustered together (a third anchor bar separates them) and as a result, the overlap between the two bars creates a significant resistance zone—a price zone that will not easily be overcome.

Clustered anchor bars are similar to congruent anchor bars in that it is the price overlap between the anchors that creates a support or resistance zone of importance. The difference between them is that cluster anchors come as a group of adjacent bars. Congruent anchor bars can occur over large periods of time, in which many bars separate the anchor bars.

Congruent Anchor Bars Usually the strongest anchors are those where multiple noncontiguous anchor bars create a congruent support or resistance area.

Congruent Anchor Bars

Congruent anchor bars form a pattern consisting of two or more noncontiguous basic anchor bars.

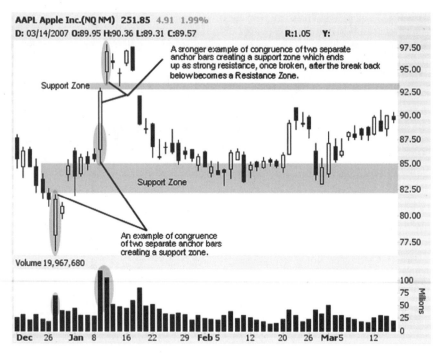

FIGURE 7.17 Resistance Zones Based on Anchor Bars—Apple Corp. (APPL), December 18, 2006 to March 15, 2007

In Figure 7.17, Apple Corporation witnessed a reversal bar in late December of 2007, where volume expanded significantly compared to all previous volume bars. A little more than a week later, another significant expansion in volume and price occurred.

The top of the first reversal bar and the bottom of the expansion bar resulted in a price zone that anchored support for Apple going forward. In this case, there is no overlap between the bars but they are reasonably close in price spread.

Additionally, clustered anchor bars appear near the price highs on this time frame (second and third shaded ovals). In this case, a price gap was created as prices spiked much higher and volume swelled. This tremendous pop higher is the case where the selling forces were overrun.

Initially, this second set of clustered anchor bars acted as a support zone. This can be seen where price retreated to the support zone, then popped higher once more for a couple of bars. After the enthusiasm wore off, both buyers and sellers began to reassess the tremendous percentage price move that occurred in a short time span (22 percent in less than two weeks). The result was that Apple's stock tumbled lower, turning the support zone into a resistance zone, in the same way that a support line turns into a resistance line. There is no difference between a support line and a support zone in this respect. Once support is broken, it becomes resistance, and vice versa.

For patient traders, the lower support zone that was anchored by the late December and middle of January anchor bars is the price area to make initial or additional purchases. Because support is anchored, it should provide good support—and it did. At this price area, there is no longer a rush to exit due to a huge percentage price increase and thus, if the initial surge of buying has a true basis in reality, then this price zone should provide a low risk entry area to purchase the stock.

As time passed, Apple stock eventually worked higher and the resistance zone around the $93 area was finally overcome. In less than a year, AAPL share prices doubled to more than $200 per share. The low-risk entry was to buy the support zone ($82–$85) based on congruent anchor bars.

Summary

Anchor bars are excellent signposts on a chart. They define areas on the chart where significance can be found. The fact that they are significant enables the technician to determine areas where lower prices are likely to be bought (support) and price areas where higher prices are likely to be sold (resistance).

Anchor bars come in varying flavors. As with most technical indicators, a trader's view and conviction are increased when multiple technical signals align with each other. Furthermore, although not addressed yet, conviction likewise increases further when multiple technical signals align across multiple time frames. With anchor bars, close proximity between anchor highs and lows on multiple anchor bars, irrespective of their proximity in time, provides increased confidence in the support and resistance zones that they create.

When huge volume occurs on a single bar, the significance of the price area defined by that bar is markedly increased. If a high-volume anchor bar is accompanied by wide price spread, then even greater importance can be placed on the price zone that lies between the top and bottom price boundaries defined by the wide-price-spread anchor bar.

More broadly speaking, combining anchor bars with trend and swing points provides a significant advantage in trying to determine entry and exit prices for stocks. In general, anchor bars provide an excellent way to implement a trading plan for exit and entry on both winning and losing positions. Naturally, the objective of trading is to lose less money than you make, and an important piece of that puzzle is to reduce your realized losses in losing positions. For example, if a trader finds herself on the losing side of a trade, then knowing that the most you can expect to get back out of a losing trade is defined by the price zone resulting from a set of anchor bars will help a trader to minimize her losses.

Although anchor bars are reasonably easy to identify, there are no hard rules about how much volume is needed, or how much price spread is required. Although guidelines are suggested, the identification process is interpretative, and over time, each technician will form his own ideas about what the identification parameters are with respect to their trading style and visual acumen.

Combining Swing Points and Anchor Bars

Swing points, in the majority of cases, define areas of the charts where a price boundary exists. Anchor bars identify chart price areas where significance exists. Swing points and anchor bars, either in isolation or in complementary positions, can define support and resistance zones.

There are times where swing points end up clustered, just like anchor bars. Clustered swing points are similar to clustered anchor bars, although usually not as valuable. The fact that multiple swing points tend to cluster in the same price vicinity lends credence to the idea that the price area has more relevance, but unless volume was significant at the swing point, a cluster of low-volume swing points is only slightly more valuable than a single swing point without volume support.

Figure 7.18 shows a clustered swing point support zone where two swing point lows align relatively closely in price, but neither has significant volume. The result is that they do provide weak support.

As prices retreat to the clustered swing point area, the key will be to examine the volume characteristics when the clustered swing zone is hit. In this particular case (and in general) the trader should always err on the side of caution. In this particular chart, the most recent swing point low has more than 10 million shares traded for the week. To break through this cluster swing point support zone, more than 10 million shares will be needed to provide confidence that even lower prices are likely. The next most swing point lows has 7.3 million shares, which adds additional support and makes it slightly more difficult to break through this area.

If there is one underlying concept that bears repeating, it is that many technical patterns are strengthened—they give more confidence—when multiple technical patterns complement each other. This only makes sense and has been thoroughly discussed in the technical literature for a long time.

For support and resistance zones, there is overwhelming evidence that this concept applies as well. Figure 7.19 is the same chart of Interactive Brokers as shown in Figure 7.13, with the small exception that the support

FIGURE 7.18 Clustered Swing Points—Cooper Industries (CBE), July 6, 2009 to July 6, 2010

and resistance zones have been redrawn to include anchor and/or swing bars. The picture presented is quite different and enlightening.

The value of combining gap, anchor, and swing points when creating support and resistance zones is that in real trading, you need guideposts—something that will tell you when to get in and when to get out. "Getting in" is a one-sided trade because it is the beginning or initiation of a position. "Getting out" is two-sided; a trade exit occurs because either profits or losses are being taken. Recognizing both types of exit criteria is important, and having support and resistance zones that encompass the majority of the *future price points* is a critical part to being able to successfully navigate the markets over time.

Looking back at Figure 7.19, when adding multiple criteria to create the support and resistance zones, it clearly offers more value than Figure 7.13, which used the gap area only. It is more valuable because it encompasses a price zone that captures the majority of the future price highs and lows. The ability to construct the lower resistance zone was possible once the large gap-down bar was created. Without the lower resistance zone,

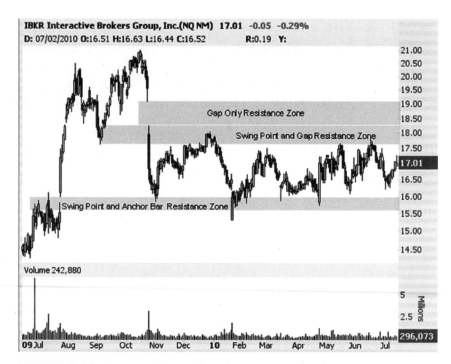

FIGURE 7.19 Common Gaps and Anchor Bars Combined—IBKR, June 15, 2009 to July 14, 2010

a trader trying to exit a losing long position or attempting to establish a short-sell position would never have the opportunity to make the trade, since the gap resistance zone is never penetrated.

Regardless of whether the trade taken is to exit a winning or losing position, having support and resistance zones that actually *predict* future turning points is critical. That is what support and resistance are for. By combining multiple criteria, more useful support and resistance zones can be constructed—and again, it's zones, not lines.

Channels and Channel Zones

One other way to define entry and exit points that can be derived from anchoring is the use of horizontal channels. Loosely defined, the classical definition of channels is that they are technical patterns where a line is drawn across the tops and bottoms of multiple bars, forming a channel. The top and bottom lines are equally spaced and can be up, down, or horizontal in their slope.

FIGURE 7.20 Channels—Dell Corp. (DELL), January 2, 1997 to July 1, 2010

For illustrative purposes, Figure 7.20 is a very long-term chart of Dell Corporation that exhibits all three channel formations. From left to right, there is a very steep uptrend channel followed by a horizontal channel, and finally a downtrending channel that overlaps with the horizontal channel lines.

A lot has been written about channels and they do have their value, but their application is somewhat limited. They are limited because up- and down-trending channels can't be anchored to anything of significance. There isn't, for example, any method for anchoring a channel to a high-volume bar if it has a slope. In classical technical literature, channels are just an extension of trend line. Their primary use is to determine price boundaries. As has already been shown, there is a better way to do that.

So is there any value in channels? Yes, there is, and it is in horizontal channels. Horizontal channels can be established congruent to anchor bars, gaps, and swing points. Figure 7.21 is a chart of Western Refining, Inc., that displays a fairly well-formed horizontal channel.

FIGURE 7.21 Horizontal Channels—Western Refining, Inc. (WNR), July 27, 2009 to July 26, 2010

In Figure 7.21, the channel captures the majority of the price action. If anchor bars and swing point highs and lows are incorporated (gaps could also be used if they existed), then a separate set of channel lines is created, as shown in Figure 7.22.

Stepping back to look at Figure 7.22 and reconsidering the idea of support and resistance zones, it isn't very hard to extrapolate the horizontal channel into a channel zone, as shown in Figure 7.23.

Channel zones, like support and resistance zones, provide a zone where it becomes difficult to trade beyond. The primary difference is that a trading zone usually captures the majority of the trading action on the time frame under examination while support and resistance zones may or may not. Zones are crucial trading tools. Channel zones are simply an extension of the previously covered concepts of support and resistance, if they are viewed with boundaries that are constructed with zones rather than lines. Channel lines with slope are not valuable as there is nothing to anchor them to.

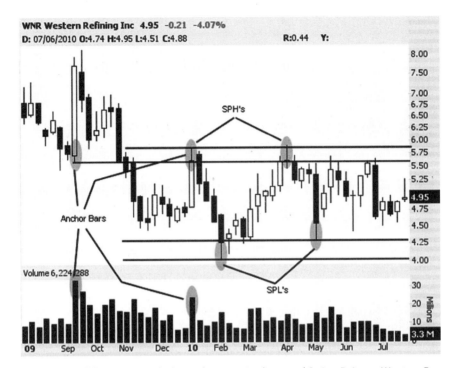

FIGURE 7.22 Horizontal Channels Using Anchors and Swing Points—Western Refining (WNR), July 27, 2009 to July 26, 2010

A TRADING EXAMPLE: COMBINING TECHNICAL EVENTS

The most significant support and resistance zones are those zones created as a combination of more than one of the support-and-resistance charting patterns discussed previously. Whether it is the combination of an anchor bar with a swing point or channel zones built from swing points and anchor bars, any time more than one pattern coexists with another, the odds are that the pattern is strengthened as a result.

Figure 7.24 shows how a combination of support zones can be both identified and utilized to aid in trading. Each technical event is labeled on the chart as it occurs.

Starting from left to right, there are 10 events to observe:

1. The first technical note of interest is the large volume bar with wide price spread. The fact that it has both of these attributes makes it more

FIGURE 7.23 Channel Zones—Western Refining (WNR), July 27, 2009 to July 26, 2010

important than just a high-volume bar, for example. This bar becomes an anchor bar going forward. It was a significant sign of strength in the stock, meaning that one or more larger buyers decided that they wanted to purchase shares and they wanted to do so in a big way. When a large buyer begins to purchase and is unwilling to wait for prices to retrace lower before buying more, they are signaling that their interest in acquiring shares in reasonably intense. From this, a trader can surmise that more than likely something good will happen reasonably soon in the stock. Large buyers typically do not flip a coin about what to purchase next. Either they know something that others do not know or they have put together enough clues to make them believe there are better than even odds that something is about to happen that would be beneficial to the stock.

2. The very next bar exhibits follow-on buying, which creates a gap higher in price. Once again, volume is significant and the price spread is wide. In fact, volume on this bar is higher than volume on event number 1. This creates the second anchor bar in a row. Once again, that is significant and makes this bar a stronger anchor bar. Again, the buyer/buyers

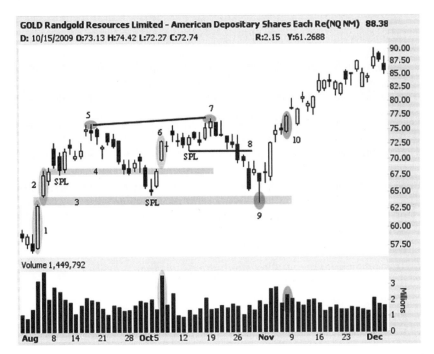

FIGURE 7.24 Trading Combined Technical Events—Randgold Corp. (GOLD), August 28, 2009 to December 3, 2009

have made a conscious decision to accumulate shares. In addition, there are probably a significant number of short-term momentum traders piggybacking the move at this juncture. This anchor bar when paired with the first creates a clustered anchor bar formation. The combination of large price spread, gaps, and high-volume clustered anchors creates strong support going forward.

3. The gap up adds to the strength of the two back-to-back clustered anchor bars and becomes the natural place to draw in a support zone.

4. Once the SPL actualized, it, too, is combined with highs from the anchor bar (number 2), creating another support zone. This support is higher than the support zone created in number 3, but is a place to begin purchases or add to an existing position, if already long. Naturally, the desire is to buy the bulk of any added positions at the support zone defined as number 3. As it turns out, the lower support zone will not be reached on the first price retrace.

5. This is the swing point high created off the initial surge. Although it is not actualized until six bars have passed, once actualized it becomes a benchmark for comparisons going forward.

6. After a retrace in price that falls just shy of the lower support zone, buyers step in with another large volume push higher with wide price spread. The problem with this type of day is that it is roughly in the middle of the price range. The range is the gap and anchor bar support zone and the swing point high that was registered. This bar is a sign that the buyers are still interested. It signals the trader to continue to expect higher prices, not lower ones.

7. A new swing point high is registered. Buyers push prices over the previous swing point high but volume is only 1.4 million shares as compared to the previous swing point high's 1.9 million shares. That transitions the trend from confirmed bullish to suspect bullish. Shorter-term traders might reduce their holdings to some degree as a result of this downgrade in trend quality with the idea of buying back in at lower prices on a retrace if volume supports that notion, once it occurs.

8. The suspicion surrounding the higher high that transitions Rangold's to a suspect bullish trend is well founded and prices immediately retreat. From a trend perspective, the suspect bullish trend is displaced by a confirmed sideways trend as prices retreat substantially. If more aggressive traders did not lighten up when the suspect bullish trend was created, it is likely that many are likely forced out of their positions here.

9. The selling exhibited on the way to event number 8 pushes prices to the point where a test of the prior swing point low occurs. This becomes a critical test, as it would change the trend to bearish if price were to break this swing point low. At the same time, it offers significant opportunity because it is at the lowest support zone where significant support exists. As it turns out, opportunity trumps risk in this case and the chart provides a trader with the signals to take advantage of the good fortune. In particular:

   • Volume registered on the test bar ends up being less than the volume on the swing point low bar. Price goes under the swing point low and closes over it. That is a full test and the test indicates that the sellers of Rangold apparently do not have the ability to push prices lower at this time.

   • If a comparison is made between volume of the test bar and volume of the two anchor bars providing cluster bar support, then there is simply no comparison. Volume on the test bar is 1.9 million compared to volume at the anchor bars of 3.2 million and 3.8 million shares.

   • Given these indicators, a trader should either increase their holdings or initiate a long position because the inability to push prices lower suggests that the support zone will hold and prices should turn higher again. Note that there are three technical events pointing to higher prices at this time: swing point test failure, gap support zone, and cluster anchor bar support.

10. Since there were an insufficient number of sellers at the swing point low, prices turn and head higher once more. This eventually results in a test of the previous swing point high (the one that created the suspect bullish trend transition). The test succeeds on price and on volume as a higher close is registered and volume expands. This event transitions trend, again moving it back to confirmed bullish from confirmed sideways. The purchase made on the swing point low test now looks brilliant.

The above exercise is a brief example of how to combine anchor bar support with qualified trend to determine turning points for a stock and to position the trade consistently with the prevailing trend. Identifying a potential turning point in a stock is huge for both entry and exit of a position, because it is typically at the point where a stock turns that the greatest amount of money can be made in the shortest period of time with the least amount of risk. Think about that for a second.

In the example above, by identifying that the test of the swing point low was unlikely to carry prices lower, it is at that point that a trader could purchase Rangold and place a protective stop just on the other side of the support zone. The risk is minimal and, if prices do reverse, the potential gain is large because the chart has already indicated in numerous ways that Rangold wants to trade higher, and potentially much higher.

SUMMARY

Determining true trend enables a trader to get on the right side of a trade for a given time frame, but it does little to help a trader time their entry and exit. Entry and exit timing is dependent on understanding the technical road markers that are evident on the charts. Those technical events are largely centered on the concepts of support and resistance.

Support and resistance are not abstract ideas but instead concrete notions. Unfortunately, over the years, support and resistance have been considered from the standpoint of lines and points on a chart. The reality is that it isn't possible to pinpoint such a price point with consistency over time. Treating support and resistance as a zone offers a better representation of reality; moreover, the construction of price support and resistance zones based on significant events offers the best bet of "getting it right" most of the time.

To that end, anchor bars and prior swing points are utilized to anchor support and resistance zones. The greater the number of technical formations that form around a given price area, the stronger the support or resistance zone becomes. It is in this way that greater confidence can be had and a trader can short sell or buy retraces into resistance or support. The result is the minimization of risk exposure and maximization of potential rewards.

Combining improved entry and exit criteria with trend recognition and qualification provides the trader with a set of tools that offer a significant trading edge. No, they will not work all the time but, over time, they offer the consistency needed to improve a trader's performance and to do so in a significant way. There are some additional timing measures that can be taken to improve performance even further, and the next chapter considers these.

CHAPTER 8

Reversals and Price Projections

In the previous chapter, the key concept of support and resistance anchors was considered. Lines were turned into zones to better reflect reality and to emphasize that the real way to trade is to scale in and out of positions *in the zone*. When combining support and resistance zones with trend, a trader can better time his or her entries and exits, increasing the odds of consistent profitability.

In the same vein, the incorporation of the idea of price reversals into a trader's lexicon can provide the trader with a leg up on the competition. Price reversals can occur anywhere within the context of a chart, but their real value is at the tops and bottoms of longer-terms moves (as judged by the time frame they are observed on). Their correct identification allows the trader to not only reduce or eliminate exposure to the stock but to actually turn and trade the stock back in the other direction as well, in some situations. Price reversals are not always identifiable, but when they are, they should be heeded.

In a different vein, price projections are another piece of the puzzle used by a trader in estimating the reward side of the reward-to-risk equation used when determining whether to enter a trade. Support and resistance zones as well as expected swing point tests can be used when computing the reward-to-risk equation, but there is another tool that works quite well and appears abundantly on the charts. That pattern is the AB = CD price projection equation, and its identification and use provide a tremendously valuable trading aid.

Lastly, there is a final price projection pattern that, although its timing characteristics are notoriously vague, bears consideration. This pattern is the concept of magnets. Magnets are high-volume highs and lows. They are worthy of consideration because they provide price targets on both short- and long-term time frames. In spite of their less-than-valuable timing characteristic, when a stock begins to head in the direction of the magnet, the magnet provides a valuable price projection characteristic.

PRICE REVERSALS

A price reversal is, as it sounds, a place on the chart where a directional move reverses and begins to trade in the opposite direction. Over the years, numerous derivative indicators have been created that attempt to pinpoint reversal points. Price reversals based on a simple read of the chart reveal two types of reversal patterns. One is a reversal pattern that plays out time and again, called the two-bar reversal. The other pattern involves a high-volume price reversal that occurs at the top or the bottom of a chart. The former is a short-term indicator suggesting that a reversal is likely on the very next bar and is applicable to any time frame. The latter warns of an impending price change of longer-term duration.

Two-Bar Reversals

Swing point and support and resistance tests, as has been shown, provide a high-probability methodology for identifying reversals in stocks. There is another common occurrence of a reversal that doesn't require a swing point, support, or resistance to change a stock's direction. This reversal signal can happen at those particular areas and, when it does, it makes it even stronger, but it can also happen outside of these chart areas and it commonly does. The reversal is called a two-bar reversal and it happens whenever, after an extended move, price exceeds the previous bar's high (uptrend) or low (downtrend) then closes back under it/over it with lower volume. This sort of price and volume behavior usually portends that a reversal has occurred. These failure patterns are actionable.

***

Two-Bar Reversal
A two-bar reversal involves two adjacent bars and is indicative that a reversal in directional movement has occurred. The two-bar reversal pattern occurs if, after an extended directional move (both in terms of time and price), price pushes past the previous bar's high (uptrend) or low (downtrend) then closes back under/over the previous bar's high/low with lighter volume. The longer the extension and the lighter the volume, the better the signal.

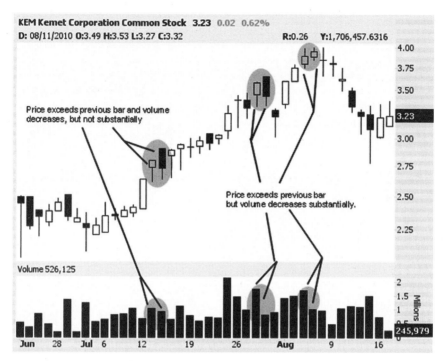

FIGURE 8.1 Buying the Retrace/Retest on Kemet Corporation (KEM), June 22, 2010 to August 17, 2010

The two-bar reversal patterns are simple to spot and, depending on when and where they appear, can be used to profitably trade both with and in opposition to the prevailing trend. There are two patterns, one being the inverse of the other. They are called the "under-and-over" and the "over-and-under" reversal patterns.

Over-and-Under Reversal Pattern Both the over-and-under and the under-and-over patterns utilize the exact same fulfillment criteria. In the under-and-over pattern, consider two adjacent bars where the price of the second bar trades under the low of the prior bar, then closes over it while volume decreases simultaneously. Figure 8.1 is an example of three apparent over-and-under setups on Kemet Corporation. The result of the first isn't favorable.

In this chart, the first under-and-over reversal setup failed while the second succeeded for a day. The latter was an actual retrace of substance. The first occurrence of the pattern was deemed a failure because price did not immediately reverse the following day once the signal was given. Without an extended move, two-bar reversals do not have the same predictive

FIGURE 8.2 Over-and-Under Reversal with Added Signals—Apple, Inc. (AAPL), May 17, 2010 to August 17, 2010

power. In all cases, if the two-bar reversal comes after an extended directional move, it has a much better chance for success.

Compare the two-bar reversal in Figure 8.2 with the one in Figure 8.1. In Figure 8.2, there is anchor bar resistance and a reasonably extended move to get back to that resistance zone. The two-bar reversal that comes after this has a much higher probability of actually working, since it is combined with an additional technical signal that has significance.

In this chart, the first failure pattern was the exhaustion gap that filled as price declined from the highs. That created a resistance zone. The second failure pattern was the high-volume anchor bar in late June as prices sunk lower. That anchor was tested in the third week of July, creating another anchor bar on the failure to trade higher. The tops of those two anchor bars were part of the test that occurred in conjunction with the over-and-under reversal signal. Although volume was reasonably light on the over-and-under pattern, when the other technical patterns are taken into consideration it is shown that it succeeded more as a result of the other indicators than because of the over-and-under pattern itself. It did provide, however, yet another signal that prices probably were heading lower again.

Under-and-Over Reversal Pattern The under-and-over reversal pattern is the exact opposite of the over-and-under pattern. Its application comes when the stock is moving lower and then reverses back to the upside. Figure 8.3 shows the under-and-over pattern in Intel Corporation, where prices had declined for some period of time and volume shrank dramatically as price went under and then closed over the previous bar. Note that the longer the extension in terms of price and time creates a higher probability of success when the two-bar reversal pattern occurs. The same is true of lighter volume. If volume on the second bar, as compared to the first, is significantly lighter, then the odds of a reversal markedly increase.

In Figure 8.3b, a prior two-bar reversal occurred around the same price. Volume was lighter and price went under, then back over. That reversal added to the probability of a potential price reversal.

Under-and-Over or Over-and-Under Patterns in Which Volume Expands Consider the case where all conditions are met for an over-and-under reversal pattern save one—volume increases rather than decreases. In such a case, the over-and-under reversal pattern is not triggered because the chart now shows a higher price high with higher volume. If higher volume is attached to the higher high, then even though prices ended lower, the market typically will eventually retest the higher high that has volume attached.

The same is true of an over-and-under reversal pattern. If volume expands as part of the two-bar reversal pattern, then the pattern isn't triggered because the result leaves volume at the lower lows on the second bar of the potential two-bar reversal pattern.

Figure 8.4 is a chart of Monsanto Company showing three potential two-bar reversal patterns. The first and the last have the correct volume attributes while the middle one doesn't. Even though it turned out in this case to work in all three cases, there are many examples where the pattern fails if volume isn't lighter on the second of two bars. Trading this and other patterns explained in this book is about putting the odds on a trader's side, and that means watching and waiting for the best possible setup, not simply swinging at any pitch that comes over the plate.

High-Volume Reversals

Sometimes a technician observes a pattern where, at the top of a chart, price reverses and volume expands. The high-volume bar isn't the highest price bar but close in proximity. Similarly, at the bottom of a chart price

FIGURE 8.3 Over-and-Under Reversal with Added Signals—Intel Corp. (INTC), May 17, 2010 to August 17, 2010

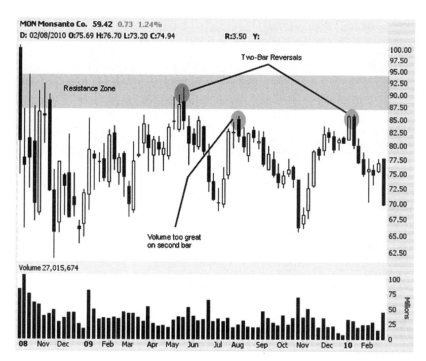

FIGURE 8.4 Over-and-Under Reversal Patterns for Monsanto Co. (MON), September 29, 2008 to February 22, 2010

may reverse and head higher with an accompanying large expansion in volume. Again, the high-volume bar isn't the lowest priced bar, but close in proximity. These two reversal patterns typically identify intermediate- to long-term significant trend changes and are characterized by high-volume moves in the opposite direction of the prevailing trend, either immediately or almost immediately, after a new high or a low occurs.

Volume off the Top   Volume off the top is the situation in which a price reversal occurs almost immediately after an ongoing bullish uptrend registers new highs. The pattern can occur on any time frame and is effective for the time frame on which it occurs. Many times a volume-off-the-top pattern permeates multiple time frames and thus becomes a longer-term trend changer.

In Figure 8.5, there are two annotated ovals. Both could be interpreted as volume off the top but the first one really isn't. In this chart, Monsanto exhibited a correctly formed high-volume top price reversal pattern (second set of shaded ovals), as compared to a potentially mistakenly identified volume off the top seen in the first shaded oval. The difference between the

FIGURE 8.5 Volume off the Top (MON), September 24, 2007 to September 2, 2008

two patterns is that the first actually made a higher high *with volume.* The second of the two ovals did not. Volume came out of the stock the very next bar after the high. Follow-through becomes key once volume off the top occurs. If prices continue to push lower the day after volume comes out of a stock that suggests that larger traders were repositioning (either taking profits or starting to short the stock).

Almost any technical breakout or breakdown signal requires follow-through. Follow-through says that larger positional trades are being placed by larger players. Those positional trades are usually not reversed in a matter of days, but instead over weeks and months. You generally want to trade with the elephants, not the antelopes.

Volume off the Bottom   Volume off the bottom possesses the same characteristics as volume off the top, with one major exception. Volume off the top always happens faster and more furiously than off the bottom. The difference is that at the top, fear drives the selling while at the bottom it is greed driving the buying. Fear is a much stronger motivator than greed, so price declines always happen more quickly and with more urgency than price appreciation.

The end result is that volume off the bottom typically plays out over several trading sessions rather than just a few successive ones. By the time the market or the stock takes off, there are few real believers who are holding stock who are willing to continue to hold it for the longer term. Like volume off the top, volume off the bottom comes after a long series of declines. The market participants are reasonably apathetic at that point, and many false rallies have probably already occurred. Figure 8.6 is an example of volume off the bottom using the Standard and Poor's SPY ETF as a proxy for the S&P 500 index. This was the classic bear market bottom in 2002.

In this chart, volume off the bottom isn't the case in either of the first two large bounces off the lows, but instead on the third attempted try. Notice how volume and price escalated on the second day of the bounce rather than the first, and that price continued to move higher afterward. That is the follow-through that is needed on both declines and advances when considering volume-off-the-bottom or -top patterns. Because it came

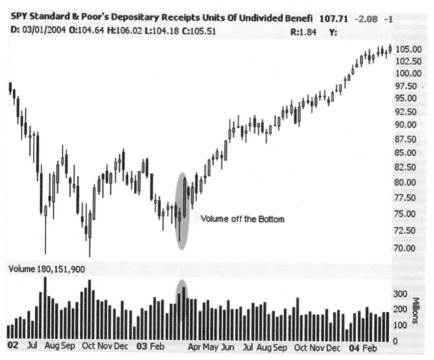

FIGURE 8.6 Volume off the Bottom (SPY), May 20, 2002 to March 1, 2004

on the bar after a low, it wasn't volume at the bottom. The latter case would create a magnet as discussed later.

Trading Isolated Signals versus a Combination of Signals

To emphasize the point one more time, an underlying principle of all technical analysis is that technical signals stand a greater chance of succeeding if they occur in multiples, not singularly. Multiple signals that overlap in price and time are especially valuable. Figure 8.2 (previously shown) was an example of two bearish anchor bars backed up by a resistance gap when an over-and-under reversal signal occurred. The reversal signal wasn't ideal by itself, but when a trading signal is given and multiple technical signals are in congruence, a trader can have greater confidence that the stock will do what is expected. It is in those circumstances that a trader may take a larger position size. So much about trading out-performance is about getting a greater amount of money on the table when you have increased odds for success.

PRICE PROJECTIONS

Price projections are derived from trading signals providing the opportunity to assign a target price to an expected move higher or lower. Just as a fundamental trader might put a price multiple on a stock based on their expected fundamental earnings power over some period of time, a technical trader can look to certain patterns to project the future price for that same stock.

Some price projections are not nearly as time-sensitive as others. Magnets are an example of a time-insensitive pattern. Other patterns, like the AB = CD pattern, are rather specific in terms of time and price. Both have their value and both are considered below.

Magnets

While reversals are valuable technical signals because they provide the technician with knowledge of an impending change in direction, price magnets tell the technician about an eventual price continuation target. Price magnets are high-volume bars found at the top or the bottom of a chart on a given time frame. They are called magnets because they magnetize future price action.

When a high-volume high is evident on a chart, the trader should make a mental note that eventually price will attempt to get back up to that high. Likewise, a high-volume bottom is an invitation for prices to return to the lows for a revisit. Magnets become valuable tools *once price begins to trend in the direction of the magnet.*

High-Volume Low Magnet In Figure 8.6, not only is volume off the bottom on display in the chart, but a high-volume low magnet appears as well. Figure 8.7 is the same chart with differing annotations to highlight the high-volume low that magnetized prices lower.

In this particular chart, the low of the high-volume low bar was tested, which represents a full test. In those cases where the retest occurs reasonably soon, a full retest is required to put the magnet to rest.

In those cases where a reasonably immediate test occurs and a full retest doesn't take place, then the magnet lives on and continues to pull price back toward it weeks and months into the future. Exxon Mobil Corporation is an example of this latter case.

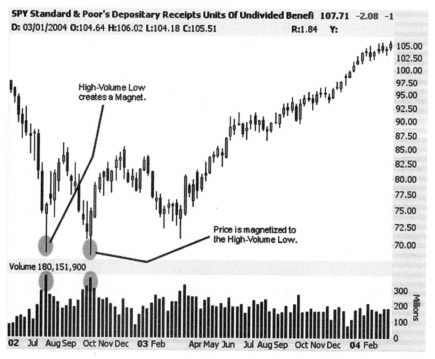

FIGURE 8.7 High-Volume Low Magnet—SPY, May 20, 2002 to March 1, 2004

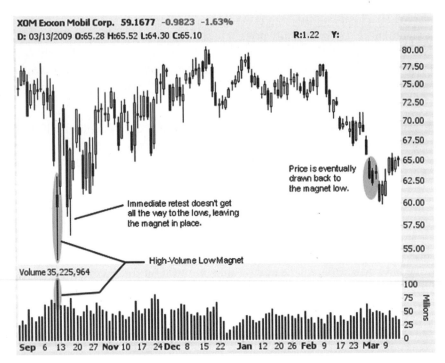

FIGURE 8.8 High-Volume Low Magnet—Exxon Mobil Corp. (XOM), September 24, 2008 to March 13, 2009

In Figure 8.8 a huge magnet is created that is partially retested within days, but a full test does not occur. Price works higher, then sideways, for multiple months until the change in trend finally reestablishes the allure of the magnet once more. Eventually, prices are pulled right back into the top of the magnet bar once more.

When considerable time passes before the retest, the bottom of the bar no longer has to be tested (although many times it in fact does get tested fully), and a test of the high of the high-volume low magnet top is sufficient. That doesn't mean prices will necessarily stop and turn once the test occurs, but the need to retest the magnet bar is fulfilled and the usefulness of the indicator has passed.

High-Volume High Magnet The high-volume high magnet is the more-often used of the two magnets, because most traders will typically purchase and stay invested in a stock a lot longer than most will stay short a stock. Because magnets many times require an extended period of time to finally get tested, there is no reliable way to project the timing. Knowing that a high-volume high remains on the chart, however, acts eerily similar to an insurance policy. A trader "knows" that the stock will most likely eventually retest the high-volume high magnet bar sometime in the future.

Clearly the intent of this statement is not to suggest that if the high-volume high magnet exists, then all risk and money management should be ignored. What it does suggest, though, is that a trader can enter a trade with the idea of having less sensitivity to price swings against the position than would normally be the case as a result of a high-volume high magnet. In other words, the time frame for the trade should be longer-term, not short-term.

Figure 8.9 is an example of a high-volume high magnet. The stock is Visa and the chart is a monthly view of that stock. The high-volume high occurred in May of 2008. From that price point, Visa declined steadily in the wake of the 2008 market meltdown, losing more than half of its value.

By the fall of 2009, however, Visa had reclaimed all those lost points and was magnetized right back up to the top of the chart again. Although a trader has to use other technical indicators, and in particular qualified

FIGURE 8.9 High-Volume High Magnet—Visa (V), March 3, 2008 to August 2, 2010

trend, to trade such a stock, the fact that a high-volume high remains on the chart is a clear and concise broadcast. What it broadcasts to everyone who cares to listen is that eventually the stock will be magnetized back to the high bar either to touch at least the bottom of the bar or to do the full 360-degree trip and tag the top once more.

AB = CD Price Projections

The AB = CD pattern is a price projection pattern most recently popularized by Tom O'Brien in his book *Timing the Trade*,[1] and by Larry Pesavento and Leslie Jouflas in their book *Trade What You See*.[2] As Larry Pesavento describes it, H. M. Gartley was the originator of the pattern back in 1935, although the name "AB = CD" was ascribed to it much later. In fact, the names vary, as O'Brien calls it the "ABC" pattern.

Essentially, the pattern reflects the ebb-and-flow nature of the market, in that it advances then retraces, advances further, and retraces again. Examples of the AB = CD patterns are everywhere on the charts and can be AB = CD patterns higher or lower. One simple example of an AB = CD pattern is shown in Figure 8.10.

In this chart, the A to B leg is the decline from the high of $31.37 to the low of $26.41, creating a $4.96 price spread between the high and the low of the A to B leg. That is the initial thrust down.

The retrace, or pause, is where price works its way back in the opposite direction of the initial thrust. That retrace forms the B to C leg of the overall AB = CD pattern. The C to D leg of the pattern comes into play once price crosses over the B point. According to O'Brien, the pattern is valid only if volume expands on that crossover. Although I agree with O'Brien that the likelihood of the pattern playing out completely is more likely if the B point is crossed with volume expansion, I disagree that the pattern is invalid if it doesn't. If a B point is crossed with "suspect" volume, it can continue on just as a suspect trend can continue on. Naturally, you have greater confidence that it will continue if volume expands but it doesn't have to for the pattern to play out. You just have to be more careful with the trade if volume doesn't expand.

Most technicians such as O'Brien, Pesavento, and Jouflas use Fibonacci ratios to estimate and project the extent of the retrace move as well as to project the subsequent C to D leg or expansion move that follows. Fibonacci ratios were introduced by Leonardo Bonacci in his book *Liber Abaci* at the turn of the thirteenth century (1202). The series of ratios that Bonacci introduced to the world include the .618, .50, and the .382 ratios that have subsequently found their way into the world of trading through countless books, papers, and charting packages.

FIGURE 8.10 AB = CD Pattern—Wells Fargo (WFC), September 23, 2009 to December 15, 2009

The most common projection espoused by followers and practitioners of the AB = CD pattern is the 1:1 extension, meaning that length of the A to B leg equals the length of the C to D leg. The very name of the pattern implies this.

Referring back to the Wells Fargo chart displayed in Figure 8.10, since the A to B leg was $4.96, a trader should expect that once prices move beyond the B point as part of the C to D leg, then the end of the C to D leg can be projected to complete at $24.07 (C price point high minus $4.96).

As seen in the chart, that projection was left unfulfilled, with price hitting a low of $24.92 on December 15. The moral of the story is that like everything in life and trading, nothing is perfect. Perfection is found in finding value in those things that are not perfect. How could value be found in this imperfectly fulfilled AB = CD pattern?

Using AB = CD Price Projections in Trading To consider how a trader could find perfection and profit in the Wells Fargo trade, Figure 8.11 pulls the chart back a bit in time to what a trader would have

FIGURE 8.11 AB = CD Pattern—Wells Fargo (WFC), August 20, 2009 to November 18, 2009

seen as the B to C leg was being formed. Assuming that the AB = CD pattern is recognized as a trading possibility on this time frame, a trader could use the skills covered in Chapter 7 (Trade Entry and Exit) to determine the likely area where the retrace would stall and reverse. Short-selling Wells Fargo stock into the resistance zones would have provided a profitable trade setup.

Although the chart is a bit busy, each annotation is made as if a trader were making mental notes on the trade possibility. To start with, each trade setup needs to offer a minimum of 2:1 reward-to-risk. In other words, for every unit of risk, at least two units of reward are required to make the trade even worth considering. Anything between 3:1 and 5:1 are considered optimal trades as long as the probability of the trade succeeding is greater than average (refer back Chapter 6, "Preparing to Trade," for additional insight).

Prior to considering the reward-to-risk ratio, however, what a trader should do is quickly determine what the probable trade parameters are for the trade. That can only be done after a possible trade is identified (in this case it is to short Wells Fargo on a retrace as near as possible to the eventual C point of the B to C leg). The trade parameters always have to do with entry and exit, where exit entails both winning and losing sides of the trade. Since the C point is an unknown because its potential remains in the future, a trader must use other tools to estimate the probable location of the C point before it is known.

As considered in Chapter 7, support and resistance zones provide excellent estimations of where the difficulty of continuing farther in price becomes greater. Other technical chart formations such as swing points, gaps, and anchor bars are used to construct the support and resistance zones.

When examining Figure 8.11, there are two anchor bars on this time frame. The leftmost anchor left volume at the bottom of the chart. That defines a high-volume low magnet and tells us that price should eventually be magnetized toward that price area again.

The high of that anchor bar is $27.63 and the B point of the possible AB = CD down is $26.41, making the high of the anchor bar a possible resistance point on the retrace higher. So, what can be combined with this anchor bar to create a resistance zone?

One possibility is that a second anchor bar exists at the October 21 trading bar. On that day, a high-volume, large-price-spread anchor was created on the way to lower prices. This is the "Bar of Interest" on this chart because it tells us that, for whatever reason, large amounts of stock were sold indiscriminately that day at successively lower and lower price points. It will be very difficult for Wells Fargo to trade higher than the high of this bar on this time frame. This knowledge is confidence-boosting with respect to the short-sell trade idea. The bar immediately following the "Bar of Interest" is also a high-volume, large-price-spread anchor as well.

Combining the second of the two high-volume, wide-price-spread anchor bars with the leftmost anchor bar creates the first of two resistance zones (the lower one as annotated). There is also a swing point high that can be used in conjunction with that same high-volume, wide-price-spread anchor bar to create a second and higher resistance zone (the higher priced resistance zone). A third resistance zone is to use the bottom of the Bar of Interest anchor bar along with the swing point high to create yet another resistance zone (not shown as it is overlapping with the prior). Note, resistance zones can come in multiples and can overlap. They are just price and volume action after all. Also note that resistance zones do not act as resistance lines—price can and does move into a zone. Sometimes it just barely gets into it. Sometimes it gets deep into the zone. Sometimes it blows right through it and the resistance zone ends up being a false read.

So, the question becomes "Which resistance zone should be used to initiate a short sell entry, or should both be used?" Should a trader make one short sell or multiple short sells? As to the latter question, multiple entry points are almost always advisable, as described in Chapter 7. The entire reason to consider price zones rather than lines or points is because humans simply do not have the tools or knowledge to pinpoint entry and exit price points. The best that can be done is to determine a zone where prices should trade to and then have difficulty continuing further. Think of a resistance zone like walking in loose sand where, once entered, the ability to continue to move forward gets progressively harder. A resistance zone wears on price as it pushes forward. It slows the advance down and usually causes price to reverse.

As for which resistance zone to use, some additional clues are available to the trade if they care to look. For example, "What was the trend prior to the Bar of Interest day?"

It turns out that it was confirmed bullish. The day the Bar of Interest printed, however, it changed to confirmed sideways. Again, this increases conviction in the possible trade, but it also tells the trader that the stock was strong and only now has begun to weaken. A strong stock usually does not suddenly turn weak without a subsequent attempt to rebound to a strong state again. At the same time, a stock that has changed from bullish to confirmed sideways will find it more difficult to turn bullish again on the current time frame.

Taken altogether, the general rule of strong stocks not giving up easily is very helpful in trading. First, strong stocks generally do not become weak stocks overnight. There is usually a window of time in which the stock gyrates. That gyration can be utilized to escape an existing position that no longer appears worth keeping. Second, the window of time can be used to establish the next trade in the reverse direction of the trend.

Given the prior strong nature of the stock, that suggests the trader should err on the side of trying to establish the trade in the higher resistance zone. Additionally, the reward-to-risk parameters also argue strongly for the higher resistance zone, as shown in the following.

For example, assume an average entry price near the top of the lower resistance zone (let's use $28.30). The risk in the trade is the top of the Bar of Interest plus a little cushion so as to not accidentally get stopped out of the trade. Assume the stop order is placed at $31.19. Furthermore, assume a trader times the entry perfectly and the exact bottom of the bar following the Bar of Interest is the extent that prices retrace on the B to C leg of the AB = CD down pattern. From that C price point, a 1:1 extension of the AB = CD pattern would target a price decline to $23.73.

In this hypothetical example, the price parameters are as follows:

- AB = CD known and expected price points
  - A = $31.37
  - B = $26.41
  - C = $28.49 (the top of the lower resistance zone)
  - D = $23.53
- Expected risk is $2.89 ($31.19 – $28.30)
- Expected reward is $4.30 ($28.30 – $24), where $24 is used to make sure that the trade is exited as it extends toward the AB CD price target extension.

Using the above parameters to compute the reward-to-risk ratio, the result is an unappealing 1.49 to 1 ratio, which is a trade that is simply not worth taking.

Looking back to Figure 8.11 once more and recalculating based on an average entry price of $29 (middle of the range of the higher resistance zone) and with the assumption that the C point ends up being the top of the higher resistance zone, a second hypothetical short-selling opportunity is examinable. In this revised case, the price parameters are as follows:

- AB = CD known and expected price points
  - A = $31.37
  - B = $26.41
  - C = $29.41 (the top of the SPH)
  - D = $24.45
- Expected risk is $2.19 ($31.19 – $29)
- Expected reward is $4.30 ($29 – $24.70), where $24.70 is used to try to make sure that the exit on a profitable trade is taken.

Using the above parameters to compute the reward-to-risk ratio, the result now approximates a trade that could be considered. The ratio stands at 1.96 to 1 and that assumes that the average entry price is the $29 that is the middle of the range for the higher resistance zone.

In practice, the average entry price would be higher if the trader scales into the trade properly. Essentially, when scaling into a trade, the desire is to do so in three uneven increments that gradually increase in size. The first entry is for 20 percent of the total expected size of the trade, while the second entry entails the next 30 percent of the trade. The final scale in order takes the remaining 50 percent of the desired trade size. In this way, the larger positional entries into the trade occur at the better price points. This reduces risk naturally, increasing the overall trade reward-to-risk ratios.

Revisiting the example above and using proper scale trading parameters, the average entry price improves to $29.14 ($28.50 × 20 percent; $29.00 × 30 percent; $29.50 × 50 percent). When plugging the $29.14 back into the reward-to-risk equation, a ratio of 2.17 is reached, as shown below:

- Expected risk is $2.05 ($31.19 – $29.14)
- Expected reward is $4.44 ($29.14 – $24.70), where $24.70 is used to ensure that the exit on a profitable trade is taken.

Implications of Scale Trading

The implications of scale trading are enormous. Revisiting the Wells Fargo trade once more (Figure 8.11), a scale trader would have ended up with only 50 percent of the desired trade size, but that is a positive, not a negative, result. If the full size of the trade is never realized, success is guaranteed,[3] because it is impossible to lose on the trade when the final short sell is never realized, which guarantees that the stop loss order also never executes.

Now, some might argue that having only 50 percent of the money involved in the trade is itself a problem. That may be, but with literally hundreds of other stocks to consider as possible trades, the extra money can easily be placed in another trade. It doesn't have to remain idle. Having guaranteed winners of smaller sizes is always better than holding unknown winners and losers of larger size when all the capital can eventually be allocated, irrespective of which particular trades are made.

Another critical point in scale trading is that as a trader averages into the trade on the retrace, they can measure whether the trade is progressing as it should with respect to how the stock trades. To visually consider this important point, Figure 8.12 looks at the Wells Fargo trade once more with a focus on measuring how the resistance zone and the bars anchoring the zone were tested. Notice the three bars that pushed high enough to test the two high-volume, wide-price-spread bars, which anchors the higher resistance zone.

Each of the three test bars exhibited much lighter volume. In fact, volume was significantly less, with the heaviest day registering in at more than 50 percent lighter volume. Notice also that each subsequent attempt to push higher showed even fewer participants in terms of volume. As a short seller of Wells Fargo stock, that is exactly what needs to be seen. It provides confidence that the trade is working and emphasizes the need to be patient and to allow the trade to continue to unfold.

FIGURE 8.12 Volume Characteristics of the Retrace—Wells Fargo (WFC), August 20, 2009 to November 18, 2009

SUMMARY

In trend trading, understanding the theoretical concept of true trend is not enough. A pragmatic approach that blends the theoretical with the practical is what allows a trader to succeed. Although it is necessary to understand true trend directions on the varying time frames, that does little to fatten the pocketbook if it cannot be combined with entry and exit criteria that maximize returns.

In the previous chapter a significant effort was made to marry the concept of support and resistance to the idea of significance. Lines were replaced with zones and the thought of scaled buy-and-sell orders was touched upon. In this chapter, some additional thoughts on trade entry are discussed along with the idea of price reversals, but those patterns also reveal the possibility of focusing on the trade exit, as well. If a trader is long a stock and it exhibits a price reversal, that clearly is a reason to consider a trade's exit (not to mention that the true trend will quickly shift to offer the same conclusion).

Price projections are primarily focused on trade exit, with the prevalent AB = CD pattern being one of the most widely used price projection technical patterns today.[4] The AB = CD pattern, with its expansion component, is a predictive tool that stands in stark contrast to most derivative indicators that are solely dependent on historical data to project future outcomes.

The commonality between all of the technical indicators discussed thus far—whether they be true trend, support or resistance as derived from swing points and anchor bars, reversal patterns, or price projections—is that all of these indicators are rooted in the concept of significance. Significance is what defines each of them and sets them apart from what is currently practiced in most technical trading literature. Significance is defined through volume expansion and is measured as part of price and volume characteristics not in isolation, but as a comparison to prior points of significance. The urgency exhibited with volume escalation is typically not an isolated event. Independent of the direction that the urgency is expressed in terms of bullish or bearish price behavior, the fact that urgency is exhibited is significant, and is a data point for all future price action to be compared to on that time frame.

Volume reads are the key. It isn't about average volume. It's not volume in isolation. It's volume as a comparison to something else. With swing points, it is volume at the swing point compared to a previous swing point in tandem with price. The same is true of crossing the B point of an AB = CD pattern. It is comparative volume of the bar that crosses the B point with the B point itself that gives confidence or creates suspicion. With support and resistance, it is about volume at the anchor bars. The emphasis is on picking the places on a chart where urgency was revealed. It's an attempt to ascertain whether conviction was part of that urgency. It is the discovery of the battle lines on a trading chart, an uncovering of the important price points and their significance. Military battles are typically not won or lost in a day. The battle that occurs over the price of a stock is no different. It usually takes more than one bar. The battlefields of the past many times become the battle zones of the future.

Price reversals, like support and resistance, provide early warning signs of impending change. When combined with all the other indicators considered so far, price reversals provide the trader with additional data points that offer the ability to either escape a potentially bad position or seize the opportunity and participate in a trend change. As witnessed with support and resistance, there are trade opportunities that present themselves outside of just swing point tests.

Price projections seek to explain where price is likely to extend to. AB = CD patterns are very specific in their projections, using the Fibonacci number series for expected expansions with the one-to-one extension being the most common. Magnets, though a bit vaguer, are markers to keep an eye on because they tend to pull prices back toward them.

The next chapter takes all that has been presented thus far and applies it to time frames. Unfortunately, the market doesn't trade on just one time frame and, though time frames are arbitrary, it is indeed necessary to consider all time frames before entering a trade, even if you are only trading on just one of them. A more powerful approach is to trade multiple time frames for the same stock, and that idea is examined as well.

CHAPTER 9

Time Frames

Time frames are arbitrarily chosen time slices on a chart. It's best to look at a chart, any chart, as consisting of a reasonably equal number of bars. The bars could represent minutes, hours, days, weeks, months, or years. It doesn't matter. Doing this removes the element of fixed durations, allowing for chart abstraction. Abstraction is beneficial as it allows one set of rules to apply to all charts for all time frames.

What is the value of a time frame and how should it be chosen? The answer to the question lies in the definition of a time frame—they are arbitrarily chosen time slices. Thus, there is no correct time frame to examine since any given time frame can be right today and wrong tomorrow. But isn't that a problem? Well, not really.

Here's another way to think about it. Think about sound waves and how they travel through the air at certain frequencies. Now think of a stock traveling through time at a certain frequency. Although there is no proof of it, the harmonic frequency for a given stock over time probably does exist. Attempting to accurately map it, however, is virtually impossible because the frequency changes over time and is an amalgamation of a significant number of variables, many of which are poorly understood and some of which are exogenous and unknowable.

So, if the perfect time slice cannot be known, then how can a trader have any confidence in any chosen time frame? The answer is that he or she cannot—not in isolation, that is. That is why it is important to look at multiple time frames, not just one. Three time frames are suggested: the short-, intermediate-, and long-term time frames. They are recommended because experience has shown that they work across all stocks most of the time.

If constructed with roughly the same number of bars, they provide a reasonably consistent view of differing time slices that, when combined, provide a reasonably consistent and accurate view of the trading instrument being analyzed. That view can be thought of as a trading bias. A trading bias is as it sounds: an inclination to buy or sell over one or more time frames.

Trading Bias
A trading bias represents a trader's underlying inclination to buy or sell over one or more time frames.

A successful trader requires a bias whether it is conscious or unconscious. Without a bias, trades are made at random. A bias provides direction, and direction is a reflection of the confluence of the trends expressed over the differing time frames.

TIME FRAME ANALYSIS

Circling back to many of the thoughts presented so far in this book, when a trader examines a stock with the idea of trading it, there are certain preparatory procedures that must be carried out prior to entering the trade. They include, but are not necessarily limited to, the following six steps:

1. Choose a time frame to analyze the stock on.
2. Determine true trend for that time frame.
3. Determine support and resistance zones.
4. Look for any technical red flags that would alter your bias, such as volume off the top or bottom or the possibility of a pending reversal.
5. If the stock warrants further attention, then determine the reward-to-risk ratio based on expected entry and exit. This entails the formulation of a trading plan for the stock.
6. Execute the trading plan.

Given the above, successfully trading the markets seems so easy. Correctly differentiating between good and bad trades is nothing more than a matter of following these steps and connecting the dots, right?

The following trading example steps through each of the six items outlined above. At the conclusion of steps one through five, a trading bias is formulated and a plan is ready to execute. That plan is to initiate a short-sell position in a sector ETF for bonds. This short position is established using the Ishares Barclays 20-Year Treasury Bond Fund ETF (TLT). The following sections show the analysis.

Choose a Time Frame

For most traders, the time frame chosen is the time frame that they trade on. In some cases, it is happenstance, but for most, despite whatever method is made to initially choose a time frame, it typically becomes the default when analyzing both existing and potential trading opportunities.

For argument's sake, let us assume that the trader in this example is a short-term trader. As such, the short-term time frame (three months) is chosen. The chart is shown in Figure 9.1.

Determine True Trend

On this time frame (see Figure 9.1), there are four trend designations. The initial trend transition for TLT was a confirmed bullish trend but it lasted for only three bars. It then transitioned to suspect bullish, and then toward

FIGURE 9.1 True Trend Determination—Ishares Barclays 20-Year Treasury Bond Fund ETF (TLT), May 13, 2010 to August 13, 2010

the end of this time frame the suspect bullish trend was reaffirmed not once, but twice.

Notice that throughout this time frame, there is an absence of a swing point low test. Lastly, also note that the final thrust higher actually tested and failed to make it over the previous high for this time frame. That swing point high is from the first week of July 2010 and volume was comparatively heavy there. Price went over that high and closed under it with less volume. That marked a failed test of a swing point high. Failed swing point tests can lead to price reversals.

Determine Support and Resistance

Figure 9.2 is the same chart for the TLT with annotations showing support and resistance. The obvious resistance level is at the top of the chart and it looks to be a reasonably good one since the swing point high was tested and both price and volume failed.

FIGURE 9.2 Support and Resistance Determination—Ishares Barclays 20-Year Treasury Bond Fund ETF (TLT), May 13, 2010 to August 13, 2010

The support zones are also rather obvious. They are discovered by locating the anchor bars then drawing in the zones that they create. The lower support zone utilizes the anchor bars to the left of the chart and the swing point lows to the right.

Look for Red Flags

The obvious red flag in considering a short position is that the trend is bullish, but only suspect bullish, not confirmed. Short selling TLT on this time frame would be going against the trend. When trading against the trend, the timing required to be successful has to be almost perfect.

Determine the Risk-to-Reward Ratio

Risk on a short sell at the current price point is minimal. The high for the last bar on the chart is $102.45. Assuming $102.66 as the risk for a buy stop and reward set at just inside the first support zone ($101.05), the reward-to-risk for the trade is 6.19—much more than what is needed to make the trade.

Execute the Trading Plan

The trade execution is to short sell some number of shares of the TLT at the close, placing the stop-loss and limit-buy order to profit, assuming a test of the swing point high occurs and both price and volume fail to confirm a break. At the close of trading day, price and volume do not confirm a swing point break. Thus, a trade is entered to short the TLT.

Trade Result and Analysis

In trading, anything that can go wrong will go wrong on occasion—and in this limited example it went very wrong. Here is the same TLT chart five days later (see Figure 9.3). As can be seen, the risk parameter utilized was completely wrong because the TLT ETF didn't just trade higher the following trading session; it opened much higher, creating a gap.

The expected risk of $.21 didn't consider the possibility of overnight risk and a gap higher in price. The result in taking this trade is that, unless a stop was already in the market and executed at the much higher than anticipated price, the trader is now faced with immediate and sizable percentage losses and faces the hard decision of whether to cut his or her losses immediately or hope for something better. As is widely known, hope is not a good trading strategy.

FIGURE 9.3   Failed Short Trade—Ishares Barclays 20-Year Treasury Bond Fund ETF (TLT), May 13, 2010 to August 19, 2010

Unfortunately, overnight risk was not the only thing that was missed when considering this trade. By focusing only on the single time frame, a large number of other factors were overlooked. For example, on the intermediate-term time frame, the TLT ETF was clearly in a confirmed bullish trend. Shorting a confirmed bullish trend is a very difficult way to make money on a consistent basis, and in this case the short sell was placed in opposition to both the intermediate- and short-term trends (see Figure 9.4).

At the outset of this book, the idea of trading with the trend was introduced. Trading with the trend doesn't mean that all the time frames must be in congruence but the trades made do need to consider the trading bias derived from an examination of trend expressed across all three time frames. Not doing so means that an incomplete bias is necessarily being used. As seen in the TLT example, that can be a costly error. In this trading example, a trader examining all three time frames would most likely not have traded the TLT short, since all three time frames are in opposition to the short sell trade.[1] Figure 9.4 displays just how strong the trend was in the TLT on the intermediate-term time frame.

FIGURE 9.4 Considering Additional Time Frames—Ishares Barclays 20-Year Treasury Bond Fund ETF (TLT), August 10, 2009 to August 9, 2010

The point of this exercise is to underscore the importance of looking at all time frames *before entering a trade*. Think about it this way. Would you agree to step into the boxing ring with Muhammad Ali when he was in his prime? Well, if you didn't know anything about boxing, then maybe so. Traders who know nothing about trading routinely make bad trades.

Put another way, what if you were asked to fight the world's greatest boxer in his prime with one hand tied behind your back? I am sure you would decline. To fight the market while looking at only one time frame is no different from boxing with one hand and against the best in the trade. It is a guaranteed loss over time.

TIME FRAME INTEGRATION

Time frame integration is the act of examining the three time frames to formulate a technical trading bias. The integration process centers on understanding true trend for each time frame and using that to establish an overall trading bias. Both the immediately prior trend as well as the present trend is examined. The resulting overall trading bias (where there is one) alternates between varying degrees of bullish, bearish, or sideways bias. Bullish implies that you want to initiate long trades at the appropriate time, while bearish implies short sell trades initiated in the same manner. A sideways trade implies a range trading opportunity that may or may not involve trading both the top and bottoms of the range.

Within this concept of a trading bias, there appear two gating factors to determine whether a trade is taken. In some cases the bias simply doesn't support trading the stock at a particular point in time. In other cases, the stock is positioned appropriately and the bias supports the trade but the reward-to-risk ratio of the postulated trade is not favorable enough to make the trade. Experience shows that the best trading returns are generated by avoiding trades with a marginal reward-to-risk bias, while embracing those exhibiting a strong one.

Rest assured that the process of developing a trading bias can be made excessively complex. Consider the following facts. There are three time frames. Each time frame can assume one of six possible states. The combined product of the overall state diagram produces 216 possible overall states. That clearly is an unwieldy number.

Fortunately, most of these states are ambiguous and can be disregarded. In other words, the majority of the possible state combinations cast no insightful light on whether a trade should be taken. They are the marginal potential trades. A later section considers these thoughts in more detail. But for now, let us consider a more detailed examination of developing the trading bias.

To that end and to better crystallize these thoughts, the following few pages examine the Standard and Poor's Depository Receipts (SPDR) ETF (SPY) over three time frames for the same constant period of time. This is done with the idea that the preparatory procedures for trade entry need revision. The major modification of the procedure is to consider all time frames in order to formulate a more realistic trading bias. The revised steps (now seven steps) are to:

1. Examine all time frames for the stock being considered to formulate a trading bias.
2. Determine true trend for all time frames.
3. Choose the appropriate time frame to trade on, given the bias and the true trends on the three time frames.
4. Determine support and resistance zones for the time frame being traded.
5. Look for any technical red flags that would alter your bias, such as volume off the top or bottom or the possibility of a pending reversal.

6. If the stock warrants further attention, then determine the reward-to-risk ratio based on expected entry and exit. This entails the formulation of a trading plan for the stock.
7. Execute the trading plan.

Note that the SPY ETF tracks the 500 largest capitalized companies in the United States, a benchmark comparison that is used by most money managers for their trading performance. An analysis of true trend, how a trading bias is created, and the trading bias changes over time are portrayed. In this exercise, true trend for each time frame is determined and the evolution of a trading bias is observed.

Long-Term Time Frame

Figure 9.5 is the long-term time frame view of the SPY ETF with annotations specifically focused on identifying true trend for this instrument. It is a five-year chart where every bar represents one month of trading.

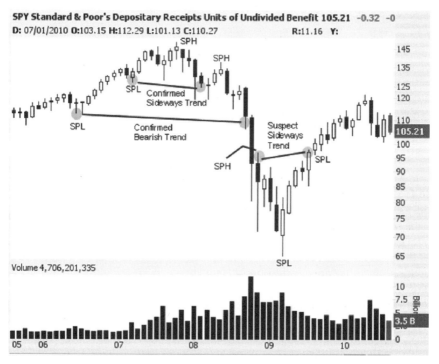

FIGURE 9.5 Long-Term Time Frame of SPDR SPY (SPY), August 1, 2005 to August 2, 2010

When investigating a perspective trade, all traders should typically start their analysis with the longest-term time frame. The reason for doing so is to understand the big picture trend before diving into the details. It's no different from a builder taking an aerial view of the land mass they are considering building on. The long-term chart offers a macro perspective of a stock, sector, or index's trend. In most cases, it drives the trends witnessed on the shorter-term time frames.

Starting at the left side of the chart, the SPY was trading in a bullish trend up until the beginning of 2008. The trend changed from a long-term perspective because prices penetrated and closed below the previous swing point low. The qualification was confirmed because volume expanded as the trend transitioned. A confirmed trend change from bullish to sideways is a significant milestone on the long-term chart. Again, this is a five-year chart and events do not occur rapidly on this time frame. In fact, in the five-year period depicted in this chart, only three trend changes are recorded. This fact emphasizes the importance and long-term implications for each trend change recorded. Every one of them is significant, although the message from each is slightly different.

The move from bullish to a confirmed sideways trend tells a trader that, from a longer-term perspective, this ETF is unlikely to regain its bullish bias on this time frame. That is a very significant statement. Again, the implications are tremendously large because the view on this time frame is broad. Such a statement should, at a minimum, persuade a trader to consider the possibility of a higher trend as reasonably unlikely, not only now, but for a long period of time. That is the whole point of qualifying trend—to not simply signify that the trend has changed but to qualify the tenor of that change. In this case, the qualification is confirmed and the time implications are long.

The very next trend state change is even more dire, because it tells a trader that the trend is no longer even sideways, but instead that it has shifted from a sideways trend to a bearish one. The trend transition has occurred with confirmation. Underscored once more is that this is the long-term trend, the most influential of all time frames.

As an aside, because this particular ETF is a reasonable representative of the general stock market, if the long-term trend changes from bullish to bearish, then the implication for all stocks is dire. An analogy is probably worthwhile. When the long-term trend is bullish, a trader throwing darts at a wall of stock symbols can buy whatever the dart strikes and probably end up making money. The reason for this, of course, is because the long-term trend of the overall market will probably bail the trader out. Assume a trader throws the dart ten times and strikes five good stocks and five bad ones. With a confirmed bullish trend for the broad market, the five bad stocks will be pulled higher while the five good ones will outperform the market. The end result is that the trader looks like a genius. This is what happened in the late 1990s when anyone with a brokerage account and pulse enough to place a buy order simply could not help but make money.

In a bear market, the opposite is true and every trader begins to look as if they are bordering on ignorant. In this situation, the five bad stocks perform even worse than the bad market and the five good ones only as bad as the general market. The trader loses money and swears to never trade stocks again. The 2008 bear market crash is an excellent and extreme example of this behavior.

By looking at the longer-term qualified trend of the broad market, a trader has a much better understanding of which side of the trade they should be on. This is true of both the broad market sectors within the market and individual stocks. Because Figure 9.5 is a long-term chart of the broad market, it has implications for the market as a whole.

Continuing with the chart interpretation, it isn't until nine months later, in July of 2009, that the trend transitions once more. Prior to the transition, the trend was confirmed bearish. Afterward, the trend changed to suspect sideways. A suspect trend is indicative of indecision. Given that the trend transitioned to lacked conviction when the transition took place, it has to be viewed with suspicion. Suspect trends can persist in the direction of the trend for some period of time once the transition occurs, but a retest of the transition area almost always occurs. The likelihood of an immediate retest is dependent upon a number of factors, of which the more significant are summarized below:

- How fast and how far the stock moved in price prior to the suspect breakout.
- How significant or insignificant the volume disparity was between the breakout bar and the swing point high or low that was broken.
- The existence of other technical signals in the breakout area that may serve to resist a further move in the direction of the breakout.
- The tenor of the sector that the stock trades in. Was it supportive? How about the general market?

If there is one thing to take away from the analysis of the long-term view it is this: "The long-term trend is the overriding trend. It is the primary trend and must be respected."

That doesn't mean that a trader can't trade counter to the long-term trend—they can. But if he or she does trade against the long-term trend, the trade necessarily has to be of shorter duration and the timing needs to be good—otherwise, it will almost certainly fail.[2]

In Figure 9.5, the current long-term view of the SPY ETF is suspect sideways, and although the ETF could work sideways to higher for an indeterminate period of time, a trader needs to exercise caution with respect to the long-term time frame. For this reason it reflects the need to trade carefully when trading from either a bullish or bearish trading bias. For a trader, that means that this is not a buy-and-hold environment but a trader's market on this larger time frame.

There are other technical signals in this chart such as the high-volume decline off the highs reached in 2010, but the emphasis presently is to restrict the discussion to understanding the trend across multiple time frames and how those trends interrelate.

Intermediate-Term Time Frame

On the intermediate-term time frame, a chart consisting of one year of data expressed in weekly bars is used (see Figure 9.6). As in the prior chart, annotations are included to show each trend transition.

In this chart, there are also three trend transitions. The first is a transition to a suspect bullish trend, although it wasn't really a transition but

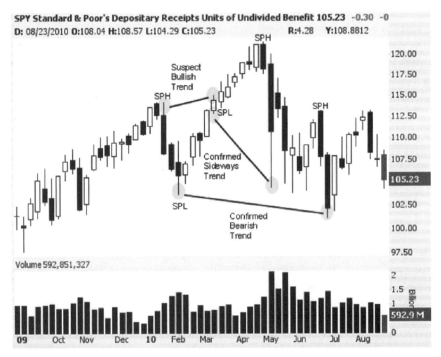

FIGURE 9.6 Intermediate-Term Time Frame of SPDR SPY (SPY), August 24, 2009 to August 23, 2010

instead an affirmation. Although not shown on this chart, the existing trend was suspect bullish already and thus, all that happened is that the SPY ETF reaffirmed that the bullish trend was suspect.

As prices moved higher, additional swing point lows were necessarily created underneath. The last one created is the first one hit when prices move lower. That swing point provides a vantage point where a trader can ascertain the true trend of the market. In this particular case, two questions were answered when prices dropped like a brick and broke through the swing point low. The first was that when the swing point low broke, it broke with volume expansion. These events force a trend transition to confirmed sideways.

The second question answered has to do with how the retest and re-generate sequence would play out as prices came back to test the suspect bullish reaffirmation area. To create a bullish bias, as prices retreated to test the top of the swing point high bar that was broken when the suspect bullish trend reaffirmed, volume needed to contract—not expand. That did not happen, as volume coming back was twice as great as the bar being tested. Thus, this ETF spoke volumes about the problems facing it. If a trader needed a wake-up call about the risk in the ETF, they received two simultaneous calls, both saying the same thing: "Big problems!"

On this time frame, it would take two more months to get the confirmation that the early warning signal was indeed valid. That came when the lower swing point low was tested and broke with volume expanding once more, transitioning the trend from confirmed sideways to confirmed bearish. Any time a trend confirms, it strongly suggests that the trend has the potential to continue and is likely to do just that. It is the strongest attribute you can ascribe to a trend.

Short-Term Time Frame

On the short-term time frame, the SPY ETF (see Figure 9.7) experienced a total of six trend transitions for the time period examined. This is not uncommon as the price points on the short-term time frame typically jump around a lot more than the longer-term time frames. Greater volatility on shorter-term time frames typically creates a greater number of trend transitions.

Starting with the two transitions to the left of the chart, notice the erratic price behavior. In traditional technical analysis of chart patterns, this type of behavior many times signifies a major trend reversal for the time frame being examined, and is called a broadening top. On this time frame and for this time slice, it provides a very misleading read on trend. In this case, trend transitioned to a confirmed trend only to reverse four days later

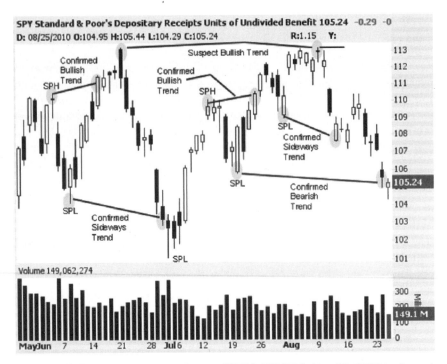

FIGURE 9.7 Short-Term Time Frame of SPDR SPY (SPY), May 25, 2010 to August 25, 2010

with a fast and unrelenting decline. That led to a trend transition of confirmed sideways as volume expands and the swing low is broken.

Immediately after the swing lows break, price reverses once more and heads higher, eventually creating and breaking another swing point high on the way to even higher highs. This third trend transition is also confirmed bullish as the price and volume characteristics meet the requirements.

At this point, anyone trading the SPY ETF on a short-term basis would probably be thoroughly confused, but it doesn't end there. The next trend transition actually gives a good signal as it reaffirms the bullish trend, but with a quality downgrade to suspect. That turns out to be the perfect notification, as it was all downhill after that. Depending on the risk- and money-management rules a trader was employing, that would have been the place to lock in some short-term profits or to tighten up the trading stops, which is easy to say in hindsight when examining this one time frame. The erratic behavior leading up to this event was reason enough to be cautious.

Just three short days later, the prior swing point low was overrun and volume expanded. At this juncture the trend has moved from confirmed bullish to suspect bullish and now to confirmed sideways. Clearly trend is weakening. If that isn't enough, with a little more passage of time another trend downgrade occurs, moving the trend to confirmed bearish.

Integrating Three Time Frames

Every trader has the opportunity to trade any time frame he or she so chooses. Each time frame traded in isolation has advantages and disadvantageous, although trading in isolation is arguably the least effective. Take the long-term time frame, for example (refer to Figure 9.5). The occurrence of a trend change takes a minimum of six bars—or six months—on this chart. A lot can happen in six months. In this particular charting example, the change from a bullish trend to confirmed sideways trend produces a relatively steep 16 percent decline.[3] The switch to a confirmed bearish trend isn't recognized until an almost 29 percent decline completes.[4]

A trade based strictly on this time frame that removed and added exposure based on trend changes would have been profitable, but not nearly as profitable as it could have been. Assume that the first downgrade in trend resulted in the trader removing 40 percent of the exposure. Further assume that the second downgrade results in the removal of all exposure. With these simple rules, a tremendous amount of pain would have been avoided when the market plunged to a low of $65. That low represents a 62 percent decline from the absolute highs. But that is only half the story—the positive half, so to speak.

If a trader used the previously discussed rules to exit the market, then what set of rules would be used for reentry? The best case (in hindsight) reentry point would have been the first upgrade in trend, but that didn't give an entry signal until a 33 percent gain has already occurred from the lowest price point of $65. Even an entry at that point would be questionable since the buy signal would have to be based on a change to a suspect sideways trend, not a confirmed one. These hypothetical thoughts also are only applied to this particular stretch of time. There are many situations where the same thoughts would perform much worse.

The point of examining this hypothetical entry and exit criteria is to underscore the fact that the long-term chart is not very granular. A trend change requires six bars at a minimum—a full half year of trading. Although the long-term chart is unlikely to give false reads, it isn't granular enough to offer entry and exit criteria in and of itself. It is great for understanding the overriding trend, and that is how it should be used.

Switching to the other extreme, the short-term view is very granular and is much more apt to give false trend readings over time. This isn't to suggest that it is useless but instead to simply recognize its weakness. It is very useful for timing entry and exit for longer-term trades. The more volatile the trading instruments being examined (large price ranges), the greater the probability of false signals.

On a short-term trading time frame (refer to Figure 9.7), if a trader had bought the first trend change to confirmed bullish, within days the trading account would have registered losses. In fact, buying or short selling the change in trend on this time frame yields worse financial results than doing the exact opposite.

The intermediate-term trend (refer to Figure 9.6) is a compromise between these two extremes. In this example these bars represent one week of trading. The trend changes are less frequent than the short-term time frame, yet more frequent than the long-term, but the problem of entry timing here is just as elusive as in the other charts.

ESTABLISHING A TRADING BIAS

The confusion illustrated in each of the previous time frame examples is a direct result of the attempt to use a change in trend to initiate a trading position. A trend change is typically not used to initiate or remove trading positions as much as to signal a possible modification in the trading bias. Said another way, a trend change on any time frame should be seen as an interruption in the existing tranquility of the stock. It's like throwing a stone into a placid pond: It causes a ripple. Sometimes it's a large stone and it causes a large ripple or even multiple waves. Other times the stone is small, yielding a ripple so minor as to barely be noticeable. It is seldom the case that any single stone is enough to cause waves great enough to create significant havoc, yet both kinds create ripples that have consequences and both can be a prelude to something larger.

Note that a single trend change does not necessarily result in the change of a trader's bias. The shorter the time frame, the less likely a bias change. Whether a trader chooses to change their trading stance immediately after a trend change occurs typically depends upon more than just the trend change. Such factors as the duration of the time frame, the trade size, the magnitude of the trend change, and whether the trend change is felt on just one or more than one time frame are all relevant. Other factors that have great bearing are the technical constructs discussed in Chapters 7 and 8.[5]

To consider the formulation of a trading bias further, Table 9.1 expresses the trends displayed in Figures 9.5 to 9.7 in a tabular form.

To illustrate how the trading bias is affected as trends change, the following analysis is provided in reference to Table 9.1. What this exercise demonstrates is that a trading bias is composed of two components: risk

TABLE 9.1 Observed Trends for SPY across Multiple Time Frames

Row Number	Time Period	Short Term	Intermediate Term	Long Term
			Trend Time Frame and Qualification	
1	08/01/05 thru 01/31/08			Confirmed Bullish
2	02/01/08 thru 08/31/08			Confirmed Sideways
3	09/01/08 thru 07/31/09			Confirmed Bearish
4	08/01/09 thru 05/05/10		Suspect Bullish	Suspect Sideways
5	05/06/10 thru 06/14/10		Confirmed Sideways	Suspect Sideways
6	06/15/10 thru 06/29/10	Confirmed Bullish	Confirmed Sideways	Suspect Sideways
7	06/30/10 thru 07/22/10	Confirmed Sideways	Confirmed Bearish	Suspect Sideways
8	07/23/10 thru 08/06/10	Confirmed Bullish	Confirmed Bearish	Suspect Sideways
9	08/09/10 thru 08/11/10	Suspect Bullish	Confirmed Bearish	Suspect Sideways
10	08/12/10 thru 08/23/10	Confirmed Sideways	Confirmed Bearish	Suspect Sideways
11	08/12/10 thru 08/23/10	Confirmed Bearish	Confirmed Bearish	Suspect Sideways

and trade direction. Trade direction is the simple part to uncover because it more discrete. If the trend is bearish on all three time frames, then the direction of the bias will necessarily be to short stocks, not to buy them.

The risk portion of the trading bias, however, is not discrete but instead continuous with varying degrees of risk recognition. There are no absolute rules for the risk designation but one of relative valuation, where a significant portion of equation is dependent on the trader. This statement may sound like a lawyer's cleverly designed contractual escape clause, but it is a fact that some traders are more comfortable with risk than are others. They come to understand just how much risk they can take and how fast they can move into and out of positions. As such, some are less risky in their approach to trading than others. Nevertheless, the following paragraphs provide the thought process that goes into an evolving trading bias based upon ever-changing trends on the various time frames.

Starting with row 6, the first time period in which all three trends can be examined together, the big-picture view is one of caution. The prior trend involved a bearish trend that had been in place for 10 months, stretching from September 2008 to July 2009. When it transitioned to sideways, it came on suspect volume and has remained that way since. Remember, a suspect trend can continue for a long time as suspect. That is the big-picture view, and that is why a cautious long-term view is needed. Based on just the long-term view, the trading bias would likely be one of sideways. What that means in trading terms is to trade both long and short.

The intermediate-term view is supportive of the long-term view that it is a trading range. On this time frame, the trend has transitioned from a suspect bullish trend to a confirmed sideways trend. That indicates that prices should continue to work sideways indefinitely. The confirmed qualification indicates that a return to a bullish trend is unlikely near term. Taken together with the long-term trend, it increases the confidence in trading both long and short in the trading range.

Finally, the short-term trend is a confirmed bullish trend. Again, this supports the notion of trading both long and short but with a bullish bias in the short term. Thus the trading bias in the time frame depicted in row 6 is a sideways trading range. Essentially, the integration of the three time frames suggests a broad trading range with the potential to trade higher short-term.

In the next time slice, depicted by row 7, both the short-term trend and the intermediate-term time frame trends degrade. This turns out to be significant on the trading bias because now the intermediate-term trend is bearish and confirmed. With the prevailing bias of a sideways trading range, the need to revise the bias to include a more bearish leaning is needed at a minimum. The change in the short-term trend also underscores this need. The only item that keeps the bias from being outright negative is that the short-term trend is not bearish.

As time passes, it turns out that not abandoning the possibility of buying longs in the range trade bias is a reasonable decision. In row 8, the confidence in the trading bias of a range traded with downside bias increases slightly. When compared with the bias that prevailed in row 7, row 8 contains a somewhat less pessimistic downside risk bias. Though the bias is stronger, it is nowhere near as strong as the time period depicted in row 6, since the intermediate-term trend has not improved.

Row 9 requires a downgrade in the trading bias as the short-term trend weakens. The trading bias returns to a state that is roughly equivalent with the state that existed during the time period depicted in row 7. That may seem odd since, on the face of it, you would think that a suspect bullish trend would invite greater confidence than a confirmed sideways trend, but it doesn't. Why? Because of the time factor as discussed below.

To wrap up this analysis, the bias of a sideways range trade with a bias to the short side prevails in row 9 but the concern grows. In row 10 the desire to trade only the short side of the prevailing range trade increases further, and by the time row 11 rolls around, there is no longer any desire to trade the long side of the range trade—only the short side if a trader wishes to trade at all. The risk level for trading longs has grown too great when considering all three time frames.

The Effect of Time

A trading bias isn't limited to the consequences of a trend change on a particular time frame. There are times where the *inability to witness a trend change on a time frame* results in a trading bias change. In the above example, the inability of the intermediate-term time frame to re-capture a sideways trend designation by the time row 9 rolls around be-comes more concerning. Note that roughly seven weeks had passed since the intermediate-term trend changed to a confirmed bearish trend. During those seven weeks, the short-term trend oscillated from confirmed bullish to confirmed sideways, back to confirmed bullish, and finally to suspect bullish. Not once did it turn bearish, yet the intermediate-term trend was unable to improve. The unequivocal axiom is to never forget the effect of time on the trading landscape. A positive behaving trend on the short-term time frame should eventually reflect positively on trend in the intermedi-ate term. If it doesn't, then the intermediate-term trend will necessarily be-gin to reassert its influence on the short-term time frame. The longer-term trends have more weight but realize that it is the short-term trend that even-tually turns the long-term trend. It's just that it occurs less frequently.

Sometimes it is the subtle broadcasts that a stock transmits that are the most important to hear. It is often said of trading that "If the traders cannot take a stock up, then they will take it down." In this case, there were seven weeks of trying to take it up—just to take it back to where it was previously. That was not accomplished. The longer that remains the case, the more risk increases. That is almost always true. Six to eight weeks is not an excessive amount of time to have witnessed trend improvement, but it is certainly enough time to test and recapture the previous trend. The longer it doesn't, the greater the risk that the shorter duration time frames are pulled in the direction of the longer-term time frames.

The Effect of Trading Floors

A trading floor refers to a definable area on the chart where a trading range stops and another starts.

Trading Floor
A trading floor is a definable area on the chart where one trading range stops and another starts.

Trading floors are essentially consolidation patterns as defined by Edwards and Magee,[6] although the term floor is more colorful because it evokes a more striking visual image. Floors have bases and ceilings and can be visualized as a cross-sectional view of an apartment building. Floors begin with a first floor followed by a second, a third, and so forth. The transition from one floor to another typically is accompanied by a trend transition or reaffirmation on the time frame for which the floors appear. The base and ceiling of two adjacent floors frequently separates one trend from another. It is common to find swing point highs and lows at the ceiling and base of the floor. Figure 9.8 takes the same SPY ETF weekly chart of the intermediate-term time frame and highlights the two floors that are apparent and visible.

In this particular chart, the boundaries between the first floor's ceiling and the second floor's base are reasonably well defined, but the base of the first floor isn't. The same is true of the third floor, where the base is well defined but the ceiling isn't. Irrespective of that, though, the establishment of the trading bias for row 9 in Table 9.1 should be affected to some degree based on the increased risk that price will be unable to break through the second-floor ceiling and instead work their way lower back toward the bottom of the second floor at a minimum.

When a ceiling or a floor is reasonably well defined, it becomes difficult to break through it, and the risks of a failure increase as prices push to that area. In many ways, these concepts have already been covered in the ideas expressed regarding support and resistance in Chapter 7, but viewing support and resistance through floors is sometimes easier and more visual. The relation to a trading bias is clear though: If prices uninterruptedly march toward a higher or lower floor, the risk of a failure to move to the next floor increases. This is particularly true when combined with the ideas presented in the previous section regarding time. If a significant period of time has transpired while the price works its way to the edge of a floor, the risk of failure increases.

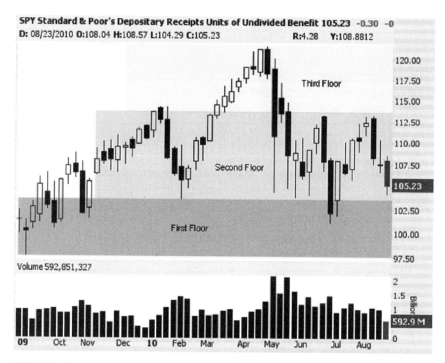

FIGURE 9.8   Intermediate-Term Time Frame of SPDR SPY (SPY), August 24, 2009 to August 23, 2010

One other way to consider all of this is to visualize a sprinter who competes in and wins a race against a group of worthy competitors. Assume that in winning, the sprinter was pushed to an extreme. Now, immediately after the race has ended, inform the sprinter that they must unexpectedly race another group of talented and well-rested sprinters. Do you expect the sprinter will win once more? It's unlikely. The harder a stock works to get to the top or bottom of a floor, the less likely it is that it will immediately advance to the next floor. The stock will more likely stop and rest, if not reverse. Stocks, like sprinters, get tired.

Summary

The establishment and evolution of a trading bias, though founded in trend on the three time frames, is more than simply trend. It incorporates the trader's emotions, the concept of time, and the notions of support and resistance as evidenced through anchor bars and swing points. Every trader

TABLE 9.2 Trade Trend Matrix Example

Current Trend

Short Term	Intermediate Term	Long Term
Confirmed Bullish	Confirmed Sideways	Suspect Sideways

eventually learns to develop a trading bias. If he or she doesn't, they typically will not be trading for very long.

The two most common mistakes with respect to a trading bias are to treat it as a stationary value and to consider it as a binary value designating whether to buy or to sell.

A trading bias is evolutionary, constantly twisting and turning. It isn't developed once but constantly massaged and changing. A trading bias attempts to take all possible inputs and create a pulse of the level of risk currently being experienced along a continuum ranging from highly risky to reasonably safe. If the trading bias is treated in this manner, it will serve the trader well.

TRADE TREND MATRIX

Earlier a reference was made to the fact that there are 216 possible state combinations that could apply to any given trading matrix representing an individual stock. Table 9.2 is an example of a trade trend matrix representing row 7 from Table 9.1.

Given that the number of potential states are tremendous, the usefulness of being able to glance at a trade trend matrix and consider whether a trade may have potential at a given point in time is reasonably limited in most instances. There are, however, some useful states that, at a glance, should and do offer interest.

Useful States

What is designated as a useful state depends on the type of trader who is viewing the matrix. A fade trader is a trader who opts to "fade" the prevailing price direction. For example, such a trader might buy a stock on a short-term time frame once it has traded lower for a few days and is approaching a well-anchored support zone. A fade trader would most likely find certain trade trend matrix states more interesting than a momentum trader who is much more interested in finding a trend and trading with it—not against it. For this reason, the trade matrix in Table 9.3 presents an additional

TABLE 9.3 Ideal Trade Trend Matrix Setups

Current Trend

Short Term	Intermediate Term	Long Term	Trading Comments
Confirmed Bullish	Confirmed Bullish	Confirmed Bullish	For a momentum trader, this is the ideal combination: a strongly trending market with no sign of weakness. They would necessarily be bullish and attempting to ride the rising prices.
Suspect Bullish	Confirmed Bullish	Confirmed Bullish	Assuming that the suspect bullish trend was a transition from a confirmed bullish state, this is the ideal scenario for the fade trader to step up and buy a stock.
Confirmed Bearish	Confirmed Bearish	Confirmed Bearish	For a momentum trader, this is the ideal combination: a strongly trending market with no sign of strength. He or she would short sell the stock.
Suspect Bearish	Confirmed Bearish	Confirmed Bearish	Assuming that the suspect bearish trend was a transition from a confirmed bearish state, this is the ideal scenario for the fade trader to short sell a stock.
Suspect or Confirmed Sideways	Confirmed Sideways	Confirmed Sideways	The fade trader enjoys this type of a market, buying weakness and selling strength at the tops and bottoms of the trading range floor.

column with a description of the trade setup provided for that combination of trade trends. Note that these are only the ideal trade scenarios.

The trend states in Table 9.3 are the more obviously useful states: the extreme cases where the odds greatly favor a trade as noted in the trading comments column of the table. Since trend qualification specifically creates a more granular view of trend, it is easy to see, for example, that values of "confirmed bullish," "suspect bullish," and "confirmed bullish" for the respective columns in the first row would work quite well for the momentum trader, too. If you add in these "less than optimal" rows, there are easily 30 rows of trend variations across the time frames that are quite tradable and do not require perfect timing. Those are the trades that a trader should be looking for when trolling for trading ideas.

SUMMARY

To truly excel in trading, a trader must be willing to view more than just one time frame when analyzing a particular stock. Examining true trend on three time frames enhances a trader's performance. Trend analysis across time frames is used to formulate a trading bias—not specifically to establish or terminate trading positions. A change in the trading bias may well result in a change in trading positions, but it is not necessarily a one-to-one relationship and there are more factors than the trading bias that come into play when establishing and removing trading positions. Many times a change in the trading bias results in a modification to the existing trading plan, forcing the reexamination of the entry and exit criteria.

The idea of a trade trend matrix is nothing more than considering the prevailing trends for each of the time frames in a more visual form. Given the abundance of possible combinatory states, the usefulness of the matrix is limited to the more obvious states.

The trade trend matrix is limited to the trends prevailing for the three time frames on a single stock. Clearly the trend of the stock is an important determinant in the future direction of the stock, but, as alluded to previously, a stock is also affected by the trend of the sector that the stock participates in, as well as the health and trend of the general market. How to incorporate those thoughts into a trader's methodology is the focus of Chapter 10.

CHAPTER 10

Markets, Sectors, and the Trading Cube

In the previous chapter the benefits of examining a stock on multiple time frames was underscored. The value derived was clarity—clarity with respect to a stock's trading bias. In this chapter, this idea is carried one step further to suggest that even viewing a stock on multiple time frames still leaves you at risk because a stock does not trade in a vacuum. The development of another superior trading bias is possible if you broaden your view a bit further.

In *How to Make Money in Stocks*,[1] William J. O'Neil states, "If you're wrong about the direction of the general market, three out of four of your stocks will plummet with the market averages." Common sense suggests the wisdom in O'Neil's statement because the general market[2] is a composite of all the stocks that constitute it. If the broad market is heading lower, then the odds are that the majority of the stocks are suffering as well.[3] If this is true, which it is, then to ignore the trend of the general market when buying or short selling a stock is somewhat suicidal.

Carrying the thought a bit further, the sector that a stock trades in, like the general market index, also exerts a drag or provides a boost to a stock as well. Market sectors are essentially indexes that are constructed to track everything from consumer goods to biotechnology, from health care providers to semiconductor chips. Every stock is representative of a company that sells one or more products or services, or both. For most companies, the bulk of their earnings is derived from one or more products that fit into an industry group or the broader concept of a market sector. Although tracking the sector can be problematic due to the weighting structure inside the sectors, they nevertheless do exert influence on individual stocks within the sector and even to the broad market indexes at times.

Just like stocks, both the general market and market sector have trends—trends that can be examined, determined, and qualified. All the tools examined thus far are applicable to the broad market indexes as well as to market sectors and, as would be expected, both are examinable across multiple time frames. The power of the neoclassical trend theory is that anything that is being traded can be studied in an identical manner using the same set of tools and procedures.

Unless the cost of examining the general market and the stock sector is prohibitive, then why would it be ignored? It isn't, and it must be examined as a result. Developing and practicing a methodology that is effective in doing this yet not too cumbersome or time consuming is valuable. This chapter presents a methodology that is reasonably streamlined in its approach.

GENERAL MARKET

In Chapter 9, the SPY ETF was examined from a trend perspective with the idea of understanding trend on multiple time frames. As stated then, the SPY ETF is a proxy for the S&P 500, the 500 largest capitalized stocks in the United States. There are other indexes as well. The Dow Jones Industrial Average, containing 30 stocks that represent the industrial might of the United States, is often thought of as representing the general equity market. In reality, though, the Industrial Average really is a sector index because it represents the largest 30 industrial stocks in the United States, not the general market as a whole. It has a significant impact on the broad market but it isn't a representation of the broad market despite being listed on the nightly evening news.

There are other broad indexes, however, that, like the S&P 500, measure a broad swath of the stock market landscape. The two most prominent are the National Association of Security Dealers Automated Quotation (System), which is known by the acronym NASDAQ, and the Russell 2000. The majority of the technology stocks (both large and small) appear on the NASDAQ while the Russell 2000 represents the small capitalization segment of the U.S. stock markets.

Between these three indexes, the vast majority of all stocks traded in the U.S. equities markets are accounted for. Through just these three indexes, the "general market" trend can be determined and qualified—nightly, if desired.

MARKET SECTORS

Although some market sector indexes have been around for the better part of a century,[4] in recent years a proliferation of tradable sector indexes have burst onto the scene. The result is that there are a number of older and more established sector indexes (many of which are not tradable instruments) and a newer brand of sector Exchange Traded Funds (ETFs) and Exchange Traded Notes (ETNs) that have been created to mimic a sector's performance.

Starting with the older and more established sector indexes, the most widely known is the Dow Jones Industrial Index as mentioned previously. It was created after the oldest of all indexes, the Dow Jones Transportation Index, which was eventually followed with the Dow Jones Utility Index. Charles Dow, along with his statistician, Edward Jones, worked together to created these venerable indexes that have stood for more than a century now. All three indexes track the performance of the three named sectors and all are composed of a select group of stocks that are admitted to and removed by overseeing committees or boards. Each of these indexes is truly an index and is not tradable. They are tradable, however, through ETFs that have come onto the market, many of which have arrived within the past few years.

Historically, all publicly traded companies were categorized into one of nine broad sectors. Those sectors are listed in Table 10.1.

These nine sector indexes also double as tradable ETF instruments. But it doesn't stop there, because each of these broad sectors has been sliced and diced into additional subcategories that are then also divided into even more sub-subcategories, *ad infinitum*. All are represented via tradable ETF and ETN products.

The proliferation of sector ETFs and ETNs over the past few years has created a rich set of tradable sector instruments, but at a cost. The downside cost for having all these instruments is finding the right one to use as a sector proxy for a stock. The term "right one" implies the use of a sector ETF that has influence on the stock being traded.

Fortunately, most ETF products are reasonably representative of the sector, with an obvious exception being the leveraged ETF products. The leveraged ETF products reset on a daily basis, which distorts the mapping between the ETF and underlying sector being tracked. Leveraged ETFs are to be avoided when searching for an appropriate ETF product to use as a proxy for the sector.

The other two items that must be examined thoroughly to qualify a particular sector as usable is the volume that the sector ETF trades and the internal structure of the sector ETF.

TABLE 10.1 Broad Sector Categorization and ETF Equivalents

Sector Name	ETF Symbol	Sector Description
Consumer Discretionary	XLY	Industries such as automobiles and components, consumer durables, apparel, hotels, restaurants, leisure, media, and retailing are primarily represented in this group.
Consumer Staples	XLP	The companies in this sector are primarily involved in the development and production of consumer products that cover food and drug retailing, beverages, food products, tobacco, household products, and personal products.
Energy	XLE	Energy companies in this Index primarily develop and produce crude oil and natural gas, and provide drilling and other energy-related services.
Financial	XLF	A wide array of diversified financial service firms are featured in this sector with business lines ranging from investment management to commercial and investment banking.
Health Care	XLV	Companies in this sector primarily include health care equipment and supplies, health care providers and services, biotechnology, and pharmaceuticals industries.
Industrial	XLI	Industries in this Index include aerospace and defense, building products, construction and engineering, electrical equipment, conglomerates, machinery, commercial services and supplies, air freight and logistics, airlines, marine, road and rail, and transportation infrastructure companies.
Materials	XLB	This Index is primarily composed of companies involved in such industries as chemicals, construction materials, containers and packaging, metals and mining, and paper and forest products.
Technology	XLK	Stocks primarily covering products developed by Internet software and service companies, IT consulting services, semiconductor equipment and products, computers and peripherals, diversified telecommunication services and wireless telecommunication services are included in this Index.
Utilities	XLU	The Utilities Index primarily provides companies that produce, generate, transmit, or distribute electricity or natural gas.

The volume characteristics are reasonably straightforward. Unless there is enough volume associated with the sector ETF, then the ability to analyze the chart of the sector is compromised. That is a relatively easy assessment. Just look at the chart and see if the instrument trades efficiently. If the bid-to-ask spreads are huge, then volume is insufficient. If the total volume per day is less than 50,000 or 100,000 shares, then one should probably find a different sector ETF to use.

As for the internal structure and weightings, this is also a reasonably simple process. A quick Internet search easily yields a listing of the ETF sector components in tabular format, showing which stocks are represented within the ETF along with their weightings. The weightings are critical because there are ETFs where one or two stocks dominate the index. The Retail HOLDRS Trust ETF, which is supposed to represent the retail sector, is heavily influenced by just one stock: Wal-Mart Store. Wal-Mart accounts for almost 20 percent of the ETF. That is too great an influence. In those cases, a substitute needs to be found. With the Internet as your guide, search for others. In this particular case, the SPDR Retail ETF (XRT) provides a substitute that is more equally balanced.

Assuming the weighting structure is reasonable, the next step a trader takes is to look at the top five or 10 holdings to see that they are representative competitors for the stock being examined. Table 10.2 is an abbreviated listing showing the internal structure of the financial sector ETF (XLF) from Table 10.1.

In some sector ETFs, there can literally be tens or hundreds of stocks represented in the sector ETF. Without fail, almost all can be narrowed down to the top five or 10 holdings, because those top holdings account for the bulk of the movement in the index. For example, in Table 10.2, roughly 40 percent of the movement of the index is concentrated in just five stocks. Even though there are 80 stocks covered in the XLF, a quick look at the top weightings shows that just five stocks account for the majority of the index. That is important to know, as well as useful. For example, to try to determine the trend of a particular sector, a trader might just examine the sector ETF, but they could also get inside it and take a look at the few stocks that have the largest weighting. If, like the XLF, five stocks constitute almost half of the ETF and four of them appear ready to pull back, then that provides an early warning system of what may be about to happen to the sector.

THE TRADING CUBE

Knowing that the general market and the sector affect the stock, the question becomes: How can a trader make sense of all three? Especially if the

TABLE 10.2　XLF Internal Component Structure (as of September 2010)

Stock	Symbol	Weight
JPMorgan Chase & Co.	JPM	12.4%
Wells Fargo & Co.	WFC	10.1%
Bank of America Corp.	BAC	9.4%
Goldman Sachs Group Inc.	GS	6.7%
Morgan Stanley	MS	3.6%
Bank of New York Mellon Corp.	BK	3.2%
U.S. Bancorp	USB	3.1%
American Express Co.	AXP	2.6%
MetLife Inc.	MET	2.3%
Travelers Cos. Inc.	TRV	2.3%
State Street Corp.	STT	2.1%
CME Group Inc. Cl A	CME	1.9%
PNC Financial Services Group, Inc.	PNC	1.7%
Citigroup Inc.	C	1.6%
Prudential Financial, Inc.	PRU	1.6%
Charles Schwab Corp.	SCHW	1.5%
AFLAC Inc.	AFL	1.3%
BB&T Corp.	BBT	1.3%
Chubb Corp.	CB	1.3%
Simon Property Group, Inc.	SPG	1.3%
Allstate Corp.	ALL	1.2%
Northern Trust Corp.	NTRS	1.2%
Marsh & McLennan Cos.	MMC	1.0%
Franklin Resources, Inc.	BEN	1.0%
AON Corp.	AOC	1.0%
T. Rowe Price Group Inc.	TROW	1.0%

Note: Additional stocks with a weighting of <1 percent were omitted.

need to consider each in terms of time frames is added to the mix as well. The answer is to use a visual aid: the Trading Cube.

The Trading Cube provides a comprehensive view of the qualified trend of the general market, the sector, and the stock over the three time frames and does so at a glance. Figure 10.1 is a generic example of the Trading Cube.

This visual aid combines time and qualified trend across multiple instruments. The three time frames for the stock, stock sector, and the general market all contain a qualified trend and are all identified on the face of the cube. Color is typically used to qualify trend but, given that this book is printed in black and white, regular font is used to represent a confirmed trend while *italics* are used to represent a *suspect trend*.

Each trend represented on the Trading Cube reflects the current trend state of the instrument across all time frames. No previous trends are

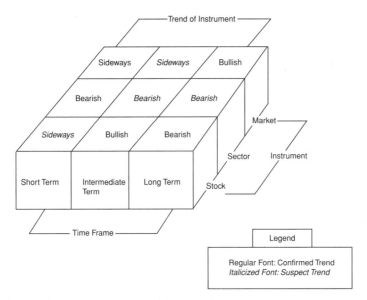

FIGURE 10.1 Generic Trading Cube Example

noted, although they can be easily tracked through software automation. The Trading Cube provides a snapshot of the market, stock sector, and stock at a given point in time, much like the balance sheet provides a portrait of a company's financial health at an instant in time.

Although it could be argued that the value provided by the Trading Cube is mitigated by the effort involved in constructing the trend states for the various instruments, the counter to that argument is that the cost of not doing so is inordinately high. A trader should trade with the best information available, and from a technical perspective, the Trading Cube provides that information in a compact and visual form. As has been emphasized, qualifying trend on the varying time frames can be accomplished algorithmically, as done on www.tatoday.com. The same is true of trend qualification through trend transitions. Finally, all of these algorithms are equally applicable to the general market and stock market sector instruments as well. In essence, the Trading Cube is the end result of a programmatic examination of trend for varying instruments across all time frames. As such, it is an indispensable tool.

Interpreting the Cube

The snapshot view of the Trading Cube is definitely valuable, capturing a lot of information in a concise visual representation, but how is it used? As with most things in life, the Trading Cube doesn't offer black-and-white solutions but varying shades of gray.

The Trading Cube, once mastered, is a time-saver. A quick glance at the output provides a snapshot of the stock, the stock sector, and the general market in one concise and easy-to-read format. Depending on the information it conveys, along with a trader's current investments, it is used to quickly determine if further investigation of the charts offers value. In essence, the Trading Cube offers a trader the ability to form a more holistic trading bias by stepping outside a singular "stock only" view.

Another valuable result derived from the Trading Cube is the recognition of divergences. Divergences provide an early warning for impending change, and their appearance in the Trading Cube is easily detectable.

When a trader is first introduced to the Trading Cube, the typical reaction is mild confusion. The confusion stems from the fact that there is no frame of reference in which to interpret all the data presented. The Trading Cube is packed with a significant amount of data in as condensed a manner as possible. There is the trend for each of the three time frames with qualifications. Additionally, the trend focuses on the stock, the stock sector, and the general market. All of this data is presented without the benefit of a chart to look at, which is what technical traders are accustomed to. It is a big transition on how to "view" the market, to say the least.

With a little practice, though, a glance at the Trading Cube provides the trader with a quick view of whether a trade is worth investigating further. Leaving aside the more detailed work of finding support and resistance or calculating reward-to-risk ratios, the quick view provided by the Trading Cube indicates whether it is worth even looking. How is that possible?

Take the following example: To keep it simple, assume that the exact same trends appear on each of the three different instruments (the general market, the sector, and the individual stock). In Figure 10.2, a snapshot of the three instruments is provided through the Trading Cube. It depicts the qualified trend for each of these instruments across the three time frames. The stock is Apple, Inc. It trades in the technology sector of the NASDAQ; a representative sector for this stock is the XLK Technology SPDR ETF. Finally, the general market is NASDAQ.

The Trading Cube provides a real-time sketch of the trading bias. Trading biases come in two flavors. One bias applies to existing shareholders while the other applies to bystanders with a desire to become a shareholder.

Trading Bias for Existing Shareholders   Starting with the trading bias for existing shareholders, the snapshot presented in Figure 10.2 is that of indecision and suspicion across all time frames for all instruments. The long-term trend is suspect bullish. The implication is that, on the long-term time frame, there will likely come a time where the stock retraces to retest

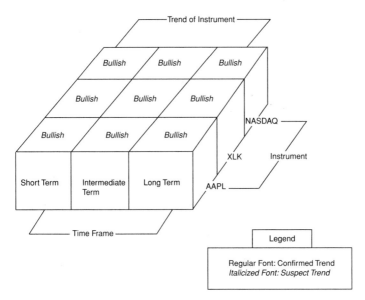

FIGURE 10.2 Trading Cube Example—Apple, Inc.

and regenerate. Therefore, from a long-term perspective, a trader should exhibit some degree of caution but, since it is the long term, there isn't a compelling reason not to trade the stock from a bullish perspective, assuming the other time frames support that notion. A common misconception in trading is that crashes come out of nowhere. They somehow suddenly appear on the landscape without any warning whatsoever. This is patently false. They provide early warning signs in all but the rarest cases. There may not be a lot of warning but warning signs do appear.

On the intermediate-term time frame, the trading cube exhibits the same trend, namely, a suspect bullish state. As indicated above, the fact that it is suspect bullish isn't a reason to avoid the stock, as suspect bullish trends can continue for long periods of time prior to a retest and regenerate sequence.

Finally, the short-term trend also exhibits a suspect bullish trend as well. Because all three time frames are bullish, clearly the bias has to be positive, but slightly cautious. When the short-term trend is suspect bullish or bearish, it has a reasonably high probability of retesting and regenerating in a few bars. For existing short-term traders, when the short-term trend changes to suspect, it is typically a time where stops need to be tightened up a bit. Swing points need to be identified and the trading plan revisited to make certain that an exit strategy that maximizes gains or minimizes losses is ready and in place.

Traders who are trading on longer-term time frames hold tight and wait for retraces to add additional shares with a Trading Cube like the one shown for Apple. Their goal is for a longer-term trade more typically exhibited by the intermediate-term time frame and, from that perspective, there is no reason to sell with this type of Trading Cube view.

Trading Bias for Nonshareholders   For traders who have no existing position in Apple, Inc., the fact that the short-term trend is suspect bullish suggests patience. Traders typically do not buy stocks that are short-term bullish yet suspicious; they wait for the expected retrace to buy. On the other hand, a suspect bullish trend could potentially be a short sell trade if the intermediate and long-term trends were bearish—but they aren't. Furthermore, given the assumption that the sector and the general market are exhibiting the same trend as the stock, there isn't any broader reason to consider a short sell in this example.

This stock is currently a wait-and-see situation for traders on the outside looking in. The Trading Cube quickly relays that information—at a glance.

Now, to see the actual charts that created that trading bias as expressed through the Trading Cube, Figure 10.3 is a long-term chart of Apple, Inc. Remember that the assumption is that everything that applies to this stock also applies to the technology sector (XLK) and the general market (NASDAQ). Naturally, this isn't always the case, but rather than examine nine different charts, the point of the exercise is demonstrated with just three.

In the case of Figure 10.3, for the long-term perspective, notice how the swing point high from January 2006 was surpassed in November 2006. The test was a success in that price traded higher than the previous high and closed over it, yet it was a failure when comparing November's to January's volume. The fact that volume was considerably lighter (494 million compared to 782 million) indicates that the trend has transitioned with less strength. Although the trend remains bullish, it must be qualified as suspect bullish because volume did not confirm the breakout.

Moving to the intermediate-term chart, in Figure 10.4 the most recent year's worth of data is displayed using weekly bars. It is eerily similar to the picture broadcast by Apple, Inc., on the long-term time frame.

In this chart, the trend is also suspect bullish, having transitioned to that state in April of 2007 and reaffirmed the state again in October of the same year.

As for the short-term trend, Apple, Inc., price behavior has become more erratic. It turned confirmed sideways in early November on a large and fast price decline, only to work higher and actually confirm a bullish trend (just barely, but confirmed nevertheless). The final trend transition

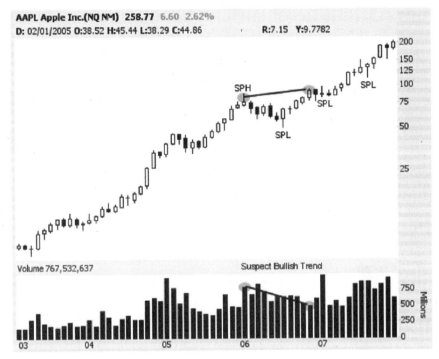

AAPL Apple Inc.(NQ NM) 258.77 6.60 2.62%
D: 02/01/2005 O:38.52 H:45.44 L:38.29 C:44.86   R:7.15 Y:9.7782

FIGURE 10.3 Apple, Inc. (AAPL), February 3, 2003 to December 3, 2007

was to a suspect bullish trend right at the end of December as shown in Figure 10.5.

Assume these three charts are reasonably representative of the sector and the general market as well. As an existing short-term trading shareholder, it would be wise to tighten up stops and become more cautious. On the other hand, all three time frames for all three instruments remain bullish, although suspicious. Never forget that suspicious trends can remain suspect for long periods of time. Depending on a short-term trader's position sizing (how much stock they hold compared to the cash size of the account), they might consider taking some partial profits with the idea of buying back in on a successful retest. Of course, that represents a trade-off because, even though caution is being broadcast, there is no breakdown of serious consequence yet on any time frame.

This short example is indicative of what the Trading Cube offers. A quick examination of the cube would tell you, the existing shareholder, to be wary and monitor your positions carefully. If heavily invested, a closer look at the charts is needed to see if some profit taking is in order.

FIGURE 10.4 Apple, Inc. (AAPL), December 4, 2006 to December 24, 2007

To a trader wanting to buy or short sell this stock, the message would be that there is nothing worth pursuing in this stock at this time. This is not a configuration requiring further examination until the short-term retrace occurs.

Trading Cube Divergences

A divergence is when two somewhat related items diverge. One item signals one possible outcome while the other signals a very different potential outcome. Divergences are particularly valuable when a stock, stock sector, or the general market have trended in a particular direction and there is no indication of an impending trend change. With multiple related instruments there is the possibility that one or more of the related instruments might begin to show a divergent view of the current trend. When this happens, many times it can serve as an early indication of an impending trend change.

Consider the following hypothetical example. Using Microsoft as an example, assume a long position was purchased and since then the stock

FIGURE 10.5 Apple, Inc. (AAPL), October 1, 2007 to December 31, 2007

has happily trended higher. The Trading Cube at the time of the purchase appeared as shown in Figure 10.6.

In this view of the Trading Cube, the general market trend was confirmed bullish on the short- and long-term time frames and suspect sideways on the intermediate term. That offers a bullish outlook and bias to all stocks that trade in the NASDAQ.

The sector that Microsoft trades in is the technology represented by the XLK Technology SPDR ETF. Microsoft represents the largest weighting within this sector ETF. The sector trend is not nearly as bullish as the general market trend because, as can be seen in the Trading Cube, all three time frames exhibit suspect trends. It is noteworthy that the short-term trend is the most bullish of the three, however.

Finally, the individual stock's (Microsoft) trends were excellent at the time of purchase because they were confirmed bullish on the long and intermediate term, and suspect sideways on the short-term time frame. In other words, the stock was trending higher and had retraced on the short-term time frame.

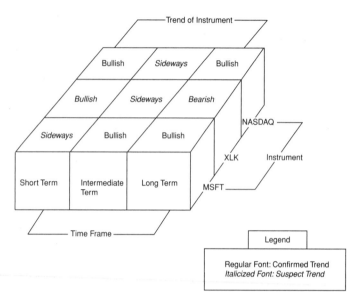

FIGURE 10.6 Microsoft Trading Cube at Time of Purchase

Now, for the sake of argument, imagine that the Trading Cube configuration appears as shown in Figure 10.7 a month later.

In this figure it is clear that things have deteriorated in the sector and the general market. That decreased bullishness isn't reflected in stock, though. In the Trading Cube, Microsoft still exhibits the same trends, and this is the essence of divergence. The trends have diverged. Either the stock's trend or the sector and general market trends are most likely wrong. Given that the general market is typically stronger than an individual stock, the better bet is to assume that Microsoft is inappropriately priced—not the general market.

The additional confirmation that Microsoft is likely to weaken and to do so relatively soon is the fact that the sector that Microsoft trades in has weakened as well, and it has done so on the short-term time frame. These are warning signs. That is what divergences provide: red flags. They can represent opportunity as well as risk. It depends only on your position as to how you will react to the divergence.

Divergences can happen on any time frame and their implication is typically applicable only to the time frame in which they occur. Do notice, though, that time frames overlap where the short-term time frame represents the most recent trading for the intermediate time frame.

Another situation where divergence works quite well happens when the sector begins to diverge from the general market. Markets typical

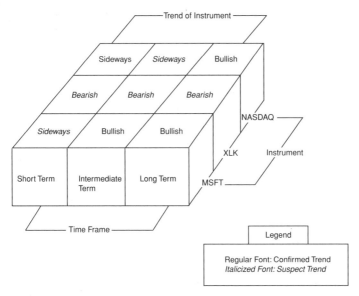

FIGURE 10.7 Microsoft Trading Cube One Month Later

rotate through various sectors when they are trending strong. When a sector begins to strengthen prior to the general market strengthening, then the divergence suggests the general market may strengthen as well. The same holds true in reverse.

Trading Cube Configurations

The Trading Cube provides a trader with a quick hit trading bias. It also identifies potential trend divergences. These advantages translate into actionable trading opportunities. This idea was explored in Chapter 9, but only in a singular fashion. The stock was considered in isolation and without regard to the stock sector and the general market.

In Chapter 9, the overwhelming number of qualified trend combinations that were possible across the three time frames yielded 216 possible states. Well, it just got a lot worse. With the Trading Cube, the number of combinations grows exponentially and amounts to a grand total of 7,776 possible unique states when all instruments are considered across all time frames. If 216 combinations was a problem, 7,776 possible combinations is more than a problem: It's impractical. Impractical because any attempt to have a trading bias or trading plan for most combinations is simply not possible. In fact, it wouldn't even be valuable.

Whether it is ideal or not, 7,776 possible states is simply a reflection of reality. Reality is not necessarily simple and easily comprehendible. That is true of many realities we humans deal with. The typical approach to complicated realities is to reduce them to useful and nonuseful states. If that approach is taken with the Trading Cube, then it has significant value.

In the next section, the displayed configurations represent the strongest possibilities that, anytime they surface in the Trading Cube, they require a trader to take notice. Only the strongest configurations are shown but, as can be imagined, there are myriad slightly weaker configurations for each.

The reality is that traders do not trade just the absolute best trades. They instead trade a vast array of trading setups that range from something less than perfect to something dramatically less than perfect. Successful traders alter their allocation size and their trading time frames and strategies to adjust for the less than ideal situations. It is a somewhat dubious process, but a process nonetheless. If there were only ideal trades to be had, trading wouldn't be quite so demanding. The ideal cases do come around, but rarely. Cases slightly less than ideal show up a bit more frequently, but the general offerings of trading setups are significantly less than ideal. That is the reality of trading, but that doesn't mean a trader can't be successful. The truth is far from that, because solid risk and money management, combined with excellent reads on trend and augmented with well-timed entry and exit strategies, leads to consistently profitable trading results.

When trading, the most important consideration is to view the market from a top-down perspective. This approach forces a trader to consider the long-term time frame for the general market as the primary trend determinant. The broad market's long-term trend is the key trend determinant in all trading affecting all sectors and stocks. If it is bullish, then a trader generally wants to be bullish. The opposite holds true if bearish. The only time this isn't true is during the period when the short-term trends run counter to long-term trend and the shorter-term trends end up changing the long-term trend. This happens infrequently and usually comes after a long period during which the trend was moving higher or lower.

The change of a secular bull market to a bearish one or vice versa does start with the short-term trends and gradually changes the long term. In all other cases, you want to be trading with the long-term trend. Exactly how to do so and how to recognize a long-term bullish or bearish reversal are discussed in the following paragraphs. Long-term trend changes occur infrequently. Timing the exact turn is not possible with certainty. Most of the time possible long-term trend changes end up being false. The need to stick with the trend until it is reasonably certain to have changed is critical to long-term success.

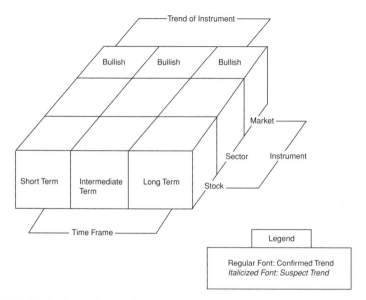

FIGURE 10.8 Strongly Trending Bull Market

Strongly Trending Market When the market shifts to a strongly trending market, almost any trade works. It does so because a rising tide tends to lift all boats. What does a strongly trending market look like in the Trading Cube? Figure 10.8 shows what the strongest trending market looks like.

As would be expected, the trend is bullish across all three time frames for the general market and, what's more, they are all confirmed bullish trends. This is as bullish as a market can be. Naturally, the same would be true for the opposite case—a strongly trending bear market appears as shown in Figure 10.9.

In a strongly trending market the ideal buy or short sell point isn't when the Trading Cube appears as it does in Figure 10.9. Ideally a trader would want to initiate a position during temporary short-term weakness, not extreme strength. That is because the ideal time to purchase (strongly trending bullish market) or short sell (strongly trending bearish market) is during a retrace, since the reward-to-risk equation is much more in the trader's favor. A high probability retrace stock purchase configuration in the Trading Cube is displayed in Figure 10.10.

In this configuration, all trends for all but one time frame are maximum bullish. The only weakness shown is the suspect sideways trend on the short-term time frame for the stock. Imagine what that would look like on the nine charts that the Trading Cube summarizes. All would be strongly

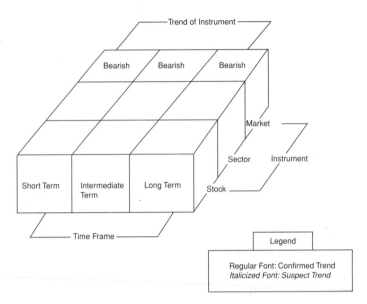

FIGURE 10.9   Strongly Trending Bear Market

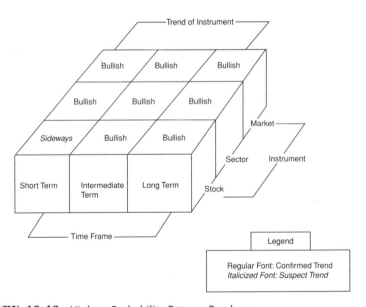

FIGURE 10.10   Highest Probability Retrace Purchase

bullish with the exception of the stock's short-term time frame. The chart would show a small dip in the stock's price on the short-term time frame. The dip would result in a suspect sideways trend transition because decreasing volume accompanied the test of the swing point low. That is an ideal Trading Cube configuration to step into the stock. With respect to timing, it doesn't get much more bullish than that. A trader would be hard-pressed to find a more bullish entry point than this.

Lastly, consider that it is extremely rare to see this configuration, but when it does occur, you want to get as much money into the trade as possible. What is much more common is that weakness in the stock or the stock sector or even in the general market persists at the same time that a retrace occurs. For example, assume the exact same configuration with the general market's intermediate-term trend being qualified as suspect bullish. This, though not the most ideal case, is still very bullish. The long- and short-term trends are confirmed as bullish, which, for a reasonable period of time, should keep the intermediate-term bullish. It wouldn't become a concern until the long-term trend changes. Remember, the long-term trend is like the great ocean tide: Where it goes, most boats go as well.

Trading Range   Trading ranges offer great opportunities for traders because prices move back and forth on a regular basis. If the range is reasonably wide, the opportunity is great. Figure 10.11 displays what the Trading Cube looks like when a trading range is in effect.

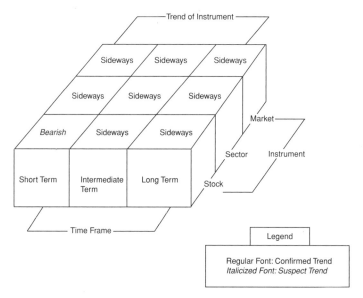

FIGURE 10.11   Trading Range Configuration

In this configuration, the market is sideways on all time frames for the general and sector trends. The stock trend is sideways as well, with the exception of the short-term time frame. Figure 10.11 describes a situation where the short-term trend is suspect bearish. In a sideways market, this indicates that the stock's chart has undergone a bout of selling without volume confirmation. The result is that a retest and regenerate sequence is likely, and given the trading bias of the sector and general market's long-term time frames, the retest is likely to fail. If this is true, rather than head lower, the stock is bound to bounce higher. That is how a trading range opportunity appears on the charts and through the lens of the Trading Cube.

Had the short-term been suspect bullish, then the opposite situation would apply: an opportunity to short sell the stock on the idea that it will trade lower as forecast by the trends in all the other time frames and instruments.

Trading ranges can also have upward and downward biases. In such a situation, the general market or the sector may show a suspect or confirmed bullish or bearish trend rather than a sideways one. Assume a confirmed bearish trend as an example. That implies that the stock will be tugged lower by the larger macro trends. Although the stock can still be bought at the bottom end of the trading range, a trader has to be more careful in that situation, since the larger trends are against the trade. Thus, a trader could buy fewer shares or make sure to maintain a reasonably tight stop-loss order.

Other strategies might include the use of options or hedging strategies. The simplest strategy, however, would be to trade just one side of the range—the one exhibiting the trading bias. In this particular example, that would mean to only short sell the stock, not to buy it at the bottom of the range.

Trading Cube Reversal Configurations

The ever-present temptation to try to buy the bottom or sell the tops is a constant force in trading. Unfortunately, on a long-term time frame, this is practically impossible. Realistically, the best that can be done is to get on the train early enough to get a good ride, but not so early as to be involved in the next train crash. That is true at the end of bear as well as bull markets, although the patterns are slightly different.

The primary difference between these two stock market extremes is centered on the notion that fear is a stronger motivation than greed. Greed is what holds a bull market at highs even though it is ready to fall. Greed tends to play out over an extended period of time because greed is necessarily supported and abetted by the larger stock market operators: investors or investment pools that control literally millions and millions of shares. The large stock operators have a vested interest in maintaining the appearance of a bullish market as long as possible to enable them to sell their shares at the best possible prices. Large operators tend to disseminate information as well as rumors and innuendos to cast those stocks in which they hold large positions into as favorable a light as possible. Taken as a whole and given the size and breadth of their ranks as well as their holdings, large operators work diligently to encourage late buyers to make purchases of shares that they more than willingly sell.

Look at any major top in the stock market. It is not a single bar event. It usually plays out over many bars (monthly bars) for a long period of time. During that time period, price works back and forth but makes little progress in moving higher in any sustained way. Might it be suggested that price cannot rise substantially because the largest holders of the stock are busy selling their shares to the late-coming buyers?

Wall Street sells hope and stories. Wall Street is composed of many large stock operators. They make and lose fortunes through the buying and selling of stocks. It's true that there are stories broadcast by each publicly traded company, and it is reasonable to believe this as it is definitely in the company's best interest to put its best foot forward. But what about all the stories passed out by analysts who work for the firms that hold large positions in the stock being touted? These large operators trade for both their own books as well as for large clients, who pay huge fees to have the brokers manage their vast investments. They also have a vested interest.

The period of trading that marks a market top is referred to as distribution. It's a common word that, when taken literally, means to distribute stock from one shareholder to another. Since large operators have huge stock positions, distributing these shares takes a considerable amount of time—months, usually. That is a large part of why tops take a long time to develop.

Toward the end of the distribution process, the liquidation (markdown) phase begins. Liquidation is another name for a fire sale: a process where any remaining shares of large operators are sold at a discount and as hurriedly as possible. This is when the smaller stockholders find that the stories sold were light on truth and long on hope. The rosy forecasts turned out to be pie in the sky. Eventually, disbelief on the part of the later purchasers gives way to fear. In the stock market, value is not an absolute; it is only a perception. Sometimes that perception is vastly different from the reality. There were plenty of stocks that sold for $100 and $200 a share at the height of the 2000 NASDAQ highs that, within a couple of years, were selling for single digits. Some sold for pennies. Many went out of business. Dreams were lost and irreparable harm was done to many a small trader's portfolio. The losses sustained during the rampant fear at the height of liquidation were great, and always are.

Panic-type selling is the hallmark of rampant fear. Panic sell-offs in the stock market do not happen frequently, but they are a necessary part of the system because Wall Street sells stories—not reality. As long as there are buyers, the stories just keep coming. Selling perception means that any price is a fair price. If a trading house can convince potential buyers that a stock should be valued by how many eyeballs view the company's products rather than how many actually buy the product (as they did in the dot-com bubble), then nonsensical valuations are possible—for a while. When the stories collapse, though, the fear drives prices lower and very quickly.

Many refer to bottoms in markets as washouts. That is seldom the case, though. Usually bear markets simply wear buyers out on subsequent probes of the lows created during the washout. When the sellers are finally exhausted, then the market can begin to trade higher again. The primary difference, though, between bull and bear markets is that bull markets take an extraordinary amount of time to work stocks to higher prices while a bear market, in comparison, makes value rapidly disappear.

Bearish Reversal   The following description of a bear market reversal is provided in the light of how the Trading Cube transitions while the reversal occurs. Although bear markets are associated with the collapse of share prices, the fact is that once the washout is done, the transition back to a bull market or at least to a sideways market typically occurs over less time than is taken by a bull market reversal.

A turn in trend implies a trend transition. Bear-to-bull trend transitions always follow the course from bearish (suspect or confirmed) to sideways (again suspect or confirmed) and eventually to bullish. A reversal of a long-term trend is necessarily preceded by a reversal in the intermediate-term trend, which itself first witnesses a reversal in the short-term trend. This is true of bull and bear markets, with one being the inverse of the other.

The problem with a reversal is whether the reversal can be trusted. Qualified trends are all about how much trust to place in a trend transition. If the qualification of the transition is suspect, then not as much trust is extended. If it is confirmed, then there are increased odds of the continuation of the transitioned-to state. Figure 10.12 is a state diagram of the stages that the Trading Cube transgresses through on a bearish reversal—moving from a bearish long-term trend to a bullish one. It depicts the transition stages of the Trading Cube as a bear market bottoms, attempts to lift, retests and reveals divergence with lower prices but lighter volume (suspect bearish), then reverses again with confidence (confirmed sideways). The final confirmation that the long-term general market trend has reversed occurs when the intermediate-term trend confirms a sideways trend or a bullish one.

There are a number of caveats regarding this state diagram. First, there is nothing to say that the state diagram will always resemble the one

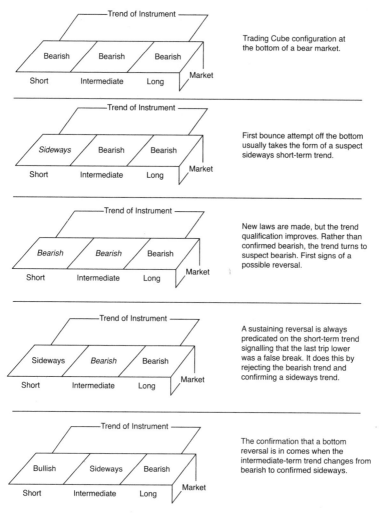

FIGURE 10.12 Bear Market Reversal Trading Cube Sequence

shown in Figure 10.12. It will probably be some variation of it. Figure 10.12 represents a common set of state transitions as expressed through the trading cube, but there are many other variations. For a bearish reversal, however, there are two critical components to watch for. First, after the washout, there needs to be a retest of the washout area. In some bear market reversals, the retest on the short- and intermediate-term time frame is only a test and not a change in trend.[5] In others, as depicted in Figure 10.12, a trend transition occurs and results in an upgrade in trend (from confirmed bearish to suspect bearish). Without a retest, the lingering possibility of an eventual retest removes the confidence that a reversal has indeed occurred. Ambiguity and uncertainty are the death knell to sustained rallies.

The second important characteristic is that one never knows if the bottom is really in, until the intermediate-term trend turns to at least confirmed sideways or, in its absence, a suspect sideways trend undergoes a retest and regenerate sequence proving that price has no intention of trading lower again.[6] Without confirmation, or a retest-and-regenerate sequence, then an eventual retest and regenerate sequence remains the most likely possibility. Retest-and-regenerate sequences imply that the probing for a bottom is not complete. If the trend turns to suspect sideways, wait for the retest-and-regenerate sequence to occur and prove that the bottom is in.

Stepping through the state transitions expressed in Figure 10.12, notice how the probing for a lower low occurs. There is an attempted move higher that succumbs to additional selling pressure. To determine how much selling pressure remains requires a trader to examine how the selling pressure manifests itself at the prior swing point low. If the pressure subsides (lower volume as compared to the swing point), then at least a temporary low is in. If it expands, then the bottom is likely not in yet. This is visible on a chart and through the state transitions expressed via the Trading Cube.

After the first real bottom possibility is expressed, then there is the need to see the short-term trend to transition to a confirmed sideways trend. If that happens, and if it can be sustained long enough, then the intermediate-term trend should follow suit. It is at that point that the trader knows the bottom is most likely in.

From a trading perspective, traders can attempt to game the turn at any point during the reversal process. The issue will always be whether the trader is able to maintain their conviction as the initial probing trades are retested in subsequent selling. Naturally, the earlier a trader can position long in a rising market, the better, but many of the technical trading constructs require confirmation. Confirmation that a bearish reversal has staying power is demarcated by a change to a confirmed sideways trend or to a suspect sideways trend that successfully endures a subsequent retest and regenerate sequence.

Note that the process described above is for a long-term bear market reversal. The same general theme applies across the time spectrum. For a day trader, a long-term washout might be a plunge in price over a couple of weeks. The same process applies and the same stages occur as well—just in microcosm.

Bullish Reversal   The transition sequence from a bull to a bear market is practically a mirror image of a bearish reversal. The difference is time. Bull market tops can witness long periods of time where prices hang at

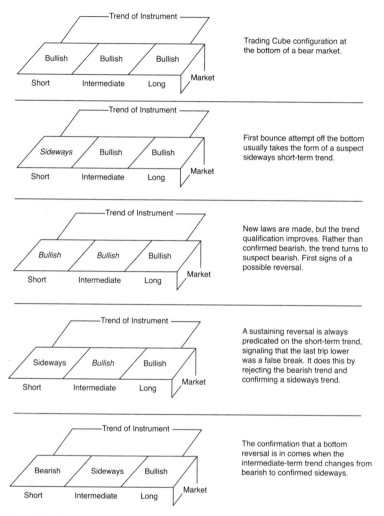

FIGURE 10.13 Bull Market Reversal Trading Cube Sequence

their highs. Figure 10.13 is a transition diagram as seen through the Trading Cube for a bull market reversal.

As was the case for a bear market reversal, two essential ingredients are necessary for the possibility of a bull market top. The first is the need to witness either a failed test at the top as part of a swing point high test or a realized trend transition to suspect bullish or sideways on a short-term time frame. That is always the first signal. Note that these signals do not guarantee a bull market top—far from it. They are, however, always evident when analyzing the tops of prior bull markets.

The second ingredient is the actual trend transition to a confirmed sideways or bearish trend on the intermediate-term time frame. Similar to a bullish reversal, this trend transition may take the form of a retest-and-regenerate sequence as part of a more complex breakdown process. The 2007–2008 top took the form of a more complex retest-and-regenerate sequence in the spring of 2008. The start of the bullish reversal began all the way back in October of 2007. That top took almost nine months to play out. The mark-down phase didn't begin until a full year had already passed.

Another general characteristic in bull market tops is that they tend to see more erratic price behavior as the top nears. Many times there are plunges in price followed by low-volume rallies back to new highs, creating suspect trends. These erratic transitions spread to the intermediate-term trend in addition to the short-term trend.

Again, from a trading perspective, there are many places where a trader can attempt to "call the top," but until the above two events take place, the idea of a top remains an idea without support. Because market tops take such a long time to develop, this usually results in the larger picture being lost due to short-term trading desires. It's almost as if the forest can't be seen for all the trees. The result is that traders tend to trade the short-term trends and forget the developing storm clouds—until it's too late!

SUMMARY

The Trading Cube offers a visual road map for trend followers, capturing a complete picture of the trading landscape in a snapshot view. The Trading Cube contains the qualified trend for the market, market sector, and the individual stock across all time frames. One look at the Trading Cube, once understood, provides the trader with a visual understanding of opportunity or peril.

The real strength of the Trading Cube is the same strength of qualified trends: trend transition. The trading landscape is pictorially evident when observing transitions in the Trading Cube. Trend transitions, whether viewed through the Trading Cube, a trend transitions matrix, or simply through the various charts represented in the Trading Cube, are the heart and soul of understanding where the market has been, currently is, and probably is going.

At this juncture, all the tools and visual aids are on the table. What remains is to use everything presented so far in an actual trading example. Rest assured that no trader is ever certain about a particular trade. They can't be. Trading involves the future and future events are outside the realm of what can be known with certainty. Trading is therefore reduced to a set of possibilities and, through trend qualification, the location of significant support and resistance, and the integration of multiple markets across multiple time frames, the trader is far better prepared than they otherwise would be. The result is a higher probability of outcomes in which the trader consistently profits through his or her trading endeavors.

CHAPTER 11

Trading
Qualified Trends

To trade or not to trade—that is the question that all traders face, each and every day. The answer is seldom in terms of black or white, but is somewhere in the shades of gray in between. With the right tools and a little practice, consistently profitable trading is quite achievable.

This book begins with the premise that the classical view of trend is outdated and in need of repair. In its place, Chapters 3, 4, and 5 introduce the neoclassical theory. Definitions are supplied and numerous examples are provided, showing how all trends can be qualified. Indeed, not all trends are created equal. A methodological approach to determining trends and examining their transitions is presented. The concepts of confirmation and suspicion are introduced, along with the notion of retesting and regenerating to alleviate the "suspect" nature of suspicious trends. Examples of trend transitions are offered to describe each of these states.

From theory the focus shifts to application, since it is with application that money is either made or lost. The presentation of some preparatory material underscores the fact that technical analysis represents just one piece of the successful trading puzzle. It is an important cog in the machine, but by no means the only one.

Chapter 7 examined the critical concepts of support and resistance. Once a trend is identified and a stock singled out for trading, the critical question is whether the trade is worthwhile. The reward-to-risk of the trade as well as timing the entry and exit are centered on the notion of support and resistance. Unless a trader can identify support and resistance that have real anchors, well-timed entries and exits will continue to be a problem, and trades that should succeed will fail.

In Chapter 8, additional work is undertaken regarding timing through the examination of price reversals and projections. Chapters 9 and 10 return the focus to trend and the integration of time frames. The need to consider the effect of multiple instruments when trading any stock is introduced, and the Trading Cube is proposed as a way to visualize multiple instruments on multiple time frames in order to quickly ascertain the trading landscape and its potential.

The objective of this final chapter is to employ the bulk of all the ideas presented so far, and to do so over a sufficiently long period of time. By choosing a long period, the focus is upon trends and trend transitions for the long- and intermediate-term time frames in both bull and bear markets. In trading, the market can move up, down, or sideways, and do all of this at the same time with different instruments and on different time frames. A successful trader must be able to make money independently of the market environment. Trend qualification and transitions when combined with proper entry and exit provide the means to do so.

EXAMPLE OF A QUALIFIED TREND

With all of this in mind, the remainder of this chapter applies the concepts presented so far and embarks upon a trade utilizing those concepts and methods. The time period examined is from January 2003 to August 2009. This seven-year period witnessed the end of a recession that sprang from the collapse of the dot-com bubble; the birth of another bull market; and finally the climatic end to that bull market run with the 2008 financial meltdown. To illustrate a realistic trading scenario, the approach taken is top down: Start with the big-picture trend and from there move to the sectors. If the big-picture trend is bullish or appears to be in the process of becoming bullish, then look for sectors that are relatively stronger in their bullishness. If it is negative or appears to be turning negative, look for sectors that are relatively weaker and more bearish. For the bullish case, proceed to find stocks that are even stronger than the sector. The opposite case applies to the market when it is bearish.

The above is what happens in trading. One determines the general market direction, forms a bias, locates opportunities, and then formulates a trading plan. At the start of this particular trading example, the market was bearish coming into 2003, but the possibility of a turn was evident. A bias of a potential transition from bearish to bullish was formed, then sectors and stocks examined. The sector chosen was one of the strongest sectors up until the crash in 2008 and, quite appropriately, one of the weakest performers during that crash. That sector was the financial sector and within it, a star performer was Wells Fargo. Since the market tends to trend higher for longer durations than it trends lower, the desire is to find the strongest sectors and stocks within them near the beginning of a bull market, get on board, and ride them for as long as possible. That is where the best gains can be had over time.

To set the framework, Wells Fargo trades on the New York Stock Exchange under the symbol WFC. The applicable general market for this stock is the S&P 500; thus, the SPY SPDR S&P 500 ETF is used to represent the general market. The most appropriate sector ETF is the Financial Select Sector SPDR ETF, whose symbol is XLF.

To get a snapshot view of the trading landscape from January of 2003 through August of 2009, two tables are provided. Table 11.1 presents a time-line of the general market, the sector, and the stock being tracked, as does Table 11.2. Each table contains the qualified trend transitions for both the long- and intermediate-term time frames for the three instruments.

Note that the second column in Table 11.1 indicates the prevailing qualified trend from the beginning of 2003.

Because a substantial amount of information is condensed into these two tables, a legend to aid in interpreting the data is contained in Table 11.3.

This chapter considers the trading landscape as signified in these two tables. Correlations and divergences are pointed out, as well as lead and lag indications.

Note that Tables 11.1 and 11.2 include only the long- and intermediate-term qualified trends. To include the short-term trends over such a long time period would have been overwhelming and useless. The trading examples examined illustrate the principles espoused throughout this book, based on the long- and intermediate-term trends. Throughout the exercise, charts for the appropriate time frame are examined in order to illustrate how qualified trend, trend transitions, and anchored support and resistance, as well as many of the other concepts, are integrated into a uniform approach to trading the market.

Before becoming immersed in the myriad details contained in Tables 11.1 and 11.2, observe the following points:

- The transition from a bearish trend to a confirmed sideways trend on the long-term time frame from the general market signaled a long and sustained period of bullishness.
- The transition from a bullish trend to a confirmed sideways trend on the long-term time frame from the general market signaled a long and sustained period of bearishness.

TABLE 11.1 January 2003 to December 2006 Timeline

Symbol / Time Frame	2003	2004	2005	2006
SPY-LT	C-Bear		C-Side Jan 04 S-Bull Nov 04	C-Bull Nov 05	
XLF-LT	C-Side	C-Bull Oct 03	C-Bull Feb 04 S-Bull Nov 04	C-Bull Nov 05	
WFC-LT	S-Bull	C-Bull Oct 03		C-Bull Nov 05	
SPY-IT	C-Bear	A-Side Apr 03 C-Bull May 03 S-Bull Sep 03	S-Side Aug 04 C-Bull Nov 04	C-Side Apr 05 C-Bull Jul 05 C-Side Oct 05 C-Bull Nov 05	C-Side Jul 06 C-Bull Sep 06
XLF-IT	S-Bear	C-Side May 03 S-Bull Sep 03	C-Side May 04 S-Bull Aug 04 C-Bull Nov 04	C-Side Mar 05 C-Bull Oct 05 C-Bull Nov 05	C-Side Jun 06 S-Bull Sep 06
WFC-IT	A-Side	C-Bull Apr 03 C-Bull May 03 C-Bull Jun 03 S-Bull Sep 03	C-Bull May 04 S-Bull Sep 04	C-Bull May 05 S-Bull Jul 05 C-Side Aug 05 C-Bull Nov 05	C-Bull Feb 06 S-Bull Nov 06

TABLE 11.2 January 2007 to August 2009 Timeline

Symbol Time Frame	2007	2008	2009
SPY-LT		C-Side Jan 08; C-Bear Sep 08	S-Side Jul 09
XLF-LT	C-Side Nov 07	C-Bear Feb 08	
WFC-LT		C-Side Feb 08; C-Bear Jun 08; C-Side Sep 08	
SPY-IT	C-Side Feb 07; C-Bull Apr 07; C-Side Jul 07; S-Bull Oct 07	S-Side Jan 08; S-Bull Apr 08; C-Bear Jul 08	S-Bear Mar 09; S-Side Jun 09; S-Bull Jul 09
XLF-IT	C-Side Feb 07; C-Bull May 07; C-Side Jul 07; C-Bear Jul 07; C-Bear Nov 07	C-Bear Jan 08; C-Bear Mar 08; S-Bear Jun 08; C-Side Sep 08; C-Bear Oct 08	C-Side May 09; S-Bull Jul 09
WFC-IT	C-Side Feb 07; C-Bull May 07; C-Bull Aug 07; S-Side Oct 07; C-Bear Nov 07	S-Bear Jun 08; C-Bear Jul 08; C-Side Sep 08; C-Bear Nov 08	C-Side May 09

TABLE 11.3   Timeline Legend

Symbol	Interpretation
C-Bull	Confirmed bullish trend transition or affirmation
S-Bull	Suspect bullish trend transition or affirmation
C-Bear	Confirmed bearish trend transition or affirmation
S-Bear	Suspect bearish trend transition or affirmation
C-Side	Confirmed sideways trend transition or affirmation
S-Side	Suspect sideways trend transition or affirmation
A-Side	Ambivalent sideways trend transition
SPY-LT	SPY SPDR S&P 500 ETF—Long Term
XLF-LT	Financial Select Sector SPDR ETF—Long Term
WFC-LT	Wells Fargo—Long Term
SPY-IT	SPY SPDR S&P 500 ETF—Intermediate Term
XLF-IT	Financial Select Sector SPDR ETF—Intermediate Term
WFC-IT	Wells Fargo—Intermediate Term

If a trader had done nothing more than to enter the market when the long-term trend of the general market transitioned from bearish to bullish and then exited when the opposite occurred, they would have entered the market at around $103 SPY and would have exited around $126 SPY for a gain of roughly 28 percent over the four-year period. The problem with this strategy is that, since the crash of 2008 and the subsequent rise back to more than $112 SPY, the market has yet to issue a transition back to a bullish state on a monthly basis. Although probable, there is no guarantee that it will offer a transition to a bullish trend and even if it does, a huge amount of potential gains will have already occurred. Fortunately, there are other time frames available that, when combined with trading strategies, can provide earlier entry and even earlier exit.

Another broad observation, and one that is quite reasonable, is that the short-term time frame will always turn before the intermediate-term time frame. The same is true of the intermediate term when juxtaposed to the long term. It has to be that way. The issue is finding a method to ferret out the many false signals that occur on the shorter-term time frames.

Again, looking at Table 11.1, notice how many times the SPY-IT transitioned from sideways to bullish and back again. From a long-term trend perspective, it didn't matter whatsoever, though, as prices continued higher. Now take a closer look again at Table 11.2. The SPY-IT finally moved to a bearish trend (confirmed as well), in September of 2008. Earlier that same year, the XLF-LT did the same. In fact, the XLF-IT first transitioned to a bearish trend way back in July of 2007.

These observations are early warning signals that an impending long-term trend change is increasingly probable. When a cluster of sectors begin to flash signs that the bullish trends are abating, that is usually a reasonably good indicator that the broad market will soon do the same. It doesn't mean that it has to, but it certainly indicates that a trader should consider the possibility and be on the lookout.

Those are the big-picture observations. The remaining pages move from the macro to the more micro (intermediate-term trend), using the information in Tables 11.1 and 11.2 augmented with select charts to interweave a story of how a trader might position their trades based solely upon the charts.

ENTERING A TRADE

At the beginning of 2003, a two-year-long bear market was drawing to a close. It was no ordinary bear market, though. For the NASDAQ, the brutality was unparalleled, with more than 75 percent of the broad market's wealth wiped out in two short years. A decade later, the NASDAQ remains more than 50 percent below the all-time highs registered in March 2000.

To get a sense of where the general market, the sector, and the stock used for this trading example were coming into 2003, refer to the second column of Table 11.1. That column denotes the qualified trend of the market, the sector, and the stock entering into 2003.

The long-term trend of the broad market (SPY) was confirmed bearish while the financial sector (XLF) and Wells Fargo (WFC) had already begun to turn (confirmed sideways and suspect bullish). That is how long-term trends change. They start from the ground up. The initial vestige of a turn in the broad index always begins with a few stocks that bottom-out first. If enough stocks in a sector bottom, then the sector will bottom. For the long-term broad market chart to change, it is imperative that some number of stocks and stock sectors begin to turn first. As 2003 began, there were small signs of that possibility brewing. Of course, at that particular point in time, after two years of devastating selling, few were interested in buying, as is always the case at a major market bottom.

Note that a bottom in the broad market is a process, just as a top is. It takes time (less time typically for a bottom than a top) and there are fits of starts and stops along the way, making it difficult to recognize. In fact, until the broad market moves to a confirmed sideways trend, there is a very uncomfortable feeling buying stocks because the probabilities of the turn materializing are greatly at risk. Remember, long-term time frames change infrequently. They inspire greater confidence as a result. Long-term trends

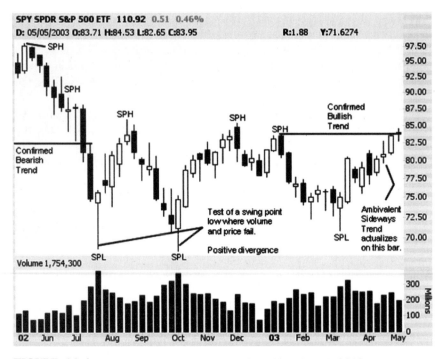

FIGURE 11.1 SPY Bottoming Process, May 6, 2002 to May 5, 2003

are slow to register a change, which is what makes their transitions so important. The problem is, their transitions occur much later in the process of a turnaround, which is why traders look to the shorter-term time frames to get a jump on the long-term ones.

Turning back to Table 11.1, take a look at the 2003 column. Notice that the intermediate-term broad market (SPY-IT) transitioned from a confirmed bearish trend to an ambivalent sideways trend in April 2003. The very next month saw it move to a confirmed bullish trend. Figure 11.1 is a chart of the SPY that covers this period. The actual bottom in the broad market was a classic test of a swing point low on lighter volume that failed on price.

The low in July 2002 was surpassed by the lower low in October of the same year, yet the volume was lighter and the price closed over rather than under the previous swing point low. That was a failed test of a swing point low. A basic rule in qualified trend trading is that if the market is unable to take out a swing point and volume is lighter on the test, then the probability that price will reverse increases dramatically. Because this was a failure of the lowest low since the bear market began in 2000, a trader has to realize that it could potentially be the bottom. It doesn't mean that it is, but it is a possibility. Another aspect of this failure to take out a swing point low is that it occurred on the broad market. That lends greater significance to all stocks and sectors and carries a broader impact.

Relative Strength

The same time frame for the XLF is shown in Figure 11.2, but here the divergence when compared to the SPY is more pronounced. The financial sector failed to even make a lower low. The significance of this event is that the financial sector was painting a portrait that it was stronger than the general market. Many times divergence is referred to synonymously as relative strength.

Another method of determining relative strength is through qualified trends. Once more, referring back to Table 11.1, coming into 2003 both the XLF-LT and WFC-LT were exhibiting relatively stronger trends than the long- and intermediate-term broad market. That too is relative strength.

FIGURE 11.2 Bottoming Process—Financial Select Sector SPDR (XLF), January 28, 2002 to February 10, 2003

Notice how both the XLF-LT and the WFC-LT turn confirmed bullish *before* the SPT-LT even turns confirmed sideways. Again, the sector and stock are expressing relative strength as compared to the broad market.

It is very simple to determine relative strength of the various sectors in the market relative to anything else. Just compare the qualified trends on the long-term trends, which are not apt to give false signals. Derivative indicators are not required, and false signals are less likely if the raw data is used in its original form. That data is the high, low, and close along with volume.

Continuing with the charts, within the financial sector WFC showed even greater relative strength than the sector as displayed in Figure 11.3.

As a recap, in 2002, divergence materialized in the broad market when a swing point low test failed on lighter volume. At the same time, the financial sector had even greater divergence on that same test, adding credence to the possibility of a bear market bottom in the general market. Inside the financial sector, Wells Fargo showed relative strength to the broad market and the financial sector as well. Although it isn't possible to assign a high

FIGURE 11.3 Bottoming Process—Wells Fargo & Co. (WFC), February 4, 2002 to February 24, 2002

degree of probability to a bottom until the long-term trend for the broad market changes from a bearish to a confirmed sideways trend, a trader need not wait until that late in the game to postulate the possibility and trade it. There is always a trade in the market if a plan exists and risk is managed. At the beginning of 2003, a trader had plenty of opportunities to position for a trade—long or short. The question was, which way.

Following the Trend

The old adage "The trend is your friend" is a true statement but, like most things in life, it sounds a lot simpler than it really is. What trend was your friend in early May of 2003, for example? Is it the bearish long-term trends exhibited in the broad market or the sideways to bullish trends witnessed in the intermediate-term trends of the financials and Wells Fargo stock in that same time period? It is always a matter of context, time, and risk tolerance. Without question, the reward-to-risk always favors those who average in at lower prices rather than at higher ones as long as a real turn is at hand. Although buying retraces versus breakouts is a matter of personal preference, over time the trading plan is what defines success or the lack thereof.

The long-term trend is always the primary trend, but it too eventually turns. That is true of all markets. Bear markets generally last from 18 to 36 months. In May of 2003, 25 months had already passed. The possibility that the bear market could soon end was growing. Probing for a turn was probably not a bad idea.

For a retrace trader at the possible conclusion of a bear market, the desire is to determine the pending change in the primary trend as early as possible, then identify the strongest stocks in those sectors. If the longer-term trend change is solid, then the same pattern can be repeated as other sectors turn.

The early warning system of a shift in the general market is first observed in the trend transitions on the intermediate term for the various market sectors. Market sectors are the components that constitute the market. When enough of them begin to turn, the market will turn. Within the sectors, there are strong stocks that lead and others that lag. As enough sectors begin to turn, finding and buying the strong stocks in the strong sectors is how a trader gets ahead of the pack and produces larger returns.

Figure 11.4 is an intermediate-term chart displaying the last six months of trading for Wells Fargo in 2002 and the first six months of trading in 2003. Wells Fargo in 2003 was a strong stock in what was becoming a strong sector.

With the general market, the financial sector, and Wells Fargo stock showing positive divergences in October 2002, a trader looking for a turn

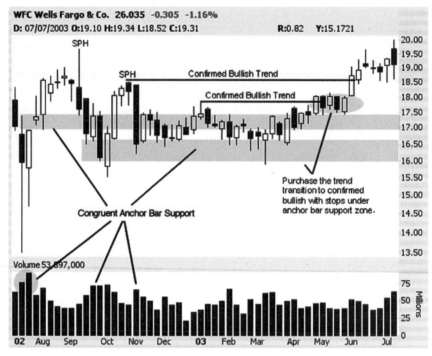

FIGURE 11.4 Buying into Wells Fargo (WFC), July 8, 2002 to July 14, 2003

had received the first solid technical signal for such an event. What was needed was a trend transition to support the notion that the general market was turning. In April 2003, the SPY-IT transitioned from confirmed bearish to ambivalent sideways. The following month, SPY-IT turned confirmed bullish. Simultaneously, the XLF-IT also turned to confirmed sideways, suggesting that it had likely turned as well. All the while, one of the strongest stocks in the financial sector, Wells Fargo, was leading the charge, turning confirmed bullish in April of 2003. The change in trend was evident, and the need to find strong stocks in strong sectors was clearly prudent.

Measuring Reward-to-Risk to Time the Entry

For Wells Fargo, the annotations on the intermediate-term chart (see Figure 11.4) clearly show several weeks where entry was potentially possible using anchor bar support for stop-loss protection. On this time frame, the apparent reward-to-risk equation appeared less than compelling at first glance. The problem with calculating a reasonable reward-to-risk equation on a stock like Wells Fargo is not a simple matter of looking to the past to find resistance areas and swing points to serve as price targets. For Wells Fargo, despite the long bear market, the stock was still near all-time highs at the beginning of 2003. In the case of this stock, the only two higher price targets on the chart were the clear-cut resistance area in the $19 range and the spike higher at $19.66. That spike was the all-time high.

What made Wells Fargo compelling as a trade was a strong sector and an exceptionally powerful stock. A clear indication of the stock's relative strength was exhibited when it registered a new all-time high in the midst of the bear market. To obtain a reasonable price projection, a trader has to use a price projection idea that postulates the following: When a trading range is broken, the new trading range is likely to be as broad as the old one. In the case of Wells Fargo (see Figure 11.5), on the monthly chart it displays a reasonably well-defined long-term trading floor during the bear market that spans from approximately $13 to $19. Assume a slightly smaller $5.50 range. Add $5.50 to the top of the range. That makes a reasonable topside price projection of $24.50 realistic.

FIGURE 11.5 Estimating Price Projections Based on a Trading Range, November 1, 1999 to September 1, 2004

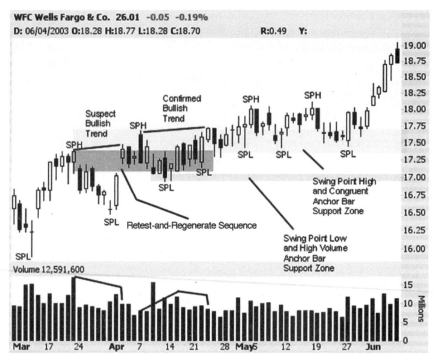

FIGURE 11.6 Using Daily Bars for Entry Timing, March 7, 2003 to June 6, 2003

Assuming a long-term price projection of $24.50, the upside potential amounts to $7 from the existing $17.50 entry price point, while the risk registers at roughly $1.50. That creates a very compelling reward-to-risk trade and makes Wells Fargo worth examining more closely.

Once the determination to buy or sell a stock is made, the trader needs to move to the micro level to time the entry. The short-term time frame in this example is the daily chart, as shown in Figure 11.6.

The annotations on this chart clearly highlight the potential buy zone that coincides with the buy signal given on the intermediate-term chart from Figure 11.4. In that figure, a confirmed bullish trend triggered a buy signal on the last week of April. Figure 11.6 exhibits multiple bars over a four-week period that was buyable once the daily chart had turned to a confirmed bullish trend and was thus in harmony with the weekly chart. The buy zone was anchored by the high of the swing point high bar registered in the middle of March and the second swing point high registered in the first week of April. Additionally, the high-volume bar from the second week of April also served as an anchor bar. Note there was a lower support buy zone, but it never came into effect.

As an aside, the previously discussed retest-and-regenerate sequence is also evident on the daily chart. When the swing point high from March 21, 2003, was surpassed on April 2, volume failed to increase as price moved higher. That created a suspect bullish trend—suspect because volume was lacking. There wasn't any indication of an increased desire on the part of the buyers.

For the stock to remain healthy, it should retrace, retest the previous swing point bar (high or low depending on how much time has passed), and do so with lighter volume. If it were to do all of these, then the retest-and-regenerate sequence would be successful and the suspicion removed. That would remove the doubt and allow the stock to work higher once more without the cloud of suspicion.

In this particular case, volume did expand on the retest, but it still wasn't greater than the bar tested. This occurred on the high-volume bar from April 9. Everything was perfect with the retest-and-regenerate sequence, with the exception of a close under the swing point high that was being retested. That close occurred April 11 but was recaptured the very next day (this is the bar labeled SPL on the chart) and highlights an important point. Stocks can and do under- and overshoot their targets on a reasonably regular basis. If the move really is a "mistake," such as an overshoot of the low from the swing point high that was under test, then it should reverse and get back inside the range immediately (within a bar or two at most). If it does, then it was just an overshoot. If it doesn't, then it is likely that something else is occurring and the interpretation is wrong.

Trading Multiple Time Frames   Continuing with the discussion of entry price, one way to easily trade into a strong stock (or any stock for that matter) is to trade it on multiple time frames. Why shouldn't a trader trade the short- and intermediate-term time frames at the same time? There isn't any rule saying that you can't employ stop-loss orders at different price levels corresponding to different time frame trades. Not only is there nothing that says you can't do it, there is everything that says you *should* do it.

In this particular example, the risk on the daily chart is a close below the swing point low from April 11 at $16.94. That represents less than a $.50 risk with a potential reward of as much as $7, whereas a trade based on the weekly chart risks about $1.50 for the same expected reward.

A basic problem with stock entry and exit is that trading is not exact, but is instead an endless game of probabilities. The probability that Wells Fargo would fall in price, closing below $16.94, is unlikely to be the same probability that it would fall below $15.99. In fact, the probability of the higher stop being triggered is, as one would expect, more likely. There are some ways to try to quantify that likelihood, but that is beyond the scope of this discussion. Common sense suggests that the higher-priced stop-loss order has a greater likelihood of being hit. The $16.94 stop is only a little over $.50 away from the entry price or less than 3 percent away. That is not a very large margin for error, whereas the $15.99 stop is more than 14 percent away. From the intermediate-term chart perspective, the lower-priced stop is two support zones removed from the current price. If Wells Fargo stock should trade low enough to remove both the higher and lower stops, then the odds are reasonably high that the stock is not really about to trend higher, which is what the entire premise of the trade was. That cannot be said about the higher-priced stop, though.

So why trade with a greater margin of error? The simple answer is because it creates a greater likelihood of gaining entry into a trade, and gaining entry into a strong stock is sometimes very difficult. Think about it this way. If the stock is one of those truly strong stocks and doesn't retrace as much as would normally be expected, then the trade will go unfilled. If a trader trades on multiple time frames, though, the entry orders will almost necessarily be higher for partial entry. If after initial entry the stock turns and runs higher, then the trader has at least a partial position, and he has a winning position almost immediately.

If, instead, prices pull back further, then subsequent entries are made with the idea of a longer-term trade. One trading plan might be to let the first entry be the entire entry for a short-term trade while the next three entries (all within the support zone) are all part of an intermediate-term trend trade. For the intermediate-term trade, the first of the three purchases is for 20 percent of the desired holding, while the second and third purchases are for 35 and 45 percent, respectively. The point of staggering entries and size is apparent once the math is completed. The resultant average entry price is necessarily closer to the stop-out price point and provides the trader with the best possible entry price, given the technical setup.

If the price fails to pull back far enough to actually trigger all four entry trades, then the trade is almost guaranteed to be a winning trade. Unless it pulls all the way back to trigger both sets of stops, even the short-term trade can end up being triggered while the intermediate-term time frame trade ends up making the overall trade profitable. This methodology is tried and true and, unless the trader has horrible identification skills for support and resistance, it is a very reasonable and successful methodology. Trading multiple time frames for the same stock makes a lot of sense.

EXPLOITING THE TREND

With every trading success comes the problem of taking profits. When does a trader exit or reduce their position in a profitable trade? There are those who equate an exit with sin. They believe that once a stock is bought, it should be held indefinitely. Unless a trader is a stock picker extraordinaire, nothing could be farther from the truth. Of the original 30 stocks in the Dow Jones Industrial Average, only one remains and the turnover rate is greater than just the other 29 original stocks.[1] These were and still are the industrial giants of the country. They were handpicked to represent the top of their class, yet many have since disappeared from the business landscape.

If the largest companies in the world can cease to exist, is it not even more likely that the lesser names that most traders trade are bound to come and go as well? Even if they don't disappear, few are likely to remain star performers. Why own a stock that isn't or doesn't have the possibility of being a star performer? Is a winning football organization satisfied with also-ran players? Do they play simply to play or do they play to win? Trading is no different. You play to win. You pick and hold star performers *while they are stars*.

Profits have to be taken either along the way or in the end, but traders often choose the time to take them without a great deal of forethought. That is unfortunate. Stocks do not go up or down forever. In almost all environments, they move up and down while trending. Eventually the prevailing trend will end. If profits were not taken prior to that point, it is necessary to take them then. Failing to do so is to risk all that has been gained. It's rather simple when thought about in this manner. The problem is determining when a trade ends.

Using Ebb and Flow to Profit

One proven approach to stock trading is to maintain a core position in a stock while trading around the position as the trending stock moves in a zigzag fashion. Referring back to Tables 11.1 and 11.2, in October 2003, the trend for the XLF-LT and WFC-LT transitioned to a confirmed bullish trend. Over the next four years, both long-term bullish trends were maintained without fail. Although they weakened a couple of times, they were not downgraded to a sideways trend until late 2007, which turned out to be prescient since the markets crashed in 2008.

During the same period of time, notice how many times the intermediate-term trend of these same two instruments (XLF-IT and WFC-IT) changed from bullish (confirmed or suspect) to sideways (confirmed or suspect). A downgrade transition in trend implies that price weakened. That is the zigzag where additional shares could be added back to the core position. To reduce holdings, a trader would need to project a price point to partial exit using AB = CD price projections, the initial hit of a magnet price point, or other timing events such as a swing point failure reversal or even two-bar reversal patterns at critical chart intervals.

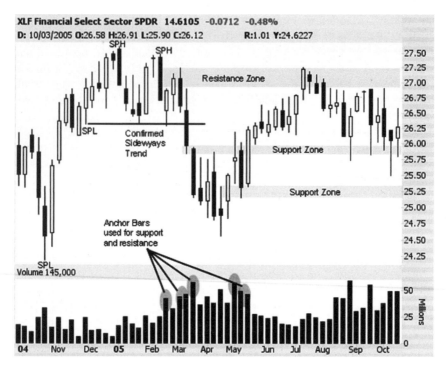

FIGURE 11.7 Sideways Trend on XLF, September 20, 2004 to October 17, 2005

As an example, consider the time period of late 2004 to late 2005 on both the XLF-IT and WFC-IT. Both the sector and the stock had oscillated in terms of strength throughout this period on this time frame (see Figure 11.1). A look at the actual charts shows this vacillation. Figure 11.7 is a chart of the XLF-IT for this time period. In March of 2005, the XLF turned to a confirmed sideways trend. By July, price has pushed back up toward the top of the sideways range.

Using anchor bars to determine resistance and support zones, it was pretty easy to see that as prices pushed back into the $27 range in July, volume was tepid as compared to the volume bars that were being pushed into. For the swing point high to be overtaken at $27.50, volume needed to expand dramatically and it just didn't happen. That suggested that the odds of a continued move higher were low.

Now, turning to the same time period for Wells Fargo and for the exact same week when the XLF was pushing into resistance on lighter volume, WFC hit a new all-time high on suspect volume.

Had a trader entered WFC back in the spring of 2003 around the $17.50 price point, he or she would have realized a 68 percent gain in a little more

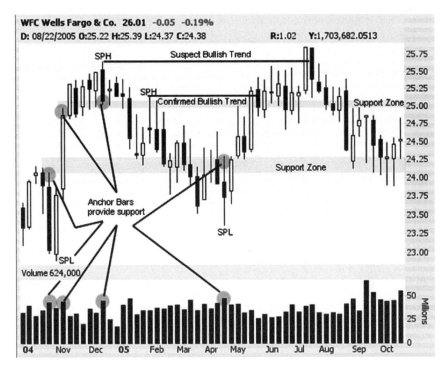

WFC Wells Fargo & Co. 26.01 -0.05 -0.19%
D: 08/22/2005 O:25.22 H:25.39 L:24.37 C:24.38   R:1.02   Y:1,703,682.0513

FIGURE 11.8 Taking Partial Profits on WFC, September 20, 2004 to October 17, 2005

than two years. In fact, this would be the first time that a real chance for an end to the bullish trend became a serious possibility. The XLF-IT had shifted to a confirmed sideways trend and it wouldn't take much more weakness to turn that to a bearish trend. Wells Fargo had remained relatively strong but, by August, it would actually change to a confirmed sideways trend as well. That was the first time that had happened since the beginning of the bullish trend that began in 2003. Not a bad time to consider some profit taking.

Examining Figure 11.7, there wasn't a classic setup for a reversal. There wasn't a two-bar reversal or the completion of AB = CD pattern. The closest thing to a good sell signal was the fact that prices were pushing higher with no volume into a reasonably significant resistance zone anchored by a high-volume cluster and congruent anchor bars exhibiting high volume and wide price spread. Volume on the anchor bars ranged from 32 million to 46 million shares traded on a weekly basis. Volume associated with the rise in price was 15 million to 22 million shares—a huge discrepancy. Clearly there wasn't any urgency to buy shares at that particular time.

Still, other than using the ebb and flow to take partial profits, there was no reason to abandon the trade at this particular point. No real warning flags had signaled.

For Wells Fargo, the volume discrepancies were not nearly as bifurcated but they were unquestionably weak comparatively. Volume at the previous swing point high from the week of December 13, 2004, registered almost 45 million shares traded. When price surged higher on the week of July 11, 2005, and created the suspect bullish trend, volume registered only 38 million shares.

As has been said previously, a suspect bullish trend does not mean that the trend must end, but it does mean one has to be more suspicious of it continuing. Combining that suspicion with a large gain over the two-year period and with the sector chart indicating a high possibility of a failure at the top of the range, a prudent strategy would be to either lock in some profits or to hedge the trade.

Locking in Gains

It never hurts to lock in some profits if the act of doing so leaves a trader with a reasonable probability of reentering the trade at a better price point. That implies that a trader needs to sell into strength so that they may buy back into weakness.

Selling into strength typically needs to occur as part of a reversal pattern or a confluence of events that, when taken as a whole, suggest that the probability of a continued climb in the near future is unlikely. The example outlined above is one of confluent events. There is nothing in the chart of Wells Fargo to suggest a discontinuance of the trend for higher prices at this juncture. Yes, the trend did change to suspect bullish, but that isn't a reason to abandon the trade.

In fact, the best trade on Wells Fargo wouldn't be to sell Wells Fargo stock but instead to sell some number of shares in the XLF as a hedge against the individual stock. The reason for this is that the XLF is in a confirmed sideways trend and at the top of the range. It has proceeded to the top of the range with declining volume, where the top of the range is anchored by heavy resistance. If a pullback should occur, it is likely to be more pronounced in the XLF than in WFC.

Locking in gains also aids the trader in achieving another important actionable goal that every trader should employ. That actionable goal is a simple one and was originally proposed in *Trade Like the Little Guy*.

> *To achieve your goals of successful trading, focus on keeping your portfolio within a few percentage points of your all-time highs and regularly achieving new highs throughout the trading year.*[2]

To be a successful trader requires that profits be taken from time to time. In those situations where profits are taken prematurely and reentry is impossible, then the money extracted from the profitable trade is redeployed to another trade that has favorable characteristics. Not all entry points for all trades are available at the same time, nor should they be. They are somewhat distributed, which is why there's always another trade.

In the case of hedging, clear-cut stop-loss orders must be deployed to limit losses on the hedge if the timing is wrong. Those stop losses could be in the form of single or multiple time frame trades, but they must be considered prior to the trade initiation and treated as if a separate trade with respect to the reward-to-risk calculations. In the XLF hedge, shorting the XLF in stages as it enters into the heavy resistance zone with a stop above the swing point highs is a favorable trade that cushions any weakness that might be experienced in WFC in the ensuing weeks. The two identified support zones were ideal places to cover the short sell. Since only the lower of the two zones was hit, the remaining hedge would have to be removed at higher levels once it was clear that the retrace was complete.

EXITING THE TRADE

Throughout the life of a trade, a trader must place a great deal of importance on monitoring the trade for trend transitions pertaining to the stock, the stock sector, and the general market. A change in trend for the general market from a bullish or bearish trend (suspect or confirmed) to a confirmed sideways trend is a strong signal to begin exiting positions that were congruent with the prevailing trend.

To exit positions doesn't require wholesale dumping of positions but it does require an exit plan to be constructed and executed to obtain the best possible prices without being too greedy.

In February of 2008, the prevailing bullish trend that began off the 2002 lows and later actualized in January of 2004 turned to a confirmed sideways trend. That was the signal to formulate and execute an exit plan on the vast majority of, if not all, stocks that a trader might have in their portfolio. It was the signal that the years-long bull market was likely drawing to a close.

Note that the general market trend change did not occur in a vacuum. As one would expect, it was preceded by a long-term trend change to sideways for the financial sector (XLF-LT) in November 2007. These two events were preceded by a transition to a confirmed bearish trend in the intermediate-term trend of the financial sector (XLF-IT) as early as July 2007. By November, both the XLF-IT and the WFC-IT were confirmed bearish in their respective trends. Something was clearly awry.

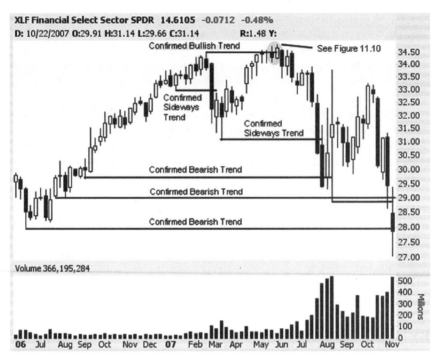

FIGURE 11.9 XLF Becomes Top-Heavy, May 30, 2006 to November 5, 2007

Figure 11.9 is the intermediate-term chart of XLF for the latter half of 2006 and most of 2007. What this chart shows is how, after a sustained move higher throughout 2006, the large price drop in February 2007 changed the tone of the market.

After the February hiccup, the XLF worked higher without fail to record a new high. This is not only expected after a long steady run higher that has lasted for years, it would actually be unusual for it not to happen. Greed is ever-present and apparent at the end of bull market movements on all time frames. The longer the bull market length, then the greater the greed and the more difficult for a final top to occur. Figure 11.10 displays that final top and, with it, a transition to a confirmed bullish trend right before the top.

Although it is a bit unusual to see a confirmed bullish trend transition at the top of the chart, there were other signs of concern on the same chart despite it. For example, the hard sell-off in February left volume at the bottom of the short-term time frame despite the candle reversal (hammer) bar. Volume at the bottom is never a good sign. It is a magnet for future prices and it clearly says that price will most likely come back down to retest at some future time.

FIGURE 11.10 XLF Problems on Short-Term Time Frame, January 29, 2007 to June 12, 2007

The other warning sign that was noticeable on the daily chart in late May was that each attempt to push higher once the intermediate-term trend transitioned back to a confirmed bullish state was met with difficulty. If the market really was that bullish and had confirmed yet another technical breakout higher, then why couldn't it take off and run much higher?

In late May, a two-bar reversal appeared and prices headed lower. As price came off the highs, volume expanded. Again, it was another subtle sign of potential problems which, by July, would become larger in size.

During this same general time period, Wells Fargo began to struggle as well. Figure 11.11 shows the same intermediate-term time frame for it.

There are a number of annotations on this chart with respect to trend transitions. The most dramatic was the price swings witnessed in August 2007. Volume expanded tremendously while prices dropped then rose like a rocket. The price plunge resulted in a high-volume test of the swing point low from March. Although price held, it created another sign of a top-heavy stock. When price and volume accelerate to the downside, it is signaling that the stock is probably undergoing institutional selling. Institutions have

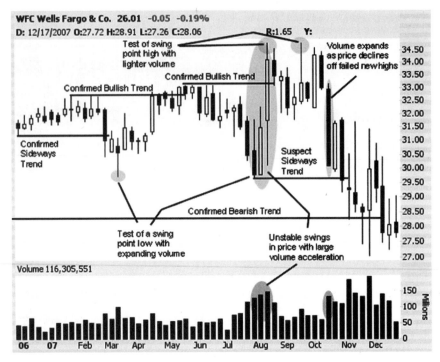

FIGURE 11.11 WFC Becomes Top-Heavy, November 27, 2006 to December 24, 2007

lots and lots of stock and they usually do not finish selling in a day or even a week. It usually takes many weeks and even months.

The institutional selling seems to have become more pronounced when the test of the potential swing point high reverses badly in mid-September. One additional sign of probable institutional selling is evident when a large anchor bar consisting of wide price spread and volume expansion occurs. That was evidence of a greater urgency to push out Wells Fargo stock at lower and lower price levels.

A short-term chart showing trading from June until October is a very informative time period because the definitive support zone that would soon turn to a resistance zone was created. Although prices would surge once more over this zone right before the 2008 financial collapse occurred, this area became the critical area on the chart to use for liquidation (see Figure 11.12).

In this chart, notice the swing point high from June of 2007, which corresponds with the two clustered anchor bars from the middle of August. The volume on the two anchor bars was tremendous and that created a

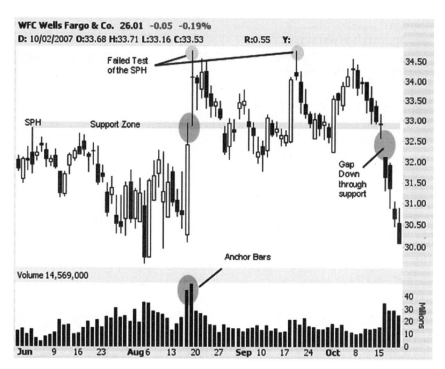

FIGURE 11.12 WFC Critical Support Becomes Resistance, June 26, 2007 to October 19, 2007

line in the sand that, if definitively broken, would be a problem to get back above. All through late August and September, it appeared that it had been broken and the stock was done. The final surge in early October ended up being the last straw, though, because if a trader needed a real dump signal, it came in late October when the stock broke in classic fashion with a gap through the support zone. That left two high-volume, high-price spread anchor bars as resistance, which was reinforced with a gap-down resistance zone. Figure 11.13 shows WFC on an intermediate-term chart with that resistance zone drawn in.

As it turns out, this resistance zone held prices lower until just before the crash of October 2008. During that period of time, the long-term trend of the broad market changed to a confirmed sideways trend (see Table 11.2), as did the XLF-LT and WFC-LT. Had a trader understood the significance of the event, a significant amount of pain could have been avoided once the support zone broke. Wells Fargo stock traded from the $34.77 highs to a low of $19.29. Taking partial profits on the break of a significant support zone was unquestionably a smart move. But the sign to sell

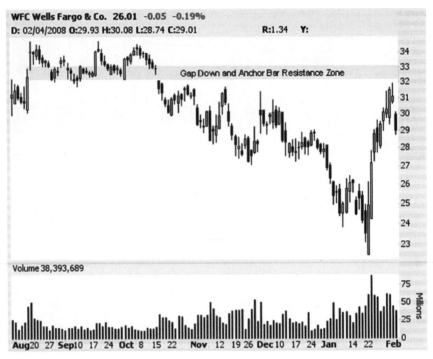

FIGURE 11.13 WFC Gap Down and Anchor Bar Resistance, August 9, 2007 to February 4, 2008

everything had not yet been given. That wouldn't trigger until the second week of January 2008.

Like clockwork, the January plunge set up the February bounce with the price of Wells Fargo bouncing back from its $19.29 low to, you guessed it, the same resistance zone, just shy of $32. It was time to dump any remaining shares that a trader might own and to thank their lucky stars for the exit opportunity. That was the exit. Eventually Wells Fargo would fall to a low of $7.65, just over a year later.

FLIPPING TRADING POSITIONS

When the long-term trend signals a change, not only should a trader consider liquidation of their existing positions, but they should also consider how to take advantage of the likely long-term change in trend. In early 2008, the broad market indicated that a trend change was likely. Utilizing the exact same principles used to determine the strongest sectors back in early

FIGURE 11.14 Confirmed Bearish Trend—ITB, May 1, 2006 to March 2, 2009

2003, a trader would be wise to look for the weakest sectors in early 2008 in order to exploit the potential downtrend.

One sector that clearly showed definitive weakness at that time was the home construction sector as exhibited through the iShares Dow Jones US Home Construction ETF (ITB). That particular sector broke to a confirmed bearish trend on the long-term time frame in June of 2007 (see Figure 11.14).

Unfortunately, by the time the impeding long-term broad market trend change was recognized, this sector had already declined almost 60 percent and did not provide the correct trading signals to indicate a further decline.

Given the weakness in home building, another related sector that was under some pressure was the iShares Dow Jones US Real Estate sector ETF (IYR). It turned confirmed sideways on the long-term chart in July 2007 and as 2008 rolled around, it traded in a broad sideways range and had yet to turn bearish. Although home construction had plummeted, real estate had declined, but not yet in any severe manner (see Figure 11.15).

In fact, this chart was set up nicely for a potential short because it had transitioned from long-term bullish to a confirmed sideways trend and had

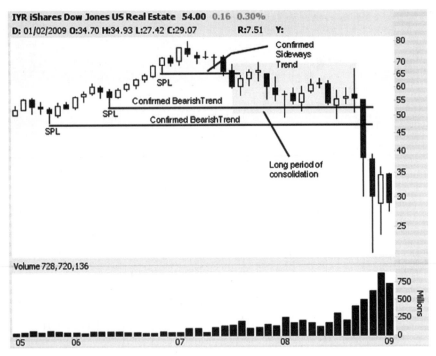

IYR iShares Dow Jones US Real Estate 54.00 0.16 0.30%
D: 01/02/2009 O:34.70 H:34.93 L:27.42 C:29.07   R:7.51 Y:

FIGURE 11.15 Confirmed Sideways Trend—IYR, June 1, 2005 to January 2, 2009

created a sideways range that had persisted for a substantial period of time as February 2008 rolled around.

Figure 11.16 drills down to the intermediate-term chart for the IYR. The annotations supply the context for resistance zones based on anchor bars. In this chart all four types of anchor bars are visible. Congruent, clustered, high volume, and wide price spread are all evident.

Using the two-tiered time frame approach to trading (trading a short- and intermediate-term time frame simultaneously), two bands of resistance are demarcated and used for entry of short sells. The stop loss would be above the swing point high of October 2007. From the longer-term chart, the target was determined to be around $33. The shorter-term projection based on the AB = CD down has a target of $47.09, as shown in Figure 11.17. All in all, the reward-to-risk parameters work when a two-tiered approach is used.

As a recap, in February of 2008, the general market has signaled a change in direction. The bullish trend that was in place since 2003 was replaced by a confirmed sideways trend. The sector index and stock that was traded since 2004 changed as well to a confirmed bearish trend and a

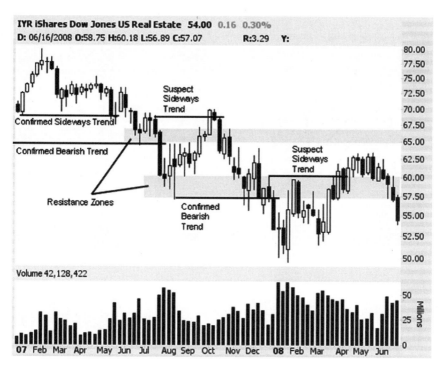

FIGURE 11.16 Mapping out Resistance—IYR, January 3, 2007 to June 23, 2008

confirmed sideways trend, respectively. The warning signs are everywhere and long positions were liquidated as a result.

The trade now was to flip around to the other side and to search for sectors that showed relative weakness. One such sector was iShares Dow Jones US Real Estate, which the long- and intermediate-term trends confirm as a potential short sell. Using the short-term chart, an actual entry was staked out. In Figure 11.18, a resistance zone on the short-term time frame forms near the top of the chart based on an anchor bar and swing point high. There are three days in May where price trades into the resistance area but is unable to break higher. That price point is around $63, which, when looking back at the intermediate-term time frame, is in between the resistance zones on that time frame. This is the first time that the short-term time frame has offered up a technical setup to get short. Everything prior to this has lacked a reason to begin a short position.

As is well known, 2008 proved to be a very bad year for stocks, and the liquidation of long holdings combined with the short selling of weak sectors would not only have saved a trader's capital base, it would have expanded it as well, in one of the worst bear markets in history.

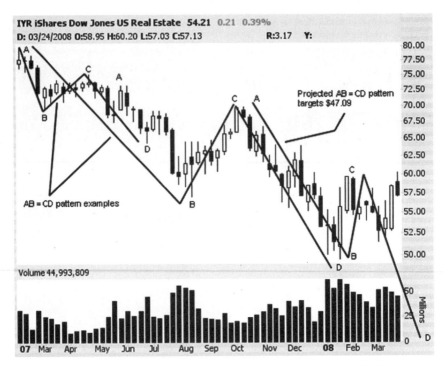

FIGURE 11.17   Short Selling—IYR, February 5, 2007 to March 24, 2008

The ability to navigate the market during a great bull market and both exit and begin to short the next phase of a market that was decidedly bullish is based solely on the ability to read the true trend through trend qualification. This ability isn't shrouded in secrecy nor is it an unattainable desire. It is right in front of each and every one of us and always has been. It's just that now it has been exposed.

CONCLUDING THOUGHTS

In closure, there are some basic trading principles that, although preached elsewhere, bear repeating here. These four principles are general guides for all trading.

1. *Keep it simple.* The more complicated it is, the more room there is for error.

FIGURE 11.18 Short Selling—IYR, March 3, 2008 to June 11, 2008

2. *Always seek the best return given the risk.* It takes time to figure out the best way to do so, but once understood, it makes life much easier.

3. *Learn to be patient, as you need plenty of patience to trade.* Many of the best trades require a trader to sit and wait, and wait, and then wait a bit more.

4. *Find and feel the difference between conviction and obstinacy.* The former is needed and the latter is dangerous. Knowing where to draw the line is critical.

With qualified trends, a new age of technical analysis has been ushered into the trading consciousness. It isn't perfect. Nothing is. It is not an end to all the studies of the discipline we call technical analysis. There never will be. It is, however, a very powerful method that, with proper identification and application, leads a trader to a more profitable conclusion.

A century after Hamilton and Dow first introduced the concept of trend, the definition has now been qualified, both literally and figuratively. It now has shades of gray. Trends never were created equal—we just thought they were.

Qualified trends are apparent in every stock, commodity, and financial trading instrument. They are apparent on all time frames and they reach every corner of the globe. Wherever humans meet *en masse* in an unfettered marketplace to exchange instruments of value, trends exist. They can be examined, qualified, and measured to determine their strength and probability for continuance. Those who understand that fact necessarily have an advantage over those who don't. Now you have the advantage. You are in the know. Use it.

Notes

INTRODUCTION

1. Robert W. Colby, *The Encyclopedia of Technical Market Indicators* (New York: McGraw-Hill, 2003), 412–415.
2. Ibid., 114–120.
3. Martin J. Pring, *Technical Analysis Explained: The Successful Investor's Guide to Spotting Investment Trends and Turning Points* (New York: McGraw-Hill, 1991), 93.
4. Curtis M. Faith, *Way of the Turtle: The Secret Methods that Turned Ordinary People into Legendary Traders* (New York: McGraw-Hill), 2007.
5. John Gallwas, Developer's Interview with Dean Hoffman, *Futures Truth Magazine*, June/July 2002, 32.

CHAPTER 1: REDEFINING TREND

1. Robert D. Edwards and John Magee, *Technical Analysis of Stock Trends*, 7th ed. (Boca Raton, FL: St. Lucie Press, 1998), 15–23.
2. Robert Rhea, *The Dow Theory* (Flint Hill, VA: Fraser Publishing, 1993), 14.
3. Vadym Graifer and Christopher Schumacher, *Techniques of Tape Reading* (New York: McGraw-Hill, 2003), 99–101.
4. Mark Douglas, *The Disciplined Trader: Developing Winning Attitudes* (New York: New York Institute of Finance, 1990), 197–198.
5. Bill Williams, *Trading Chaos: Applying Expert Techniques to Maximize Your Profits* (New York: John Wiley & Sons, 1995), 83–84.

CHAPTER 2: CLASSICAL TREND MODEL

1. Robert Rhea, *The Dow Theory* (Flint Hill, VA: Fraser Publishing, 1993), 36.
2. Ibid., 14.
3. Ibid., 11–13.
4. Ibid., 11–13.

5. Ibid., 11–13.

6. Ibid., 11–52.

CHAPTER 3: NEOCLASSICAL TREND MODEL

1. Ambivalent trends are more of an oddity and are covered in other sections of the document. Here the emphasis is on the six trends that most often occur and the transitions that cause them.

2. An explanation of the rare exceptions is detailed in later discussions.

CHAPTER 4: DETERMINING TRENDS

1. John Maynard Keynes, "BrainyQuote," www.brainyquote.com/quotes/quotes/j/johnmaynar380219.html.

2. Brian Orelli, "Juicing Up the Earnings Report," *The Motley Fool*, www.fool.com/investing/high-growth/2009/07/24/juicing-up-the-earnings-report.aspx.

3. "Celgene 1Q Profit Jumps, Hugin Named CEO," The Associated Press, April 29, 2010.

4. Note that had two actualized swing point lows already existed, then as soon as the prior swing point high was surpassed on a closing basis, the bullish trend would have been identifiable.

CHAPTER 5: QUALIFYING TRENDS

1. Note that in many of the charts, including Figure 5.2, the entire picture is not shown in order to more clearly focus on the key points being discussed. Thus, a series of higher highs and higher lows, while not shown in this limited view, are both apparent and exist on a longer time frame.

2. Edwin Lefevre, *Reminiscences of a Stock Operator* (New York: John Wiley & Sons, 1993–1994), 289–294.

CHAPTER 6: PREPARING TO TRADE

1. L.A. Little, *Trade Like the Little Guy* (Charleston, SC: BookSurge Publishing, 2009).

2. It would have been far clearer had volume on the breakout bar been higher, or if each of the retrace bars would have been lighter, because it would be preferable to compare to the breakout bar, not the bar that pushed into the swing point but failed to break it. This is a subtle but important difference and would cause a trader to trade with a bit less conviction than they otherwise might.

3. L.A. Little, *Trade Like the Little Guy*, 97–184.

CHAPTER 7: ENTERING AND EXITING TRADES

1. Norman G. Fosback, *Stock Market Logic* (Fort Lauderdale, FL: Dearborn Financial Publishing, 2004), 206–219.

2. Vadym Graifer and Christopher Schumacher, *Techniques of Tape Reading* (New York: McGraw-Hill, 2003), 137–144.

3. Koos Van der Merwe, "Projecting Price and Time with Gann Fans and Angles." In *Technical Analysis of Stocks & Commodities*, Vol. 28, No. 8 (Seattle, WA: Traders.com, July 2010), 28–32.

4. One notable exception was Tom O'Brien of Tiger Financial News Network. Mr. O'Brien's technical market reads are heavily influenced by his attempts to measure the supply and demand of stocks through volume. His ideas on large-volume bars and wide price spreads heavily influenced my desire to look deeper into their identification and application.

5. Martin J. Pring, *Technical Analysis Explained* (New York: McGraw-Hill, 1991), 86–92.

CHAPTER 8: REVERSALS AND PRICE PROJECTIONS

1. Tom O'Brien, *Timing the Trade: How Price and Value Move Markets*, Tiger Financial News Network, 2005, 51–60.

2. Larry Pesavento and Leslie Jouflas, *Trade What You See: How To Profit from Pattern Recognition* (Hoboken, NJ: John Wiley & Sons, 2007), 37–52.

3. The only possible exception to this fact is the case where the trader removes the trade prematurely for whatever reason prior to profits being realized.

4. Note that almost all of these technical patterns, such as support and resistance, AB = CD patterns, swing point tests, etc., can be used as entry or exit criteria because each of them attempts to forecast a possible turning point. Whether a trader chooses to focus on purchase or short selling, the signal is independent of the technical indicator and has much more to do with the trader's strategy.

CHAPTER 9: TIME FRAMES

1. Although not shown, the long-term chart also exhibits a confirmed bullish trend.
2. The only instance in which trading against the long-term trend would succeed is if the long-term trend ends up reversing direction while the trade is in progress.
3. Sixteen percent is the absolute worst possible number, given that the absolute high was $148.21 and the absolute low of the bar that changed the trend was $124.60 or ($124.60/$148.21), yielding .8401: the equivalent of a 16 percent decline.
4. This computation comes from an absolute low of $106.21 on the bar where the trend changes to confirmed bearish: ($106.21/$148.21) yields .7166.
5. Chapter 7 covered constructs tied to support and resistance while Chapter 8 discussed reversal patterns, such as the two-bar and high-volume reversals.
6. Robert D. Edwards and John Magee, *Technical Analysis of Stock Trends*, 7th ed. (Boca Raton, FL: St. Lucie Press, 1998), 141–152.

CHAPTER 10: MARKETS, SECTORS, AND THE TRADING CUBE

1. William O'Neil, How to *Make Money in Stocks: A Winning System in Good Times or Bad*, 3rd ed. (New York: McGraw-Hill, 2002), 48.
2. The terms "general market" and "broad market" are used synonymously.
3. This could be false if the weighting structure is such that a few stocks unduly influence the broad market indexes through an outsized weighting. If the largest weighted stocks trend differently from the majority of stocks, then the broad market trend could be in opposition to most stocks as represented by the index.
4. The earliest indexes were the two created by Dow and Hamilton covering the industrials and the transports.
5. The bear market reversal in 2002 had this characteristic. The first plunge in July of 2002 was retested on the daily chart in October of 2002. Price traded under but closed back over the swing point low from July, signaling that there wasn't sufficient force to trade lower at that time. That ended up being the very low price for that particular bear market.
6. The bearish reversal off the 2009 low is a case in point. Although the reversal pushed prices much higher than most dreamed, the reversal off the bottom was suspect sideways. That occurred in June of 2009, but was immediately retested and regenerated in July of the same year. That is what led to the sustained rally.

CHAPTER 11: TRADING QUALIFIED TRENDS

1. There have been 48 changes to the 30 stocks over the years. What used to be household names either no longer exist or are shadows of their former selves. Note that, in fairness, some of the names changed as a result of mergers.
2. L.A. Little, *Trade Like the Little Guy* (Charleston, SC: BookSurge Publishing, 2009), 147–148.

Glossary of Key Terms

Actualized Swing Point When a potential swing point low remains the low price point for six consecutive bars, then the swing point low becomes actualized. The same is true of a potential swing point high. When a potential swing point high remains the high price point for six consecutive bars, then the swing point high becomes actualized. *See also* Swing Point.

Ambivalent Sideways Trend A sideways trend that is the result of ambivalence. An ambivalent sideways trend does not result from a swing point test but instead comes about without a test as additional swing points are created. An ambivalent sideways trend occurs when there exists a series of swing points where no swing point test is involved, resulting in the actualization of two lower swing point highs and two higher swing point lows or two higher swing point highs and two lower swing point lows.

Anchor An anchor bar is, for the time frame being examined, a bar where volume expands dramatically as compared to all other bars, or the price spread of the bar is large compared to all other bars, or the bar is the result of a gap up or down in price or a combination of one or more of these characteristics.

Anchor Bottom The anchor bottom is the low price of an anchor.

Anchor Top The anchor top is the high price of an anchor.

Bearish Trend As part of the same directional move, a series of lower price highs and lower price lows (not necessarily sequential) in which price trades below and closes lower than the most recent previous swing point low.

Bias A trading bias is as it sounds: an inclination to buy or sell over one or more time frames. *See also* Trading Bias.

Bullish Trend As part of the same directional move, a series of higher price highs and higher price lows (not necessarily sequential) in which price trades above and closes higher than the most recent previous swing point high.

Channel Channels are technical patterns in which a line is drawn across the tops and bottoms of multiple bars. The top and bottom lines are equally spaced and directionally can be up, down, or horizontal in their slope.

Clustered Anchor Bars   Clustered anchor bars form a pattern consisting of two or more contiguous anchor bars.

Confirmed Bearish Trend   As part of the same directional move, a series of lower price highs and lower price lows (not necessarily sequential) where price trades below and closes lower than the most recent previous swing point low, while volume expands as compared to volume at the previous swing point low.

Confirmed Bullish Trend   As part of the same directional move, a series of higher price highs and higher price lows (not necessarily sequential), in which price trades above and closes higher than the most recent previous swing point high, while volume expands as compared to volume at the previous swing point high.

Confirmed Sideways Trend   The interruption of a bullish or bearish trend, in which sequential swing points interrupt the existing trend of higher highs and higher lows or lower highs and lower lows, while volume expands on that interruption.

Confirmed Trend   When the current price trades lower (downtrend) or higher (uptrend) than the previous swing point price and volume expands, the trend is confirmed.

Congruent Anchor Bars   Congruent anchor bars form a pattern consisting of two or more noncontiguous anchor bars.

Divergence   A divergence occurs when two somewhat related items show an outcome variation. One item signals one possible outcome, while the other signals a very different potential outcome.

Downtrend   A downtrend is synonymous with a bearish trend. *See also* Bearish Trend.

Fundamental Trader   A trader who analyzes the fundamentals of a company and uses that analysis to make investment decisions.

Gap   A gap is an area of the chart where prices simply do not trade. This could be on any time frame, but the shorter the time frame, the greater the potential for price gaps to exist.

General Trend   The general trend usually refers to the general market trend, which can be bullish, bearish, or sideways.

High-Volume Anchor Bar   In a high-volume anchor bar, volume expands dramatically as compared to all other bars on the time frame being examined.

Noise   Noise refers to random price change that has no material impact on the trend under examination.

Potential Swing Point   The identification of a swing point begins with a potential swing point. A potential swing point is any chart bar where a new high or low was established as compared to the previously identified potential swing point bar. *See also:* Swing Point High; Swing Point Low.

Price Magnet   Price magnets are high-volume bars found at the top or the bottom of a chart on a given time frame.

Price Projection   Price projections are derived from trading signals and are used to assign a target price to an expected move higher or lower.

Price Reversal   A price reversal is a place on the chart where a directional move reverses and begins to trade in the opposite direction.

Price Zone   Price zone is generally defined as a price area where price should trade to, but not beyond. The degree of confidence in the price zone is a reflection of how it is anchored, where anchoring is reflective of the expected supply of stock versus the demand for it.

Retest and Regenerate   A retest and regenerate sequence is predicated on the need to retest a swing point area where price did succeed in both surpassing and closing beyond the previous swing point, but in doing so, it created a suspect trend.

Resistance   Resistance is generally defined as a price level above which price is less likely to continue to rise, due to the expected supply of stock versus demand for it.

Sideways Trend   Sideways trends result from either conflicting consecutive swing point highs or lows or from a transition from a prevailing bullish or bearish trend.

Slope   Slope is the angle of a line. It can be measured in degrees.

Support   Support is generally defined as a price level below which price is less likely to continue to fall, due to the expected demand of stock versus supply of it.

Suspect Bearish Trend   A suspect bearish trend develops with, as part of the same directional move, a series of lower price highs and lower price lows (not necessarily sequential), in which price trades below and closes lower than the most recent previous swing point low, while volume contracts as compared to volume at the previous swing point low.

Suspect Bullish Trend   A suspect bullish trend develops with, as part of the same directional move, a series of higher price highs and higher price lows (not necessarily sequential), in which price trades above and closes higher than the most recent previous swing point high, while volume contracts as compared to volume at the previous swing point high.

Suspect Sideways Trend   The interruption of a bullish or bearish trend where sequential swing points interrupt the existing trend of higher highs and higher lows or lower highs and lower lows while volume contracts on that interruption.

Suspect Trend   When the current price trades lower (downtrend) or higher (uptrend) than the previous swing point price and volume contracts, the trend is suspect.

Swing Point   Typically thought of as a price point that is "at the edge" of all other prices points within the general time proximity. Algorithmically, a swing point low is actualized if, after six bars, the potential swing point remains the lowest price point. A swing point high is the same but opposite, where after six bars the potential swing point high remains the highest price point.

Swing Point High (SPH)   Swing point high is a common term used to qualify a swing point as signifying a high bar on a chart where prices once traded to but subsequently turned away from.

Swing Point High Test   A swing point high test occurs when the current bar's high exceeds the previous and nearest (nearest in terms of a higher price) swing point high.

Swing Point Low (SPL)   Swing point low is a common term used to qualify a swing point as signifying a low bar on a chart where prices once traded to but subsequently turned away from.

Swing Point Low Test   A swing point high test occurs when the current bar's low exceeds the previous and nearest (nearest in terms of a lower price) swing point low.

Technical Trader   A trader who primarily uses charts to make trading decisions. A broader definition, used in other texts, includes sentiment and money flow analysis as well.

Time Frame   Time frames are arbitrarily chosen periods of time during which the analysis of trend occurs.

Time Frame Integration   Time frame integration is the act of examining the three time frames to formulate a trading bias.

Trading Bias   A trading bias represents a trader's underlying inclination to buy or sell over one or more time frames. *See also* Bias.

Trading Cube   The Trading Cube is a visual aid for traders. It provides a comprehensive view of the qualified trend of the general market, the sector, and the stock over the three time frames.

Trading Floor   A trading floor refers to a definable area on the chart where one trading range stops and another starts.

Trend   Trend, as it applies to securities trading, is loosely defined as the proclivity for prices to move in a general direction for some period of time.

Trend Line   A trend line is a charting technique where a technician applies a line to a chart in order to represent the trend in a given security. The act of drawing a trend line is as simple as drawing a straight line that connects the tops and/or bottom prices of three or more bars. Trend lines are used as a visual aid to highlight an underlying trend.

Trend Qualification   The act of qualifying trends as suspect or confirmed on each of the time frames.

True Trend   True trend, as it applies to securities trading, is the act of determining the expected future direction of price and doing so with increased confidence. True trend is established as a result of trend qualification. *See also* Trend Qualification.

Two-Bar Reversal   A two-bar reversal involves two adjacent bars and is indicative that a reversal in directional movement has occurred. The two-bar reversal pattern occurs if, after an extended directional move (both in terms of time and price), price pushes past the previous bar's high (uptrend) or low (downtrend) then closes back under/over the previous bar's high/low with lighter volume. The longer the extension and the lighter the volume, the better the signal.

Underlying Trend   The underlying trend references the broad trend of the market and can be bullish, bearish, or sideways.

Uptrend   An uptrend is synonymous with a bullish trend. *See also* Bullish Trend.

Volume   Volume is supplied by each exchange where the tradable instrument is traded. It generally is presented as a total number of shares that traded during a particular time period.

Wide-Price-Spread Anchor Bar   In a wide-price-spread anchor bar, the spread between the high and low of the bar expands dramatically as compared to the price spread on all other bars for the time frame being examined.

Zone   A zone is a price area on the chart where prices should trade to and have difficulty trading beyond. It isn't a single price point but instead a price range, and is typically associated with support and resistance. *See also* Trading Zone.

About the Author

L.A. Little is a professional trader and money manager with degrees in Philosophy, Computer Science, Telecommunications, and Computer Information Systems. He is the author of *Trade Like the Little Guy* (available on Amazon.com) and writes daily columns for RealMoney.com and RealMoneySilver.com. He also contributes weekly articles to TheStreet.com, in addition to producing educational videos that appear on the same site.

His work has appeared on *Mad Money* with Jim Cramer and in regular articles in *Stocks and Commodities* magazine, as well as other industry-related magazines and conference presentations.

He operates an educational trading Web site (*Technical Analysis Today*: www.tatoday.com) that provides daily market commentary and provides a number of investment services, including qualified trends for most commonly traded stocks in addition to their recent trend transitions. Another service addresses trading signals based on the concepts expressed in this book.

His trading experience spans four decades in commodities, stocks, and options. His trading systems were developed over the course of many years, synthesizing influences from towering figures from the past as well as the present. He focuses upon simplicity and the idea that trading success is not based on an innate talent, but a learned skill.

Index